# Telos Welcoming New Earth

• • •

Master Adama
Bryan Tilghman

MU PRESS

Mt. Shasta, California

Printed in the United States of America
First Printing, 2017
ISBN-13: 9780692887042
ISBN-10: 0692887040
Library of Congress Control Number: 2017909178
Mu Press, Mt. Shasta, CA

MU PRESS
110 S B Street
Mt. Shasta, CA 96067
(530) 425-6700
Bryan@LostLemuria.com

Ordering Information:
Single sales. 'Telos, Welcoming New Earth' is available for purchase on Amazon.com.
Quantity sales. Special discounts are available on quantity purchases by resellers, corporations, associations, and others. For details, contact the publisher at the address above.

Adama's image reprinted here with permission by Glenda Green.

Cover Art – Mei Drucker
(See Acknowledgments)

Lemurian light language – Michael Lott
Notes about how we came about the light language symbols used in this book are included in the Acknowledgments section in the back.

MU PRESS

# Contents

# Preface from Adama

Dear friends,

My name is Adama. I am the High Priest of Telos. We are a city of the Lemurian race living here in the 5th dimensional city of Telos inside the mountain of Mt. Shasta, CA. It is with great pleasure that we come to address you all again. There is a great deal of activity taking place in your world now, and we have much that we wish to share. In this book, we introduce our channel Bryan Tilghman who has been chosen by myself and the High Council of Telos to be a messenger and successor of Aurelia Louis Jones. Our dear channel Aurelia worked with us for many years; and in this capacity she served not only as our messenger, but she also embodied and brought forth great light and love into the world. She has returned to her heavenly home and she visits with us often. She is also participating with us on this project. She would like to take this opportunity to let all of you know, those of you who have followed her work or perhaps who have known her in her time on the mountain, she wishes to take this opportunity now to send you her blessings and gratitude for all that you have done and all that you continue to do. She wishes for you to know that she is doing wonderfully well and that each day she is utterly amazed by the love, beauty, and grace that she experiences now. She sends her love and blessings to all.

Bryan has also had numerous embodiments in the last golden ages as a Lemurian, and one of his higher aspects, Jonathan, resides here in Telos with us yet today. He has moved to the mountain at my request and with an extension of the offer to come and do this work with us. He has gladly agreed to do so. It is our sincere hope that our messages will bring not only wisdom and understanding but also great hope and anticipation for all that is to come as we move into the next Golden Age, which we reference in these works as New Earth. For truly, we are moving into the next Golden Age and we will attempt, from time to time in these works, to give you a glimpse and a vision of all the beauty and grace that is to come for humanity, for Gaia and for all life forms sharing the planet. We bring forth this information now at this most auspicious time in your earthly history and we ask that all may be blessed by and through these works.

Throughout this book we often use analogies. We reference many times the analogy of the Project Plan for example. This refers to the great plan of Creator for Gaia, humanity and all life present and of the many events taking place in your world at this time. Our hope is that, like our messenger, our readers may benefit by the use of simple analogies and an easy conversational style. We endeavor to convey wisdom and understanding in a way that is easily accessible and enjoyable.

We wish for you to know that we, the Lemurians, are still here patiently waiting and anticipating the time when we may come forth and share additional information with you. We look forward with great excitement to the day when humanity is ready, that we may come out of the mountain and show ourselves to you and to begin working with you side by side in the creation of our New Earth. We wish for you to know that we are your family and we have always been here. We have been awaiting this time with great anticipation. Each and every one of you is most dearly loved.

I am Adama.

GOD

GAIA

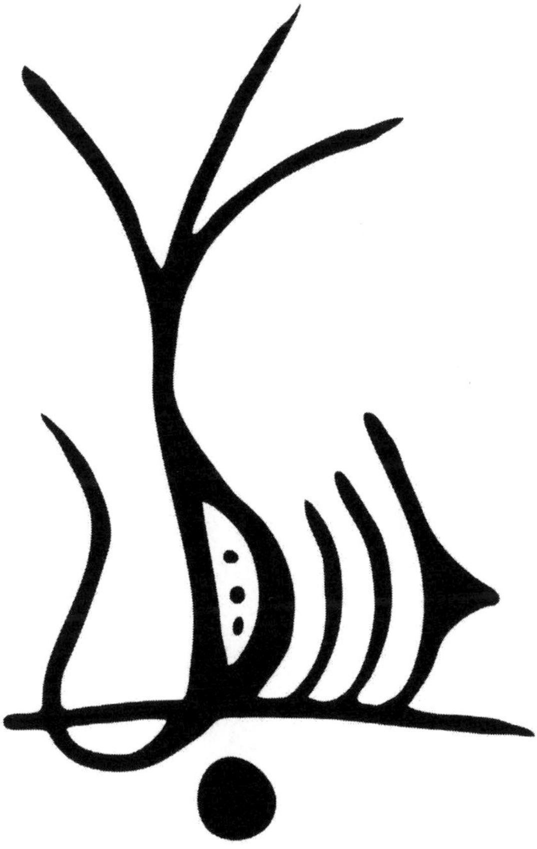

JOY

LIGHT

LOVE

OPPORTUNITY

MU

HARMONY

MOUNT SHASTA

# Prologue

## How the Author Learned to Connect with Telosians, Angels, and Masters in 5D

I am a messenger for Master Adama, the High Priest of Telos. I have a degree in business and prior to my transition to Mt. Shasta, I spent 25 years in the corporate world with a successful career in different areas of Supply Chain Management. In 2008, I also started a small business with a handful of products I developed to help horses with their hoof problems.

Growing up in the South, I came to have a great love and appreciation for the natural world. I owe that to my parents. We love the mountains and we have a great appreciation for the beauty of our Earth. I have pondered truth and wisdom and I've come to find God in the mountains and streams. I felt certain there was more to the story or meaning of life than we were aware of or being told, but my normal day-to-day life moved on like everyone else's. It wasn't until later in life that circumstances would provide me with an opportunity to step onto the path of initiation in earnest.

A course of events in my mid-forties led to something often referred to as the dark night of the soul. My marriage had failed and I was crushed. It was a sad and challenging time for both of us. These kinds of situations may be brought about by the Higher Self and are often intended to finally break through to strong willed and stubborn individuals like myself. My heart space was wide open now, but I needed to find a way back to wholeness and wellness. I decided that meditation was the answer and declared that I would sit on the couch and meditate every day until I found my balance. During this time, I read a variety of spiritual works and was particularly drawn to the angels. I would pray to God for guidance and another book would appear.

Around day 75 or 80, I called to Archangel Michael. My meditation practice had offered a glimpse of the love vibration that flows continuously in Heaven (the Light Realms), and on this day I was struggling. I spoke silently and asked Archangel Michael if I could come home. To my great astonishment and awe, he came and showed himself to me. He spoke to me. There was no mistaking, not even for an instant, who he was. His presence felt huge and his light was very bright. His presence felt imposing and strong but at the same time gentle and warm. His voice was loud. He said "Yes Bryan, you will come home, but not now. We have work to do. You will see me again." That was it. That was the message. My life changed in that moment. The realization that came with this experience was life altering, and the walls of another paradigm came crumbling down. Thus began my journey in earnest on the Path of Light back home to our Father/Mother God. Archangel Michael had not only heard my calls but he came to me and made himself known in a very real way. He came to set me firmly onto a new life path. He remains my constant companion, my most trusted friend, teacher and ally. This is where my story begins.

Over the years, I had exposed myself to a variety of spiritual and esoteric information. I felt I had an open mind about the mysteries of life and the universe. However, just a few short years ago, it's likely that I would have completely dismissed any serious attempt to discuss such subjects as higher dimensional beings inhabiting Middle Earth. I wasn't ready to hear it or receive it. The fact that some of this stuff may sound nuts to you has not escaped me. I used to refer to people like me as "Woo Woo." Now, I am one. We've been living our lives in a box that we call reality. This is our paradigm and what we think we know to be true. We can attend corporate seminars or self-help workshops and learn to "Think outside the box." This may prove to be a valuable skill in the days ahead. It's all so much bigger than most of us ever imagine. I encourage you to suspend any disbelief momentarily and just allow for the possibility. Mark Twain said, "Truth is stranger than fiction, but it is because fiction is obliged to stick to possibilities, truth isn't."

This stuff I'm talking about is pretty far out there, not just for mainstream America but for most on the planet at this time. However, I am assured in the work I do that more and more are waking up to new versions of reality each day. This is why I came back to this planet. Just as is the case with our Family of Light in Heaven, I would not abandon my earth family and Gaia. You came back for the very same reason. I am grateful that we have so many gifted earth teachers with us now and for those who continue to assist us all on our journey. Trust me, there is a big part of me that's not crazy about all of this. I would not have left a successful life and career only to expose myself to ridicule if I did not honestly believe that all I have said is truth and worthy of being shared. That doesn't mean that my truth will be the same as yours. It won't be and it doesn't need to be. However, if you can believe in angels, you can believe in the possibility of other beings of light. As it turns out, I also speak with some of the higher dimensional beings of light that we know as dragons.

My story is a living example of the expansion of consciousness in action that Master Adama speaks so much about in this book. I was most fortunate to have had the catalyst event with Archangel Michael. It created within me a great desire for spiritual growth and expansion. I came to understand that my ascension, my victory in the light, is my soul's and therefore my own priority for this lifetime. This is the silver lining and great blessing that have come from what I perceived to be a very difficult earthly experience. I have come to see it all for the gift it truly was.

In Telos, Volume 3, Aurelia Louise Jones, one of the first writers about Telos, delivers a message from Zohar, an ancient master of light from the city of Shamballa in the Inner Earth. He tells us that "Harmony should be the number one quality in your life, and rest assured that it will pave the way for your admittance into the "Halls of Ascension." Through the course of life's events, I was led to begin seeking, in earnest, the inner harmony and peace I knew were there. Soon I came to understand what it means to earn our ascension. There is no greater achievement for us. I have no greater desire than to return home, at long last, to my dear family in Heaven and to the heart of my Creator. This pursuit has led me to the mountain and to all of the wondrous experiences I've been so very blessed to have and to share with you.

Everyone's journey will be unique. Our consciousness and awareness are rising very quickly now and more and more people are waking up to their own unique experiences and remembrance of their truth. I like to say that people's love lights are turning on. There is no playbook for this stuff. We have to find our own way. This isn't a religion or a cult and I have no desire to be anyone's guru. The Veils of Illusion are thinning and it is easier now than ever before in the time of our recorded history to connect directly and personally with God and to our great and many Families of Light who make up what I refer to as "The Company of Heaven." As I have come to know these truths for myself, I continue to be utterly amazed by the levels of love and support that are always available to us. It is a magnificent and seemingly endless truth. I know that I have not even scratched the surface; yet I have been shown the most wondrous things. My Mom asked me one night at dinner as I was attempting to describe one of my experiences in a light hearted but truthful way, "Why did they choose you?" I told her I didn't know. What I did know was that everything I was experiencing was being directed by God and that I was fully protected in His Light. I also knew that what I was being shown and being told was truth. I said it was like letting the genie out of the bottle. There was no going back now and I wouldn't want to anyway.

As you make your way through this book, you will find personal examples and dialogue of my experiences being shared. I asked Master Adama about it. He said, "By sharing your personal experience, you assist others in opening their own doorway to expansion and growth". We are all going through this together and I share my journey openly in hopes of assisting others in the building of their own framework. As we go through this great shift we are each having our own unique experience. This one is mine.

Another reason for sharing personal accounts as we go along is to exemplify the fun and easygoing nature of the relationship

Master Adama and I have with each other. It's like this with all of our family across the veil. They know us better than we know ourselves because they are fully conscious and fully aware. They are our family and they are absolutely delighted when we invite them to participate in our lives. We are free will beings, so it is up us to ask them directly for their assistance if that is what we choose. "Them" meaning those Archangels, masters and avatars to whom we feel naturally drawn. For me, traveling with the angels is the only way to go. They can and do help me in so many ways just because I ask. Their blessings in my daily life are evident. It is the same for the Ascended Masters and other remarkable beings of light that I have been so blessed to know. I like to make jokes, laugh and have a bit of fun along the way, and I'm often surprised by some of the jokes and pokes I receive in return. Love is a vibration, and laughter is a beautiful expression of the love vibration. They have come to be my family in a very real way. As I began waking up, I had a real passion for these pursuits. My best achievements thus far are fully due to my very heartfelt and sincere requests and invitations for God, Jesus, the Blessed Mother Mary, the angels and many more to actually come into my life and begin working there so I could see it. I have been persistent in my intention and prayer, and my story demonstrates the many blessings that have come forth as a result. From this place, everything else continues to flow to me in grace.

Through this work, you will see that I refer to several of the angels and masters that I am blessed to know personally. However, I do not wish for the reader to get the idea that my awareness just came flooding in one day. I do not consider myself to be a natural for this work. It seems I'm often just kind of plowing through it with committed persistence and celebrating the wins along the way. There are days when my awareness is as clear as a bell and other days when things are just foggy. It's a process, but I believe that anyone who chooses can guide themselves to have fuller awareness of themselves and our Family of Light, who are always present with us just there across the Veil of Illusion.

By Veil of Illusion, I am referring to an energy layer that has limited us from remembering who we are beyond the illusion of this third dimensional construct we know as the human experience on Earth. As humans, we were originally created for and designed to remain in constant communion with God and our greater family in Heaven. We are remembering this now. New energies are guiding us to higher levels of spiritual maturity. Tidal waves of light are thinning the veil that has been partly responsible in creating within us a false sense of separation from Father/Mother God. This is most excellent news for us all.

Before moving to Mt. Shasta, I began traveling directly to the temples of Telos by following the meditations for each one through the series of Telos books that were brought forth by Aurelia Louise Jones. I don't know how it works for others, but I will quickly describe my perception of how things work for me. When I travel, of course my physical body is still on the couch or wherever it is I sat down to meditate. Everything is energy and everything is connected. In essence, our consciousness exists everywhere at all times. I felt my task was to release the old beliefs, programs and restrictions that say I/we/humans can't do X. Once I was able to break past some of the internal barriers of false belief, it became much easier to connect with my family in Heaven and to allow my consciousness to go wherever it was I was allowing/sending it to go via my focused but relaxed intention. It feels to me like bilocating in a way. I always have awareness of my body and my surroundings, but my attention or consciousness is being focused elsewhere. I've found this process to be more about accepting that these things (conscious communion with our Family of Light in Heaven for example) are possible and then simply opening the mind to all possibility and allowing them to take place.

Archangel Michael was the first to come and speak to me directly. Several years ago when I was beginning to wake up, he led me to his teachings through Ronna Herman. I learned how to create a personal pyramid in the 5$^{th}$ dimension, and this practice has been a cornerstone of my experience and development. All that I do begins and ends with Father/Mother God and I always ask for Archangel Michael's protection. The pyramid is my safe space, my jumping off point if you will. It is where I go for healing work and to visit with my Heaven Family.

I would characterize this process as meeting the Company of Heaven halfway. They will joyfully meet with us on the planes of the fifth dimension. To put it in my plain language, they are happy and willing to lower their vibration to meet with us in 5D, but that is as far down into the worlds of density as they wish to travel. This does not mean they are not assisting us in every moment wherever we are. They are. This is just a higher form of communion and work. For example, our family from the angelic realms may move out of their normal and blissful state of 7D to visit with us intimately in 5D. However, it is our responsibility to elevate ourselves beyond 3D/4D levels of consciousness so that we may access them there in 5D.

The following quote comes from the book 'Your Sacred Quest' by Ronna Herman and Archangel Michael: "By accessing your fifth dimensional Pyramid of Power, you are bypassing the negative, distorted energies of the third dimension, and the conflicting, ambiguous energies of the fourth dimension. It is time you regain the ability to function within the rarified planes of light where only perfection is possible."

This process has provided a quantum leap forward in my spiritual progression. Archangel Michael brings us these wisdom teachings so we can be assured that we are under his watchful guidance and protection as we go about our work.

In one chapter, I share an experience when Archangel Michael took me to the Fields of Telos to meet Trindletothton, a blue dragon from Venus. He picked me up from my pyramid. In this experience, I am simply keeping my energy/intention attached to or focused on Archangel Michael, and we travel to wherever it is he's taking me. I am able to have some level of perception and awareness of what I am seeing and what we are discussing as this takes place. Before I moved to Mt. Shasta and began working in the portal, my Telosian ambassador Tabiananti, a beautiful and radiant female Lemurian, would often meet me at the pyramid and take me to Telos in a merkaba light vehicle to meet with Master Adama. If he wanted to meet with me, he would send Tabiananti to come and get me. These experiences were taking place from the perspective of the higher mind or consciousness and facilitated also by the spiritual/etheric body. I've come to know and trust that the experience of what is taking place is very real indeed.

When I arrived in Mt. Shasta in May 2016, I began another series of visits to the temples of Telos to begin further integrating my energy. Through my conscious intention I was able to locate a physical portal high up on the backside of Mt. Shasta. Amidst icy crevasses and avalanche zones there is a small hole or cave that is mostly covered by large rocks. It is not likely to be found by visitors to the mountain. About ten to fifteen feet into this otherwise dirty hole, a large tunnel opens up. The floor and sides of this tunnel have a soft golden luminance. It is perfectly smooth and pristine in beauty and form. What I perceive to be about 100 yards into the mountain, the tunnel opens to a small platform overlooking a very large open space where visitors park their ships. It is like a parking garage for spacecraft. Just before dropping into meditation, I would speak to Tabiananti to let her know I was coming and she would meet me in the tunnel. Once we arrived at the platform she would have a merkaba vehicle waiting which she would navigate through the city to Master Adama's courtyard and office space or the temple I was hoping to visit.

This book comes to us from Master Adama and the High Council of Telos. I have done my very best, as his messenger, to deliver his truth and wisdom as he has intended. I invite you to feel into the messages as we go. It is my hope also that, through these words, you may feel for yourself the deep sincerity and love from Master Adama and our families in Telos. Master Adama has much more to share with us. He says we're just getting warmed up.

It is my great joy and privilege to share these messages with you.

Many blessings,

Bryan

# Chapter 1

## A Walk in Telos

In March of 2016, I sold my small business and left my corporate job. A few weeks later I sold my Maryville, TN home. I arrived in Mt. Shasta, CA in early May to begin the work I was invited here to do.

Master Emanuel of the High Council of Telos and Master Adama, High Priest of Telos told me that a portal had been opened specifically for this work and I was to find it. I was told to look for a meadow. I would know it by the wild flowers and one particular tree standing just at the edge. Sometime around the middle of May I began my search. This was to be a part of my training. Tai Chi and Reiki have been good tools to assist me in learning about energy, how to feel it and work with it. I was given a general area of the mountain in which to begin my search. The ground was still covered with hard packed snow so the clue about wild flowers wasn't going to be so helpful. I relied primarily on grounding my energy into Gaia and feeling what was there. As a new resident to Mt. Shasta, the energy lift felt strong everywhere on this magnificent mountain and I found this to be a bit of a challenge. I was learning a new level of attunement.

I began gridding out small parcels of land much like a search and rescue team would do. Through the course of the first seven days I marked three locations where I perceived a higher vibratory energy but I wasn't convinced. On day eight, as I was approaching tree line, I felt the presence of several Lemurians about seventy yards up the mountain. I could perceive them telling me to follow them which I did for a short time until I began dropping back down into another meadow. They were gone now but as I arrived the first thing I found was an Indian tree. I knew it was the snow that had caused the tree to grow this way but it was clearly the sign I was looking for. My father told me about Indian trees and sometimes we looked for them on our hikes in the Smoky Mountains of Tennessee. The Cherokee Indians would make two ninety degree bends in saplings and they would continue to grow that way. They were used as markers or signposts. I knew this was the place. The energy lift was quite noticeable. After spending some time I walked out, taking note of where I was to be sure I would find it again. The next day I came back, stilled myself and confirmed with Master Adama that this was the portal. It sits directly above what he refers to as the Great Hall of Telos. This is an energy portal, not an actual entrance to Telos like the one I described in the Prologue. Because this portal sits above their Great Hall, there is great energy radiating from it that helps me to further attune my energy signature with Master Adama and the energies of Telos for the purpose of this work.

The messages contained in this book were taken in the portal over the course of the 2016 summer season.

I asked Master Adama if he wanted this to be the first chapter or the last. He has selected it as the first chapter of the book and asked that I give you this message also. He invites us to really feel into the beauty and grandeur of life in Telos as we move through his messages. He wishes for us to have the vision of a peaceful, loving, fully conscious and beautiful society because that is exactly what we are creating now despite some outer appearances. Telos gives us a glimpse into our New Earth to come, and these are the feelings and truth that he wishes to share with us.

In these transmissions, I am sitting in the portal on the mountain and speaking my experience and Master Adama's words into a recorder. In this chapter, we have a combination of direct transmission from Master Adama along with my giving a play by play, so to speak, of what I am experiencing.

• • •

Bryan - *Master Adama is asking me if I would like to take a walk through the city with him to which I answer a resounding "Yes." As we step out of the door of this Great Hall I see we are located near the heart of the city and although I struggle to see some of the details, I am sensing and feeling that the city has a glow and a radiance about it that is soft and soothing. What is coming to me as a comparison is the kind of soft light that is emitted from a salt lamp, which has a pleasant, soft orange glow. There are a variety of different colors being radiated throughout the city. Some colors blend together and others do not. The temples here are giving off some of the radiance. Each of the seven Creator rays has a corresponding temple in Telos. The flames (violet, green, blue, gold, white, yellow, pink) rise up into the air and put off a radiance of light and color throughout the city. There are also many decorative lights that appear to be crystals emitting light. As light shines through, it takes on the quality and the color of those crystals.*

*Just standing here outside the Great Hall, my feeling is that I have just stepped into a wonderland. No Hollywood movie would compare. Its beauty is far beyond any cityscape or skyline I've ever seen. Everything is pristine and beautiful. Everything is perfect in form. There are many Telosians walking up and down the streets. Merkaba vehicles are traveling the skyways. Merkaba vehicles come in different shapes and sizes; the one I've ridden in with Tabiananti looks like a round ball made of clear crystal. It's like a half bubble that closes around you when you sit in it. The two seats conform to you right away and you can see in all directions, even under your feet. There's a kind of pop up display that comes and goes with what appear to be several controls similar to a dashboard of a car. Tabiananti would simply touch this one or that one and we would be on our way. It's like moving in a bubble. Hers is small but lightning fast.*

*As residents walk past in close proximity to Adama and me, they smile warmly and nod their heads gently in acknowledgement. I can see that just as crystals are being used for lighting, they are also being used as pathways. This is where the glow of the streets comes from. It is what I have seen in the tunnel in the physical portal on the backside of the mountain. In fact, most of the infrastructure, roadways and buildings here appear to be made of crystal. Everything is beautiful and radiant. I can see some very large archways and spires rising up to form the cityscape. We are close to the Temple of Illumination, which is near the central point of the city, as is the Great Hall.*

*We walk past a large amphitheater here in the downtown part of the city. It looks much like you would expect it to. There are many rows of seats and a large stage. The amphitheater actually sinks into the ground from this point (we are not on a hill, the ground is flat). It looks like a crater in the footprint of the city. So walking up to it you would either walk down the steps or use a device that is similar to our escalators in a mall. Master Adama tells me this is a community in every sense of the word. There is only love, support, community and cooperation here.*

Adama - In our fifth dimensional experience we are not burdened by the many struggles of duality that exist in a third dimensional experience. This amphitheater is used for a wide variety of events. We also enjoy entertainment in Telos and we see a variety of activities taking place here. We enjoy plays, music and singing just as you do. Visitors who wish to address us publicly may also use this venue. It is not an official site that would be used for council meetings or government as you might frame it. We have other locations for those activities. This is a gathering place for us.

*Bryan - We turn down another street and continue walking. I see other Telosians passing by with their very warm smiles as we turn into a courtyard that I recognize as Master Adama's courtyard. This is where Tabiananti brings me in her merkaba vehicle to meet with Master Adama. There are a variety of small trees and bushes, many flowers and other species of plants with striking vibrancy and color unlike anything we're used to.*

*I ask Master Adama, "It feels like the sun is shining here just as it would be on the surface, and I would like to know how that is?"*

Adama - Bryan, we have the technology available to us to actually capture, if you will, sunlight—the same light, rays and energy, all that is being emitted from our sun is allowed to flow freely into

Telos; and this is the same for all cities in the Agartha Network in what you like to refer to as Middle Earth. So obviously, we do not live in darkness nor do we need to rely solely on artificial light. We have spoken about how we live extended lifetimes, and one of the reasons is that we are intentionally working with, blessing and receiving, the light that comes from the sun behind the sun. As it flows through our sun here in our solar system, we have technology through the use of crystals to capture this light and allow it to radiate out through the city. Once this was established, no additional work was required. That is to say, while we are here, we are to some extent experiencing the same night and day that you do. We have within our technology, the ability to monitor and make adjustments to all manner of environmental controls and we live quite comfortably. We are not prone to the extremes of your weather patterns. We experience natural sunlight and we receive the blessings from Creator just as you do. We have many forms of technology that enhance our environment so that it is comfortable for us.

Bryan - *The courtyard is very comfortable. If you were just to sit here you may not know that you were in a different dimension aside from the many unusual and amazing multi-colored flowers and plants. It reminds me of some of the interior courtyards I've seen in New Orleans. There are buildings surrounding the courtyard that appear to be used for residence or work space. It is peaceful and quiet. It has a magical feel. This courtyard adjoins Master Adama's office.*

Bryan - *Master Adama, how do you travel from one section of the city to another?*

Adama - We often walk. We also use the merkaba light vehicles which you are so fond of. We have a system in place that resembles your subway systems. It functions in a similar way. Larger vehicles that run throughout the city service areas of heavy traffic. Our merkaba vehicles are much different than any form of transportation that you are familiar with. There are no fossil fuels in use here. We use magnetics and anti-gravity propulsion systems through the use of crystals and so on.

Many of the spires, archways and columns that you see on our skyline are there as decorative elements. Just as you might appreciate the beauty of the skyline of New York City or Hong Kong, we also wish to and do surround ourselves with beauty. We take great pride in our city and community. We have many visitors from other star nations. Our city is visited by many and now so more than ever with the events of our grand project taking place. We host a great many visitors, all manner of beings from any number of locations. We pride ourselves on being a host city and a hub for this kind of activity. We have a number of facilities that you would refer to as hotels and restaurants, and we have gone to great effort to create facilities that allow a variety of beings to be comfortable here. Also, as you know, we have here in the mountain an area just off of the city that is essentially a parking area for ships. Many who visit us choose to remain on their ships while they are here, and they will simply shuttle from their ships to the city much in the same way as would happen if you were to take a cruise. Your cruise ship will travel to a port and you'll go have your fun. Later, you will return to the ship for your meals and rest. This is a most common occurrence in our city and we have those who may choose to experience it either way according to their preference.

Bryan - *Master Adama, what is the population of Telos?*

Adama - Our population is approaching 1.5 million and I know this would not be considered a large city by your standard. We have many cities within the Agartha Network. We also have families and cities in other locations of the galaxy; and we have the ability to travel back and forth as we choose to visit those on other planets or ships. It doesn't look like a big sprawling city to you does it?

Bryan – *Yes, that is correct.*

Adama - We are quite efficient in the use of our space, and we have technology available to us in terms of the management of space that is not known yet by humanity. We have it within our ability to expand a space within a space such that on outer appearance you may observe a building that looks to be a particular size; yet when you walk into the building you experience a space that is much larger and more expansive than you expected it to be from the outside looking in.

(Bryan - *The experience of this is like walking into a typical city brownstone apartment. As you enter from the street, you might estimate the space to be 1,500 square feet. As you walk through the door you experience a space that actually appears to be more like 5,000 or 7,000 square feet*).

I understand this is a challenging concept. You are standing here with me attempting to wrap your mind around this concept and I am also looking for a way to explain it. It simply has to do with the fact that all of you are living in the illusion of space and time that exists in the 3rd dimension. There is quite a bit of discussion taking place about time. What you don't speak of as much is the illusion of space. It is also a 3rd dimensional construct that helps provide humanity with a framework and reference points. Having this illusion of time and space provides you with a framework in which you may operate comfortably in your 3rd dimensional reality. We are not limited to those same constructs, so it is within our knowledge to create space in a different way than that which you are accustomed to. Indeed, this is another complex subject. We may or may not attempt to discuss it in more detail. Suffice it to say this is something that is available to us and utilized in our city. When I say we use our real estate efficiently, we most certainly do. I understand this is all very curious to you. On one hand you see things here that look familiar and comfortable, and then you see other things that you have not seen or contemplated before.

Bryan - *Yes indeed. (We are chuckling a bit)*

Adama - My friend, let us return now to the Great Hall. This is one of many visits that we will make into the city. I thought this would be a nice break from our routine.

Bryan - *Yes sir, this has been great. I look forward to seeing more of the city and making new friends.*

Adama - Yes, we are aware of all of those who come to visit the city, so your presence here with me is not such a huge event other than to express a welcoming and loving vibration to you while you are here visiting with us.

Bryan - *We return to the Great Hall and say our goodbyes. I am excited and grateful for this experience and look forward to the next one.*

# Chapter 2

## The Great Hall
## Master Adama on Light Language

### The Great Hall and Ruby Table

The Great Hall sits at what I perceive to be about 300 feet below the portal and meadow. The hall is perhaps a hundred and fifty feet in length and a hundred feet wide, forming the shape of a large rectangle. The walls are made of white marble, but they have a pearlescent radiance or sheen about them that is difficult to describe. There is light language of gold, actual gold, imprinted in various locations on each wall. The high, arched ceiling is made of gold with ribs spaced about three feet apart and spanning the width of the hall. There are two rows of grand columns that run lengthwise. At one end there is a small pool with several small benches located inside the columns. The pool is covered with blossoms of white lotus.

At the other end of the hall sits a table made of ruby crystal that seats ten. The table is made from a single, perfect crystal that is dark ruby red. The corners and edges are rounded and smooth. Light enters the table and refracts in wonderful ways. The chairs are grayish in color with a white marbling effect. Lemurians are considerably taller than we are so the table and chairs are a bit tall for me, but I manage easily to make myself comfortable. Master Adama says the chairs are made of a combination of mineral and stone; and the table, along with everything else I might see in the city, has been created with intention and purpose.

Just off to the side of the table is a large set of double doors made of the same white marble as the walls. Together, they are perhaps fifteen feet tall and twelve feet wide. The doors contain the most beautiful works of art made from gold and gemstones. There is a great golden sun in the very center of the door with various symbols and patterns going outward which I do not understand. The patterns are outlined in gold but there are also a wide variety of colored gemstones being used strategically throughout the design.

Master Emanuel (Member of the High Council of Telos) – We welcome you to the Great Hall. You are sensing the energy and vibration of Telos, yes, but also that of this Great Hall. This is where we will be doing our work. We ask that you open to allow and receive the vibration of the Great Hall and the truth of these messages. This is the reason this portal has been opened in this special location. This is something new. This portal has not been opened before. We have awaited this day and we are just as excited as you to begin this work.

Adama - Good afternoon Bryan. I am helping you to see the image of a long table in which there are council members on either side. I am sitting at one end of the table. You will see at the other end of the table there is an empty seat. However this seat is not empty. It is your seat. When you come to this place in this portal, you are here present with us. You sit at the table among us. As we deliver these messages, we want to reinforce to you that you are not separate from us, nor are you distant from us. We want you to hold this vision when you come to sit with us at the table in the Great Hall among your family and friends. You will hear us just as if you were sitting at the table speaking conversationally with us. Our conversational way of teaching will carry forth with the work you will do with us. As you come to this place, in the energy of this special portal, you will slowly and surely begin to harmonize your vibration with Telos, with the consciousness, the energy, and with the citizens of Telos. You will begin to have a better view, as it were, of the city and all of us here. We will speak of this from time to time in our work. For we know that you and our audience will have a great curiosity to learn more about the city and the way we live and do things here. We are happy to share this information.

Adama - Bryan, can you feel the energy that is being radiated out from the ruby table?

Bryan - *I feel the energy but I can't distinguish anything in particular.*

Adama - You'll remember we have discussed that everything in Telos is created with beauty and intention. This is a very special table that is suited to our project and the activity we are conducting here in this Great Hall. The ruby crystal that makes up this table has been placed here to assist us in this work. The dark red ruby color and its emanation and radiance remind us of our own bloodline lineage. This term "bloodlines" simply has to do with our lineage or ancestry. The vibrations and energy signatures being emitted from this large, ruby table remind us and you of your lineage as a Lemurian. You have other aspects and lineages; but in this project, we will discuss primarily your Lemurian lineage and family.

This crystal also emits qualities of integrity, truth, justice and balance. More importantly, the energy signature of this table has a radiance of life force energy. Within the human body, the blood is a primary carrier of life force. It provides the transportation and distribution throughout your body of the oxygen, nutrients and life force that sustain you. This table of ruby red crystal supports us in this project with a radiance of purity. We have used it previously in other locations around Telos. We thought it desirable to have it here to facilitate our work. Its energy is one of upliftment and the radiance of life force energy of all that is. Its energies breathe new life into us and into this work, just as the life force energy sent from Creator comes each day to breathe new life for all life everywhere. Its energies also have a calming effect. These energies will carry forth through our messages for the benefit of our readers also.

## Master Adama on Light Language

Adama - There are many dialects of light language depending on whom you are speaking with. Just as we have ways of easily understanding and interpreting the many languages being used on your planet today, we can also easily understand many varieties of light language being spoken in other areas of the cosmos. Many of us have our own dialects. We have developed our own languages and cultural enhancements to the language as time has gone by. This is a natural process. The language you are working with today is specific to our Lemurian culture. Many of you, at this time, are beginning to remember that you have worked with light languages in the past. They are being allowed to come in and flow through such that many of you are finding yourselves actually speaking them now. This is certainly not a requirement or anything you need to make an assessment of in terms of what you are or are not accomplishing. However, as this is allowed to take place or if it is allowed to take place, then what is happening is you are allowing yourself to open and channel the pure vibration of the light language as it is being given to you.

It is, in essence, the same process that you and I are undergoing in this now moment; however, the vibrations being sent and received are different. There is a benefit to those who are able to receive it and speak it in the manner in which it is presented. When someone has opened themselves to receive the pure light language vibration as it is being spoken/given, it is being allowed to come into the body where it may be channeled and spoken out again through the voice. Regardless of whether it is being channeled out again through the voice or not, that language comes in as a living language of light; and those attunements and those blessings for which it was intended are now embodied. It becomes anchored in the physical body. It is typically being anchored through the subconscious mind. Your conscious awareness receives it and acknowledges it (hears it, listens to it) and you may set your good intention alongside it as it flows into the levels of your being. That is to say, it flows into and through your subconscious mind also as is the case for all your inputs in human form. However, this differs because it is a living language. It has its own intelligence and activity such that it is allowed to pass through the conscious and subconscious minds in a pure state without judgments or doubt. It will actually move into the body and integrate at the cellular and DNA levels.

Your beloved I AM Presence, which is present in every cell of your body, knows how to receive and integrate the light language for your benefit.

When I say it comes into the body, I am speaking of the four lower bodies: physical, mental, emotional and spiritual. The body knows what to do with the light language, and the light language knows what to do with the body. You need not always understand the details but simply allow and trust that it is taking place for your benefit. On this day, because you have not yet reached a level where you are readily able to receive our transmission of light language, what we have done is to allow you to integrate and share it in a different way. You have received the light language present in the Great Hall as a visual transmission rather than an auditory transmission. You have seen the shapes and recognized it as light language. You have seen that through its own activity and intelligence, you might say it floated off of the wall and literally floated into your heart space and still point so it could be integrated into the body. Your four lower bodies will receive it in this manner in just the same way and with the same effectiveness as if it had been spoken to you and therefore received as an auditory transmission. This process has the same effectiveness and outcome, just a different way to go about it.

If someone is speaking light language you may not always know where the point of origin is. This is okay as long as you have used your discernment to guide you to align with those who you know to be working in the highest light and truth. In this way, you may be assured the transmission is coming from those of higher light and those whom the channel is aligned with, their greater family in heaven. Most of you, at this point in time, are not yet able to determine the particular dialect that you are receiving or listening to, nor are you able to translate the messages fully. Again, I would like to reiterate the point that although we refer to this as light language, we are talking about the transference of energy, intention and information. As such, it has its own intelligence and activity. This is very similar to the power of your own spoken word. Your spoken word carries these same attributes and the way you choose to use them in your daily life has a great influence on your overall experience. The light languages are simply of a higher vibration and the same forces are at play, but the vibration and application are stepped up significantly.

In Telos, we utilize our common Lemurian light language. We also, more often than not, simply use telepathy to communicate with one another. In this manner, we are not required to be in the same geographic location as the one we are choosing to communicate with. We may do this at any distance with great ease. Humanity too, at some point in your future, will evolve and expand into this ability. It is your divine inheritance and one of many gifts that innately resides in each of you now. These gifts have been lying dormant for ages and they have not yet been activated. It is likely to be some time before those abilities will become activated and the reason is just as you might imagine. Each one must have full mastery over his or her own thought processes and emotional/mental/physical bodies before this would be allowed to take place. Under the current circumstances and present consciousness of humanity, you might imagine some of the disruption and imbalance, if not utter chaos (Master Adama is smiling) that may result if you were able to use telepathy to communicate at this time. Most of you are not yet fully in control of your thoughts. Most of you are still learning your lessons around judgment for example. Even you

Master Bryan. If you were to go out in public and see one of your brothers and sisters, and for whatever reason your personal perception of them caused you to have judgment about them in some way, you wouldn't want that thought and transmission to be sent to the them. You would not choose to convey to them an energy that might create disharmony and imbalance within them simply because you were unable to control the manner of your thought.

As humanity moves firmly into the upper $4^{th}$ and lower $5^{th}$ dimensional experience, one of the attributes you will gain is to have full authority and dominion over your own thoughts. At that time, these attributes, which are your divine inheritance, will be activated such that humanity will learn to communicate telepathically just as most of us at this level of awareness and above are already doing. This is part of the evolutionary process; and it will happen fairly quickly, relatively speaking, once you are all firmly planted in the New Earth consciousness. This is just one example of the many enhancements that will be coming forth for humanity. As you reach higher levels of attainment, these new levels of vibration will naturally begin to awaken those dormant attributes. We will assist each of you along the way. We would not wish that an attribute such as this become fully active from its dormant state just now because you are not yet fully prepared to receive it or manage it appropriately. You could receive, instead, a negative experience. The Higher Self of each of you will dictate the speed and timing of this for each individual.

So yes, you may also choose to receive the benefit of light language attunements through your vision and intention. Some of you are working with what you refer to as templates. Within these templates are written forms of light language which are intended for various purposes. As you softly gaze upon them and set your intention to open and receive the benefit of that light language, intelligence and activity within you, so it will be done.

I said just a moment ago, the process is that it comes in through conscious awareness in most cases and flows through the subconscious and then flows out into all other aspects of being and cellular levels within the body. The same processes take place regardless of the method in which it has come into your being. Allow it to integrate through the power of your own intention. One of your many teachers has taught, and we thought it was very well said: "Energy follows intention. Matter follows energy". This is a very basic but most useful understanding that applies in many aspects of doing and being that you will encounter here and elsewhere in your experience. It is no more complicated than that. If you are working with a visual template, you begin by setting your intention for the work. You then invite/allow the energy to come into your beingness and to express its intelligence and activity for your highest good, and it will be so. Also, as is the case with many of the activities and tools that each of you are working with, there is a compounding effect in the use of light language. The more you work with it, the more benefit you receive. The more you work with it, the stronger the vibration and the more integration takes place.

As the months and years ahead come into view, many of you in the lightworker community will expand your consciousness to the level of having more and more understanding and remembrance of the light languages. I use this as a simple example. Let us say one of your earth plane teachers is speaking light language and you know via your discernment that this is a divinely guided activity. Although you know you are receiving blessings, activations and attunements, you do not understand the words that are being spoken and often neither does the channel. In regard to this example, in a relatively short span of time many of you will have expanded such that you are able to receive and transmit or simply receive light language in a way that you will have an understanding of that which is being spoken and gifted to you. You will inherently and naturally, as your intuition is expanded, begin to understand the words that are being spoken. I say this in hopes of bringing encouragement and to give you an idea of the fast track that many of you are on. There will be many experiences, what you might call gifts, coming to you in a relatively short period of time. Many of you in the lightworker community are now on a fast track to further expansion and growth. You are in the express lane and things are moving quickly. The children who are coming onto the planet today, to some extent, already have these dormant attributes partially awakened. They are not yet fully awakened, and that will happen according to each ones Higher Self and divine blueprint. I bring this to your attention to let you know that many of the younger ones, by the time they reach your age will be fully immersed and communicative in the light language arts and particularly those that are in alignment with their lineage and dialect. This is a natural part of the process that is taking place.

I would like to say to you that all manner of light language might eventually be trusted. (A question came into your thought process earlier so I thought I would address it.) However, this is not the case at this particular time. It will shift. Again, there are many dialects of light language; and just because you hear someone speaking light language does not mean that you should open yourself to receive that which is on offer. I do not say this to create any anxiety within you but simply a reminder as always, to use your own discernment and inner guidance. This is an important quality and activity for any such work that you may choose to participate in. Just as you would not blindly trust something you read on the internet or hear on the news, we encourage the use of your discernment in regards to light languages also. Remember always that you are divine sovereign beings of light. Simply state and ask that you are always working in the highest light and truth and always under the protection of the Light of God and it will be so. Nothing more need be done.

# Chapter 3

## Ahatana and the Great Shift

Bryan - *Master Adama, would you mind speaking about the Lemurians in Hawaii and their city there?*

Adama - Yes, Bryan we can speak on this subject. This has come into your awareness on several occasions. And so you know that in our last Golden Age the surface of Gaia was much different. Through the ending of the last Golden Age, what I often refer to as the last great shift, there was the last great flood. It is the same one referenced in your Bible and other spiritual traditions. Additionally, there were a number of other shifts taking place at that time with plate tectonics moving, tidal flooding, earthquakes and volcanoes and so on. You might say everything changed in the blink of an eye. If we look at the bigger picture of your earthtime history, these changes came about relatively quickly such that the landmasses and continents underwent great change. Many of the landmasses, which contained many inhabitants, cities and communities, were lost in this great shift. It was foretold that the shift was coming. Many Lemurians at that time were given the prophecy, and we were given instructions about where to go and what to do such that we might be safe and that we might establish new communities and cities that would support us in the days ahead. That is exactly what we did.

We will not spend much time discussing the details of the last great shift. It was, needless to say, an extremely difficult and challenging time for all of us who were there; and many of you reading this book were there. Many of you have an awareness of this. Many of you had multiple embodiments both as Atlanteans and Lemurians, and also many of you were there during the time of the great shift at the end of our Golden Age as we knew it. For many of you, this has come into your awareness, and a part of your forward progress in this embodiment has included the releasing and clearing of your Akash and cellular memory of all that no longer serves you. As you go through the process of expanding your awareness, what often happens is that you tap into other aspects of your being which you may not have readily connected with before. There are any number of examples we could use to describe this situation; but for many of you, you have had or will have remembrance at some level that you were there at the time of the last great shift. Many of you still carry emotions and memories that are painful for you, such as sadness, grief, or perhaps even guilt. This is one of the reasons why many of you are drawn to these messages because you remember and you know; somehow you just know that you were there. Perhaps you have also come to know that you have friends and family today who were also there with you in those times. Many of them have been on a similar path as you. You are here today in the human embodiment, and many of you are having a knowing or remembrance at some level of your Lemurian aspects and your previous Lemurian embodiments.

Bryan - *Master Adama, for those of us who are here now and for whom it has come into our awareness that we have had past embodiments as Lemurians or Atlanteans, would it also be true that each of us has an aspect of ourselves who is also currently residing in the form of a Lemurian or Atlantean in Middle Earth or elsewhere?*

Adama - Yes, this is the case. This is the awareness that you and many others are coming into now. When we say you have friends and family members here, in fact many of you who will be reading this book will come to find in your own awareness and in your own way that you also have an aspect of your being, within the fullness of your being, that is also currently in a Lemurian embodiment. This would be one of the primary reasons why you might be drawn to this material. So yes, we chose to stay here even at that time of the great shift. We understood the importance of this decision in that we were to be of service to the next lineages and future generations of humanity. We have chosen to be in service in this way to humanity, Gaia and to all life sharing the planet. At that time, as we were coming into the great shift, that is to say as we were building up to the time of actual events and many of the cataclysmic earth changes, we were foretold of these events and we were also given instructions as to how we should proceed in setting about the rebuilding and reestablishment of our communities. We were also guided to the activities that would need to be done and maintained through the course of the great age (just under 26,000 years), which came to an end in your year 2012.

We are moving into the next great age now. Even at that time and despite the very difficult and challenging circumstances for all, we knew the importance of our role and service to Creator, which is also our service to Gaia, humanity and all life. We were guided to establish new communities in areas we were told would be safe zones for us, so we gathered together and abandoned the life that we knew. Those that could fled and moved elsewhere. It was a requirement for most of our communities and civilization that we undergo change, and there are a number of reasons for this. One reason was the coming of cataclysmic events but also of navigating the circumstances of the day if you will. At that time before the great shift, the present day islands of Hawaii were indeed the motherland. The continent of Lemuria sank and these islands are all that remain.

The capital city of Lemuria is Ahatana near the present day island of Maui. This was the greatest landmass at that time and it was the most inhabited region of Lemuria or Mu. Lemuria at that time was in a golden age and we were living a much different lifestyle than the one you know today; we had civilizations and cities all around the globe. We had the establishment of government, social systems, trade routes and cities; and let me remind you that we had higher forms of technology in use at that time so our travel and communication were different than what you experience today in your world. The city of Ahatana is still flourishing today. Telos is our largest city in the Agartha Network. This was one of the primary locations to which we were directed, at that time, to come and reestablish our civilization. Telos is where we built our largest city and this is where we reestablished what you might consider to be the capital. This is where we have moved many of our temples of light, sacred artifacts, technology and knowledge. We were not the only ones. Telos was not the only flagship city that was established at that time. Past disagreements have been set aside a long time ago. We are working here within the Agartha Network, Atlanteans and Lemurians, in the same endeavor. We are all cooperating and playing our parts according to the grand project plan and we are all working together in a cooperative manner to achieve the same goals. We travel freely as we wish. Atlanteans into Lemurian cities and otherwise; so I just wish to express to you there are no grievances or unresolved issues here. We in the Agartha Network are all in unity consciousness and service to the light.

It took about two thousand years for things to settle after the last great shift. The earth changes, shifts and the transformation of Gaia after the last Golden Age took place rather quickly compared to what your science understands as Earth's history and the cataclysmic events that have shaped her into form. What I will tell you is, yes, these events of the great flood, seismic and volcanic activities, the movement of plates, the sinking of some continents and the birth of new continents and so on took place on an accelerated scale. Your history will show and perhaps scientists would argue and say, "No, these kinds of changes take hundreds of thousands of years to complete their cycles and come about". Our last Golden Age in your linear time ended around 12,000 years ago. Just to say, we are setting the pin at the end of the last great shift at 12,000 years give or take; but let us keep in mind also, the events we are discussing also include planetary destruction resulting from the great wars that had also been taking place for thousands of years leading up to this marker that we are calling the end of the great shift. As we were coming out of the great shift, there was a period of time of several thousand years when Gaia was settling again. It was a very challenging time for all of life on the planet. Gaia was undergoing monumental change; all of the civilizations that had been experiencing life in the Golden Age were now drawing to an end. All life on the planet was affected by the shift. There was no part of this world that was not impacted by these events and they were quite severe.

These changes took place in a relatively short period of time despite what your textbooks might say on the subject. At the apex of the shift, continents sank and the face of Gaia shifted practically overnight followed by a settling period of about 2,000 years. Gaia began to settle again and while this was taking place, we had been instructed to come and build our great city of Telos here in the mountain. Those who were able, made our way to the building or further establishment of those cities where we could ride out these cataclysmic events that were to be forthcoming, and this is what has happened. There were a number of cities that were either reestablished or reaffirmed, meaning they were expanded in some way, and there were new cities also that were built. We have a network here within what you refer to as Middle Earth where our civilizations now reside, and we have cities around the globe. We have cities on most of your major continents, and they are made up primarily of Atlantean or Lemurian inhabitants. These cities have been strategically located in their geographic positions such that we could assist Gaia and humanity in holding the balance and holding the flames along with the promise of a new Golden Age to come. We have just closed one great age or cycle and stepped through the doorway of a new one. We are now moving confidently toward our next Golden Age.

There, in your present day Hawaii is the city of Ahatana where we have family and friends, and we travel back and forth regularly. This is true for our entire network of cities. We have tunnels and merkaba light vehicles and technologies that allow us to easily move back and forth. I can say that you all would be most surprised and delighted if you could come and experience this with your own eyes and your own senses. Do not despair. You will all have the opportunity at some point to experience it for yourselves.

We are your family and we have been here patiently awaiting this time. We have been holding light for humanity. We have kept the sacred fires burning on your behalf. We have awaited this time, the opening of this next great age where all of us here in the higher realms would be able to step forward and make ourselves known in a more obvious way. We knew that more and more of you would be coming into your awakening, not only to accept us and our truth, but to begin to have your own remembrance and recall of your own inner truth that you have direct ties to your Lemurian and Atlantean families who remain here in your service yet today. This is taking place now, and it is one of the reasons why we are so excited to be here delivering these messages to you.

The community of Ahatana in Hawaii is much smaller than Telos. As things began to settle down after the last shift; we began to further establish ourselves in our new environment. Many chose to go out to create new communities or to join with others. However, there were many here who had lived and had family, friends and history in the city of Ahatana; and the same is true for other cities. So as things began to settle down, there were those of us who wanted to go back to those places where we had ties and personal history. This was according to each ones choosing and so we had expansion again. In the case of Ahatana, the city had to be rebuilt. You see, through these changes and events, we were required to relocate from the surface to our Inner Earth cities such as Telos. We had the technology and we were also given great assistance that was necessary to facilitate all of this. Our brothers and sisters from other star nations came to assist us in the building and construction of these cities. It seems logical that we would want to branch out and expand our network of communities, and that is what we've done.

Although the city of Ahatana is smaller than Telos, we have a community of Lemurians living there and doing great work in participation with our project plan. Many of the oldest and wisest members of our communities live in Ahatana now. They are working with the energies of that place and with the people who are drawn there. There are many who are drawn to Hawaii just as there are those who are drawn here to the mountain of Shasta because they recognize something within. They remember these places as being sacred and they recognize their ties to them. They remember what was once the magnificence and beauty of their homeland city, and it is quite beautiful today. But it has changed. The face and structure have changed. Since we are no longer living on the surface, we have taken all that we knew and all of the beauty that we had known and we have held onto that. Although the landscape and cityscape will differ according to the preferences of those communities, what you would find is they are all most exquisite and magnificent, each in their own way. So the city of Ahatana is a most beautiful city and this is where some of our elders choose to be at this time. There is a great history there. This was our homeland city for all of Mu. It was a great and most magnificent city, and there are many who are still drawn to those energies. Even through the many shifts that have taken place, the energies of that place are still intact. They never left and they were never destroyed, so there is a powerful, reverent and beautiful energy and light there in that place. At a later date we may continue this discussion and we may discuss some of the other cities around the globe. In this way we are able to help hold space and light for your communities there on the surface. Our proximity to other geographic locations is beneficial for the whole.

Bryan - *Master Adama, are the Atlanteans and Lemurians the only beings that make up the Agartha Network?*

Adama - The Agartha Network is basically this network that we have described of the various cities and cultures here in what you refer to as Middle Earth. They are 5th dimensional cities that are physically located within the body of Gaia. We have the ability via our technology to create the most natural surroundings. They would be most beautiful and pleasing to most of you. This network is comprised of cities and communities of those of us who have established ourselves here and we are all connected by our technology and otherwise. Travel and communication to and from are easy and something we do each day.

The Agartha Network primarily consists of Lemurians and Atlanteans; however, we also have cities that serve as outposts. These outposts may be used by other beings who are coming in at this time to offer their assistance to Gaia and humanity. There are many advanced beings such as the Pleiadians, Sirians, Andromadans, Arcturians and many others coming now to offer their assistance in this way. The Sirians, for example, are very good with the finer workings of planetary bodies. They are assisting Gaia with her body electromagnetics, which affect her equilibrium and balance. They are helping to re-establish her ley lines and crystalline grids. These are her energy centers and networks that function in ways that are similar to the meridians and chakra energy centers of your own bodies. As another example, the Sirians work with her ocean currents and jet streams to facilitate further clearing. Many of your lightworker community are also being invited to participate in these activities. There are some from your lightworker community who refer to themselves as grid workers, and that is exactly the work they are being guided to do. The elementals and Devic angel kingdoms also participate in these kinds of activities. So again, I refer back to our holistic approach.

We have a number of cities that serve as scientific outposts, and we have had a number of visitors living here in Middle Earth helping us in advanced ways, specifically to assist Gaia in her ascension. Your starseed families from Sirius are advanced beings who resemble you in many ways. Many of them have also chosen to come into embodiment here on Gaia as whale and dolphin beings and consciousness. One of their primary tasks is to hold vibrations of love and joy for the planet. That is what they are doing. This is a great service to humanity and all life here even though most are not aware this is what is taking place. And so there are others who are coming in to work with us in our network, and they are specifically working with Gaia in most cases. We have those who come and go according to the needs and direction of the project plan so we work with many project teams and a variety of beings, but as far as the Agartha Network goes, we have visitors that come and go and we have scientific outposts, but it is mostly comprised of your Lemurian and Atlantean families.

Bryan – Note: *As we were wrapping up the first draft of this book, Master Adama encouraged me to go back and read the Telos books again, knowing I would find questions along the way. It had been several years, by this time since I'd read them. Therefore, you may see several follow-up conversations along the way.*

Bryan - *Master Adama, you and Aurelia mention a race of beings called Hyperboreans who also inhabit the Agartha Network, yet there is no mention of them here in this discussion. Why is that?*

Adama - What we will say, Bryan is, yes, the Agartha Network here in Middle Earth, while it is primarily made up of Lemurians and Atlanteans, some of the first inhabitants to Middle Earth were a race of beings known as Hyperboreans. They came from the Borealis star systems several hundred thousand years ago. They came here as was requested by Creator and also by Gaia. They were not the first to settle here. They were led to come and build an outpost civilization. The race of Hyperboreans is an advanced level of beings who came to hold balance and light for the planet. It was also a natural extension of their culture for them to have gone out to new frontiers to establish outposts of their homeland civilizations. They have been here off and on, as I have said for hundreds of thousands of years. Up until fairly recently by our account, they remained as some of the primary inhabitants of the Agartha Network.

They also cultivated and maintained a segment of their population here in Gaia's Middle Earth. They were of great assistance to us at the time of the last great shift as we made our pleas as a society to evolve to a 5th dimensional consciousness. Our plea was granted and we were allowed to begin constructing our own crystal cities. The Hyperboreans offered us a great deal of assistance in how we were to make our transition. They, and others, taught us how to create our own crystal cities and establish tunnel systems along with a variety of other helpful information. Much of what we have here in our Lemurian and Atlantean cities now in Middle Earth comes from that which they and others have given to us. We have taken what they gave us so long ago, and we have expanded on it greatly. We have thrived.

They along with other great beings of light such as those you know as the Holy Kumaras of Venus, established the now etheric city of Shamballa in the area of your modern day Northern Tibet.

It has had several locations over time, including the Gobi desert area, which looked much different then. It was not a desert. It is a city of great wonder and magnificence. It is one of the most glorious cities of MIddle Earth, and it is also the most ancient of cities in the Agartha Network. It was originally a surface city like Ahatana. The reason you have some reference in your mythology to Shamballa is because it is a primary energy center for Gaia. For a great long time within the interior of Middle Earth, Shamballa has been the key anchor for enlightenment for this planet. There have been many masters and sages who have come and gone through your recorded history and otherwise who had knowledge of this place. Many of the masters and sages of old expanded their awareness and consciousness such that they communed with these ancient beings there in the city of Shamballa, but certainly not all of the beings in Shamballa have been of the Hyperborean race. Our Earth history is complex and we could fill volumes and volumes. The city of Shamballa is occupied by a variety of beings coming back and forth, and we often have meetings there. Some of the traditions in your Far East––the culture, tradition and teachings–– come from the beings and masters of Shamballa. Those in the Eastern cultures generally have a greater awareness than those of the Western cultures. We have a difference there primarily due to the global position on the planet, so those cultures who have been close to the city have received some of their understanding and tradition from there, you see.

Most of the Hyperboreans have returned back to their homeland or they have gone on to new frontiers. One of the reasons for this is that as we, the Lemurians and Atlanteans, were able to elevate our societies to unity consciousness in a 5D and higher awareness, we have been able to assume the responsibilities of holding the balance of light for this world. As we have assumed these responsibilities, it has not been a requirement for them to fulfill this duty.

• • •

Yes, there has been a dark presence in Middle Earth just as there is on the surface. I am answering your question. Just as the Lemurians and Atlanteans of the Agartha Network have remained here for thousands of years, so too have those who chose to act in separation at that time. It was once a Golden Age. The time and Land of Mu. Our civilizations spanned the globe and all were living in prosperity and peace. There were segments of our society who chose to move away from the light. Things escalated quickly and continued for thousands of years. Many of the populations in Atlantis severely opposed the behaviors and activities they saw taking place. Those who were knowingly and willingly acting in dark ways did not act alone. It's more complicated than that.

Generally speaking, the surface world doesn't yet have an established terminology of many of the topics we're speaking of. You asked me if I had a preference between "Middle", "Inner" or "Hollow" Earth and I said I did not. There are many like you who enjoy the term Middle Earth that was made popular by the author Tolkien's successful novels. You enjoy using the name Middle Earth and that is okay.

Many refer to the Agartha Network as encompassing everything within the Inner Earth. It does not. The Agartha Network is made up of cities and communities that have ascended to the fifth dimension. There are places within the Inner Earth where dark activities have and continue to take place. However, they are not a part of our Agartha Network and their days are short. Those working in the lower dimensions do not have access to those of us in the higher dimensions. This refers back to one of our other discussions. We are protected in the light.

# Chapter 4

## Project Organization Chart

Adama - Bryan, on your last visit we took a walk through the city past the amphitheater where some of our entertainment takes place. It also serves as a public forum where our citizens may be addressed. I've told you that we have other facilities here that may also be used to hold formal meetings, and I thought we might speak more on this subject today.

I've described our city to you as a hub and meeting place. There are a number of locations here and around the planet where we may meet in large groups, project teams and councils to discuss many topics but those primarily having to do with the status and plans for humanity, Gaia and indeed for all life sharing the planet now. There are an almost unbelievable number of projects taking place under the umbrella of the grand project plan that has been set forth by our Creator. Within this wide variety of projects taking place, there are many, many beings who have come to participate and to assist Gaia and humanity in making this next great shift into the New Earth. There are many locations in which various teams may meet to discuss their project plans including the World Pyramid residing in the $5^{th}$ dimension, in the way you might perceive it, just outside of Gaia's atmosphere. This pyramid is a a primary control and coordination station for all that is taking place here and it is literally massive in size. It is much, much larger than any physical structure you are familiar with. There are many levels in the World Pyramid; and it has been created such that many different beings from around the cosmos, who have agreed to come and participate in the project, may spend time there comfortably. Different levels have been created intentionally to suit a particular race of being such that when they spend time there they may reside in an environment that is comfortable and natural to them.

I will provide you with a partial list of beings who are here assisting us all at this time. Gaia is guiding the way. The Devic angel kingdoms and elemental kingdoms are participating alongside Gaia. The Elohim along with multitudes and legions of Archangels and angels bless us continuously and without fail. The great Avatars, Ascended Masters, Holy Kumaras and Christed Beings of Light continue to hold the world in the embrace of their divine light. They have supported Gaia and humanity through its dark ages and planetary dark night of the soul experience with divine love and illumination. Those you know as Jesus, Mother Mary, Gautama Buddha, Master Saint Germain, Master El Morya Master Mary Magdalene, Master Hilarion, and many others work to guide humanity to their light and divinity within. Many of the ascended master councils that you are familiar with such as the Great White Brotherhood, the Order of Melchizedek, Abraham and others are all great participants in this project. There are many members from many star nations present such as the Sirians, Arcturians, Pleiadians and Andromedans. Lemurians in Telos and other Inner Earth cities have awaited this time also with great anticipation.

The dragons, unicorns and many other higher dimensional beings that you are not yet aware of are acting here to your collective benefit and greater good. Sun star planetary beings and other heavenly bodies are naturally and fundamentally involved in this great shift. Lastly and of great importance, each and every one of you are participating in this project through that which you collectively create in your moment-to-moment chosen experience. You are getting the idea that there are a wide variety of contributors all working for a common goal: primarily one of unity consciousness and love as the new paradigm for all life here, which we are referring to as the next great Golden Age and the creation of New Earth. Decrees have been set forth by our Creator. This is what we are referring to in these works as the grand project and the grand project plan.

In addition to providing comfortable lodging, the World Pyramid is large enough that many of the ships being used by our brethren are actually able not only to dock there but also to come fully into the bays of the pyramid. You have read a description from another messenger describing the Pleiadian ship New Jerusalem; and you were told that the ship is so large that if it were to hover close to the surface of Gaia that it would cover nearly the geography of the United States. This is an accurate description of how you might perceive the size of this ship. All of the star nations have craft that are suitable to facilitate meetings that might take place, and many of these star craft have also been designed to accommodate the needs of various other beings that they know may be visiting with them.

The Archangels, Ascended Masters and Seven Mighty Elohim have many etheric temples and retreats in the higher dimensions close to Gaia's atmosphere as you might perceive it. One example is the Royal Teton Retreat above the Tetons of Wyoming, which is overseen by Master Saint Germain and Master Confucius. There are a variety of activities that take place in these retreats, but they are mostly used as meeting halls for students or family of that particular master. These halls are also often used to meet and discuss our project plans. This has to do with the bringing together of those members of the master's family who may be a part of their project team. Many of you may be joining us in these locales at night while you are in your sleep time.

There are also cities such as our great city of Telos where we may hold our meetings. You might say it is a cosmically international city. We've gone to great lengths to make others feel comfortable here and we take great pride in being a host city. There are times when the Lemurian Council and/or I and others may be asked to attend a meeting in some other location, in which case we might use our merkaba light vehicles or taxi ships to travel to that location and attend the meetings. We are in constant communication with our Lemurian family in the Dahl universe and elsewhere. We have a great fleet of ships and we may travel in them also. There is no need for a fleet of ships here in Telos. So, we have a variety of locations in which we may meet, but the World Pyramid is a primary hub for the larger scale project.

Yes, although many of us residing in a 5D vibration or higher have the ability to communicate telepathically, there are different levels of communication taking place with a range of low-medium-high. This is part of your question that I'm answering here. Our Creator has issued His Holy Decrees and set forth a series of blueprints and plans representing His Divine Will. There are a great many intermediary channels from which the grand blueprint will flow down to other levels of heavenly hierarchy. The list I provided earlier does not even begin to reveal the magnitude and complexity of this subject. The appropriate information will come down through the hierarchy for which it was designed and intended. As it flows down, it reaches us at our level wherever each one is. These are the project teams that have been assembled. The grand plan from Creator is sent out from the Heart of Creator and is stepped down, so to speak, such that other levels of hierarchy may work with it, understand it and have something that you might say is tangible. There are many different levels of consciousness and activity taking place among this hierarchy that I am describing. As it flows down it reaches the level of activity taking place at the World Pyramid and those individuals with high-ranking authority and responsibility. Master Saint Germain is the sponsor of the Aquarian age and the great shift taking place now. This is where the Maha Chohan, Master Saint Germain and others will take the higher levels of the plan and break them out into smaller projects with each smaller piece feeding into the whole. I am describing this by way of analogy of how you might see a large project function in the corporate world which many of you are familiar with. This is a basic form of organization and it is taking place in a similar way here.

While we are all at different levels of awareness and understanding, many of us have the ability to communicate telepathically. However that does not forgo the opportunity that is afforded us when we all join together in a great hall and have a discussion about it. Again, it's similar to how you all see things being done. Teams are assembled. We know who the team leaders and contributors are, and everyone has responsibility to their level of the project. It is very advantageous for us to come together in the halls, retreats, cities or ships to assemble our teams.

We usually begin with a review of our piece of the project and next we will review the overall project plans to see how the various teams are making their way. We would see then, at a higher level, how the comprehensive project plan is coming together. We are all working together. We are not separate project teams running off with our own ideas and agendas. There is a method and process that must be followed. Our progress forward is event driven. It is not driven by the linear construct of time, so it is important that we all remain in sync with what is taking place in other areas of the project. We have ways to do this. Things are moving very quickly now and we are not able to predict the course of events from one week to the next. Human free will and co-creation power are always acting, and as new energies and vibratory levels bathe the planet, we see the results being played out. It is necessary for us to continually monitor the events taking place and there are a variety of ways in which we can do this. You have been shown, for example, that from the viewpoint of the World Pyramid (and other locales) that you may see through an expanded awareness the amount of light that is being absorbed, integrated and applied throughout all of humanity. That is to say, we can look from that perspective at our planet Gaia, and we can see the amount of light that is shining or emanating back from you. We can place our awareness on the God force quotient of light that is being allowed to shine through the human embodiments. We can see this, and we can calculate this to some extent. It is not a non-feeling algebraic type of calculation, but it simply allows us to observe our progress in this regard. So that is one example.

There are certain percentages of light and clearing of collective karma that must be attained globally before certain next events are allowed to take place. This is a good example of what I am attempting to describe to you. When X% of the population have balanced X% of their karma and are now receiving, integrating and distributing X% of their light quotient, we might say we have reached a milestone. By "distributing" in this case I mean a person is allowing or intending some of their light quotient to express itself out into the world in alignment with the light of Creator and for the greatest good of all. The next activity is then allowed to move forward. Our plans are in a constant state of adjustment at this time, and there is a tremendous amount of work and activity taking place here in this location of our galaxy. This is, to some extent, an oversimplified description; but it is generally the way things take place and it is a description I believe you are comfortable with.

Bryan - *Yes sir. I am just sitting here contemplating the complexity of this project, and I am curious about how the Will of Creator is expressed and how that information is actually stepped down such that those of various levels of awareness may receive it and work with it.*

Adama - Yes, there is a lot to contemplate. In the stepping down of divine energies that you are questioning and wanting to know about, our Beloved Helios and Vesta who you may think of as sun star planetary beings are the supreme rulers or Godparents of this solar system. Divine Will flows from the Sun Behind the Sun to universes, galaxies, solar systems and on it goes. Divine love, wisdom and will express through the Great Central Sun of our Galaxy and then out to our own. We will discuss later that heavenly bodies are just that. From those levels it continues to flow down through the Elohim and many other great beings of light, the Archangels, Ascended Masters, The Great White Brotherhood, the Great Divine Director, the Maha Chohan, Master Saint Germain, the Galactic Federation Council and so on. Humanity receives their information and instruction via their Higher Selves, and the elemental kingdoms receive their information and instruction from the Devic angels and the Elohim; and so it goes throughout all levels of being with the appropriate message being transmitted in the perfect way for each level of being to receive it. I am attempting to answer your question within a framework that you can relate to. The answers to all of your questions will become clear for each of you as you aspire to and reach the higher dimensional planes of consciousness and love.

I wish to add a reminder that in the higher Realms of Light we are free of the limitation that you experience in your old 3D paradigm. As fully aware beings, we access information in ways that you are not yet familiar with. I have been using the analogy of a corporate structure and project plan to help give you an idea of how things are unfolding. We are all joyful in our alignment. Everyone here across the veil, regardless of what level of the project plan they have chosen to participate in, is working the expression of their own divinity. They are working in manners and on subject topics that they have a natural interest in or that provide them with desired growth opportunities. Some may work with the environment. Some may be teaching at high levels and some may be healers. My point is, we work in a way that all are in a natural alignment and joy with their level of participation. We choose not to participate in the lower vibrational behaviors that you all have experienced. We do not allow our meetings or our societies for that matter, to become ugly or to be ruled by negative expressions such as dishonesty, greed, intimidation, etc. Now, that is not to say we will not, at times, enjoy passionate debates and discussions. We do. We are all free here to express our thoughts and opinions when we are gathered together in these meetings, and we do often have lively conversations; but we are also working within a framework that you do not experience in your old 3rd dimensional reality. We are working without the interference of ego, and we are experiencing the love vibration of unity consciousness.

All who are present and participating on this grand project plan, regardless of where they are and where they come from, have chosen by their own free will to come and be of service in this way. They have chosen to participate in areas of service that are natural and fulfilling to them. We do this with the knowledge that all will benefit in their own way and in a way that brings joy and fulfillment to them. When one expands we all expand. We come for our love and service to Creator and for all of life everywhere. We, the members of the project teams, come from the far reaches of the cosmos now to support humanity and your world at large. The responsibility lies also with each of you to create the New Earth you so desire.

# Chapter 5

## Life on New Earth, Moving from 3D to 5D
## Gaia's transition from 3D to 5D
## Follow up discussion about Gaia

### Life on New Earth, Moving from 3D to 5D

Adama - Yes Bryan, it is good to see you again also. Our city is bustling this morning as our daily activities get underway. In this regard, there are many similarities between Telos and your cities on the surface. We have days for work and days for play. We don't spend nearly as much time working as most of you do. We strive for balance. In your calendar week of 7 days, most of us will work 3-4 days and perhaps 5-6 hours per day by your time. Everyone here contributes to the greater good and everyone performs a function that is naturally suited to them. We all enjoy the work we are doing. We go about our work with happy hearts. We take pride in our work and each of us is able to see and understand the benefit and greater good that come from our individual contributions. In this way, we have an appreciation for our own individual efforts, which we set forth for the betterment of ourselves and of all of us here in the city. We appreciate the high standards of living and the quality of life that all of us in Telos enjoy.

Our work is not the same as your work. Some of the nuances of this statement may be difficult to understand simply because we are living and working in a 5th dimensional reality that is free of the constructs of duality that are experienced in your 3rd dimensional reality. As you go about your day and your work, many of you often feel trapped because you require income and financial resources to sustain yourselves; therefore, most of you work for those resources. Many of you are not in work that is joyful to you. Many of you feel that your work is not facilitating your personal growth and certainly not leading to your fulfillment; however, you continue to push on through because it is the requirement of the day.

Most of you, if you are working for an employer, a business or government agency, etc. will work between thirty to fifty hours a week and many of you more than that. The situation around your social and work environment has been created in most societies and populations around the world; and it is a part of your 3D experience, yes; but it is also a construct that has been put in place and given all sorts of fancy labels and descriptions such that you all will feel better about it. It has been established and presented in a way that makes sense for most of you; and because this is what your leaders require and because this is what all of your friends and family are doing, this is what you do also. You fit into a model of society that has its own framework and methods of operation. So when we talk about individual contributors here in Telos and the work they do, I would like to express to you that the framework of working, as it is tied to the individual and collective economic success of an individual, a family or a city, is much different.

We rely on a barter system. We have forms of currency; however, most of our work and life experiences are organized in such a way that we may take advantage of a barter system. Because we have created our societal framework in 5D, we do not require the use of paper currency to acquire goods and services as you do. Our entire what you might refer to as an "economic system" functions in a completely different way. Because we are all experiencing unity consciousness, we do not have the worry of our leaders taking advantage of those of a lesser economic status. The greed and corruption that take place within your business and government models and within the framework of work and productivity of a society do not exist here. We have been able to create a system where everyone is allowed to contribute in ways that are pleasing to them; and, as a result, everyone is also allowed to reap the benefits and rewards of the collective society.

We do not live in a society of the haves and have-nots. We are not functioning in a class system with a ruling class, elite economic class, middle class and lower class or however it is you choose to label them. These kinds of class systems have developed in all areas and nations on Earth to one extent or another, and we see a variety of social structures in between. The imbalances are severe and you all know this very well. In Telos, we have forms of governance and structure with high ranking spiritual leaders and ruling councils of various natures, but they all function in their joyful alignment with the greatest good for all. We have created social structures that are trusted and enjoyed by all of us. When I say trusted, what I mean is, again, there is no concern on the part of the average citizen that they may somehow be taken advantage of by their employer, their government or anyone else. They know that we are all working in a 5D awareness; and therefore those kinds of actions and behaviors, which are everyday occurrence in your societies, simply do not take place here.

Additionally, it is not necessary for an individual to meet certain requirements that most of you are subject to. For example, if you want to keep your job, you may be required to work 8 hours a day, 5 days a week. You must also meet certain performance expectations to keep your job and in hopes of a marginal increase in income. That is not to say we don't have any requirements for all jobs that are to be done. It is a reasonable expectation that any job must have requirements for its successful completion; but we have great flexibility in terms of how we manage the needs of the community. There are more than enough of us to perform the necessary work, and to enjoy time off or to choose a different life path is not an issue whatsoever. We do not struggle with physical imbalance so having time off for illness, for example, is not a concern.

We do also have new childbirth. Certainly, not at the alarming rate in which it takes place on the surface, but we do have children. Our developmental periods are considerably longer than yours due to the extended lifetimes we live. The development of our children and the health of the family unit are of the utmost priority for all of us. Those who choose to start a family will have spent many years together with contemplation and counseling to ensure their decision is in the best interest for all involved. Parents have plenty of time and resources to raise their children as they choose, and the community shares parenting and child rearing responsibilities. We have plenty who are available and enjoy doing the work that is required. Those choosing to work on an endeavor or project for their individual growth, expansion and enjoyment are highly encouraged to do so. There are checks and balances used to facilitate this kind of activity, but there are many opportunities available to us both inside and outside of the city. There are an almost infinite number of other cities and locations that someone may choose to travel to for higher levels of learning and service, and many of our citizens take advantage of those opportunities.

Moreover, we utilize technology here in Telos that is not yet present in your world. Much of the day-to-day work you see taking place around you that would be considered a requirement to keep things moving (your electricity and energy demands, fuels for transportation and heating, architecture and infrastructure, clothing and other manufactured goods, etc.) are being done in drastically different ways. We have technology in use that affords us great benefit in many of these areas such that workers are not necessary for many of the tasks you are familiar with.

We have many of the same types of job titles as you do that are also requirements of our society. Even though we have higher forms of technology available to us, we still need to maintain the daily operation of our city. In addition to the infrastructure of our city, we have natural places such as the Fields of Telos, which are not all that different than many of your own natural places. We have a wonderful variety of plant and animal life with us here. We also enjoy walks to get out in nature, as you would say, to have some quiet time, and to commune with other beings that share our community. We have teachers and educators at all levels. We have forms of government and administration; but as I've said, they operate from a perspective that is different than you are used to. We have many research and development projects along with higher levels of learning and experimentation. Some of our citizens delight in growing and managing our food supplies. You get the idea. This is not unfamiliar to you.

In our experience, our children do not come in with the same Veils of Illusion that are a component of the third dimensional experience. When you enter into the human embodiment in this experience of duality and contrast, the Veils of Illusion come in with you. As you come into your embodiment and begin moving through your cycles of growth and development, you will have forgotten, for the most part, all that you knew before coming here. You are starting fresh in some sense because you have forgotten most of what you knew and even who you really are. This term "starting fresh" could be misleading. You come in with a blueprint that has already been designed and which you yourselves have taken part in prior to your earthly embodiment. This blueprint comes in with you. Past life energies and memories, karma, hereditary traits, innate but dormant attributes and so forth have also come into the new embodiment with you. But outside of those types of conditions, you are essentially starting fresh and many of you will go through the experience of your full embodiment and time here without ever fully remembering what it is you came to do or even who you really are. We know that each and every one will be guided by their Higher Selves, which will attempt to lead them to their due course, activity and the fulfillment of their purpose. However, many will not have any recognition of this as they go through their life experience and they may never come into the awareness of why they have chosen to come and participate at this time. This is the way of things today. It will shift.

And so you see, when children enter into our society they come in with already a much greater level of awareness and remembrance of who they are and what they came to do. You might look at this and say that our beginning and ending is not as cut and dried as it is in your perceived experience of birth and death. There is a blending that takes place for us, so in the raising of our children we work with them and support them in their chosen goals and accomplishments for this embodiment that they have chosen. They have an expanded awareness of the fullness of their being and all that it entails. They have an expanded awareness of their families and team members for this embodiment, as well as their origins, universal law and so on. Our child rearing process takes significantly longer than it does for you. Someone here of a couple of hundred earth years is still quite young, and they are viewed as a young person much like your teenagers.

Just as we are not subject to the physical ailments present in your world today, I would like to point out that no one in Telos suffers from depression, anxiety or any of these kinds of conditions which are so prevalent in your surface world. They simply are not present. I bring this up because I believe it is a significant point of note. I am attempting to help you understand some of the differences between your current 3D and our 5D experience. The depression in humanity is really a separation issue. Most forms of suffering that humans experience originate due to your misconception that you are in separation from your Creator. You know this is not the case, but the 3D environment is thick with density and duality, brainwashing, gross misunderstandings, outdated dogma, societal controls and mass manipulation, mass produced foods devoid of Creator light, addictions to nicotine, alcohol, pharmaceutical drugs and pornography. Reports of crime or even rape, kidnapping and murder go mostly unnoticed and on and on it goes. These are all considered to be fairly normal conditions in your society at this time. If we look at the collective result of various forms of perceived separation, we can see readily the damage that has been done and the toll it has taken in your world and in the hearts and minds of your brothers and sisters. Much of this has been a matter of design by those of the dark forces who have kept humanity in enslavement for so long. You could say they have been stacking the deck in their favor, and unfortunately, they have been successful.

These dark days are coming to an end as you move into your $5^{th}$ dimensional New Earth, and many of these kinds of experiences that are considered part of your normal day-to-day challenges will simply not exist. Depression and anxiety are good examples of conditions that simply will not be present in humanity in the days to come. We are beginning to see major world structures and those who have designed these structures, which have led to the control and enslavement of humanity at large, are beginning to crumble and fall away. As you say, "The wheels are falling off." This will continue; and as these systems continue to crumble, you will begin to see all that has been hidden from you. Those who have been controlling and manipulating from the shadows will be exposed for all to see. There are entire systems such as your basic economic and banking systems, political systems, food systems, health care systems, business systems and educational systems, which include elements purposefully designed and implemented to limit humanity. You will see entire systems beginning to crumble and the dark intention behind them will become clear for all to see.

This change is happening on two fronts. Humanity is at a time now when you are being allowed certain levels of grace and assistance from the very Heart of Creator that have never been granted before. As this happens, there are joint results essentially coming from the same activity of increased light, increased love, increased vibration, awareness and consciousness that are being sent and directed to the planet now. New levels of Christ consciousness are being directed to the planet now that have not been present since the time of the last Golden Age. Through this activity, all that is not in alignment with these new levels of vibration, energy, light, love, Christ consciousness and the Divine Feminine, all that is not in alignment will begin to fall away. This is exactly what is happening within the major systems and societal frameworks that are in place today. New levels of light are affecting everything: individuals, communities, nations and all of the constructs that are in place to support those communities and nations. You will see more and more of these systems beginning to crumble.

Simultaneously, the consciousness of humanity is rising and your awareness is increasing such that you will simply know things or see the truth of things that you didn't see or understand before. You may not understand how it is you have come about knowing something; you just will. This will be a reflection of your rising consciousness and awareness. You will look upon a situation or circumstance and you will know the truth of it by way of your own inner guidance and intuition because you have placed your attention on it. It is becoming much more difficult to deceive the individual human; therefore it is also becoming more difficult to control and manipulate the individual human.

As this movement within the individual expands out into communities and nations and the planet at large, you will see a shift. You are well underway already, you see. These systems that have been designed to control and manipulate as others decide who will be the haves and have-nots cannot exist in your 5D New Earth. In the same way I might say to you an individual will not be allowed to move into New Earth if they are still choosing lower vibrations such as hatred, greed, deception and so on the same is true of your social systems, most of which are severely broken. They will not be allowed to come with you to the New Earth. Your New Earth will be just that. In some ways it will look very familiar to you, and in some ways you will be starting from scratch. You will be building a global society and building systems that are based on fifth dimensional concepts.

One of the major roles we will play with humanity is to assist you in designing and creating new societal frameworks and operational structures. There will be others participating, but this will be one of our primary responsibilities. In fact, this is one of the key reasons we have chosen to remain here in Inner Earth. We have kept the Creator flames burning in our temples on behalf of all of humanity for thousands of years. This is why we have stayed. We are just as excited as you to be here in this time when we are able to see the shifts taking place as we move confidently toward humanity's ascension in the light and the creation of New Earth. We remain in your full support.

## Gaia's transition from 3D to 5D

Bryan - *Master Adama, would you be willing to speak on the subject of how it is that Gaia's transition, or all of our transitions, from 3D to 5D will take place?*

Adama - Yes, Bryan, we may speak on this subject if you wish. I feel this will be a topic of interest for our readers. I know this has been a question and certainly you are not the only one who is curious about, let us say, the mechanics of the coming transition. We are moving confidently forward with our project and the project plans and implementations. We are moving further and further along each day into what we are referring to as the New Earth and the next Golden Age. We have relayed to you that although these events have been set forth by Creator and are therefore destined to come about, we are unable to make predictions about the particular timing of events that will lead to this next great shift or its final completion. This will be dictated by humanity and that is the consciousness, willingness and readiness of humanity will have the most influence on the timing of these events and the actual events themselves. There are multiple other factors and variables that come into the equation. The shift has already begun. It is well underway.

Let me begin by stating some general information. You are aware of our presence here in the mountain, and you have been aware of us actually coming out to the surface to greet and visit with you on the mountain. It has been through the sensory perception coming through your $5^{th}$ dimensional awareness that you have been able to observe us and to recognize that we were present with you. When I say "observe us", you have not seen us yet with your physical eyes; but you have known and felt our presence in a way that we say is empathic. You have felt us and sensed us, so you knew we were there and you were able to perceive how many of us were there. I am referring to those times when we have actually joined you on the mountain. You have been able to distinguish those who are in either a feminine or masculine embodiment, and we might say that you have seen us with your third eye vision. You have felt and sensed the connection of our energy and presence. You have been able to pick up on this, and there was no doubt about what was taking place at the time.

However, let us say you had someone joining you on the mountain who has not yet achieved a similar state of awareness. It is most likely that those, in this example, would not have been aware of our presence in the least. They would not have seen us, felt us or heard us. They would not have picked up on our telepathic communication. They simply would not have known we were there. So at the most fundamental level in this example, what we have is someone who has reached a 5D or higher level of awareness and someone who perhaps may not have gone beyond a lower 4th dimensional awareness at this time. Their sensories and third eye clairvoyance and clairsentience have not yet achieved a level that would allow them to perceive us. This applies then to all that exists in a 5D or higher vibration, and it would apply to the city of Telos itself. It would apply to all of the Lemurians and any number of other beings that may be present here in our city at any point in time. I use this illustration as we begin to discuss the transition that will be forthcoming and how you might perceive it.

What I can tell you is, there will not be what you might refer to as a mega-event or cataclysmic event. This is a cosmic scale event but, you see, this is not going to take place in the realms of your 3rd dimensional experience. I've just illustrated one example of the difference between a 3rd dimensional awareness and a 5th dimensional awareness. One person is aware of the events taking place at some levels and one is not. That does not change the fact that the event was still taking place. It does not take away from the truth of the event. So in this example, just because someone was not able to perceive that Lemurians had come out of the mountain to offer greetings and blessings does not mean it did not take place. They were simply unable to perceive it. There are degrees of perception, so we might even go a step further in this simple analogy. You may have someone who is open to the truth of our existence, and you may have someone who outright rejects and denies any notion of truth of the experience. Perhaps they draw this conclusion because they were not able to perceive it and experience it for themselves. That one was not able to perceive it and has therefore rejected the whole idea. They have now set about the attitude and belief that it does not exist. That is each one's choice to make; however, we would say just because someone has made that choice doesn't mean it is so. Each may choose whatever "that" is as his or her reality and experiential paradigm and this will be true for them. The reason I am spending time in this analogy is really to drive home the point that each one's level of awareness, vibration, perception and consciousness will govern all of the changes and shifts that will be forthcoming individually. The experience will be unique for each one. More and more of you are coming into higher levels of awareness and higher levels of vibration. More and more are working now and endeavoring, whether consciously or not, to expand themselves to at least a 5th dimensional level of awareness. This is happening naturally for all life on the planet whether they are aware of it or not.

As we move forward, there are still many milestones that must be met and achieved before such time as we are all fully present on the New Earth. What is happening now is everyone is being given a choice; however, this choice is not in the full awareness of the collective consciousness at this time. It will become more and more evident as we move forward that the environment of Earth, the framework in which you all have been working, is shifting. We are in the process now, the early stages, in fact, of this great shift. As we move forward, it will come more and more into the awareness and collective consciousness that individuals are being guided to either accept these new levels of love and light, awareness, grace and unity consciousness or not. Individually, each one will eventually have to choose to take responsibility for their own attainment and to allow themselves to move confidently and naturally into the 5th dimensional experience or they will consciously make the decision to stay where they are in some lower vibration. As we continue on this current trajectory and as more light and love flood the planet, the frequencies of light, sound, magnetic and electrical energies, Creator life force and so on are all being expanded. It is becoming more and more apparent that a shift is taking place. As these waves of momentum continue to grow and expand more and more, each of you is coming into new levels of awareness. Each one is being guided to elevate and expand. This is the natural path being set down before you. The energy, momentum and assistance from Creator and the realms of Heaven are setting their momentums in this direction. It is our desire and Gaia's desire that she bring along as many of you––and that is all life forms on the planet––as wish to come.

The first thing that is happening now is it must come into each one's awareness that we are moving closer and closer to the "choice point". Each of you is coming into the awareness for yourselves and in your own way that a new choice now stands before you. You may choose to move boldly and confidently into the New Earth and higher vibrations of harmony and love, or you may choose to stay where you are in some lower vibration. Each of you has the opportunity to make this choice for yourselves today. These shifts are in full swing now; but again, the final transition is still some time out. There are many milestones that must be accomplished before we get to this point, but I am doing my best to address your question in a way that makes some sense for you. As we move forward we will be drawing closer and closer to what I am referring to today as the "choice point". This choice is available and on offer for each of you right now, but as we move forward the time will come that all will be required to make a conscious choice as to which level of vibration they wish to participate in. This will be in the final stages of this transformational process, and our great hope and endeavor is to assist more and more individuals into new levels of awareness.

What we will see is a shift taking place over time. This will not happen in a instant. It is a transition, a shift, and we must be certain that we are going about it in the right way and in a way that allows for the greatest amount of opportunity and assistance for all of those who would make the choice to move into the New Earth environment. There will be tidal waves of awakening as more and more of you begin coming into alignment with these shifts. In this way, we will be building a new level of consciousness on the planet. The momentum will continue to build for all who allow themselves to step into a new way of living and being.

As more and more come into the 5D awareness, you will see the balance begin shifting in a big way. What we have today is a situation that, if we look just at the numbers alone with the lightworker community (we will say those who have reached a 5D or higher awareness) on one side of the balanced scale and the number of lifestreams who are still either in a 3D or working their way through the 4D experience on the other side of the balanced scale, the lightworkers would be severely outweighed and outnumbered at this particular time. Now this is simply a numbers and mathematical analogy. The great majority of energy, influence and momentum towards the light are being generated by what, at this point, is still a very small number of lifestreams on the planet. It is you, those of you reading this now and calling in the light, who are creating the momentum for this transition and holding the space for your brothers and sisters. Each and every call for the light is being multiplied thousands and thousands of times by the angelic realms. This is their great love and service to us. As we move forward, more and more will begin making the choice to move to higher levels of awareness; and as they do, in this analogy, they will be moving from one side of the balanced scale to the other.

Let us refer to this then, in this discussion, as those who are awakened and those who are presently unawakened. As we move through the days ahead, those who are currently on the unawakened scale will begin shifting in greater numbers and with greater acceleration. There will be more and more moving to the other side of the scale like tidal waves. We will view this transition both as a numbers game with seven plus billion lifestreams on the planet, and we will also view the situation energetically as light. They are both important. So as we move forward, more and more lifestreams will be shifting into higher awareness. As more and more individuals allow themselves to flow into higher awareness, the collective energy and collective consciousness of the higher 5D vibration will also grow and expand. It's building momentum. It's gaining force and it's gaining in numbers. More and more are waking up and choosing to move into this new space and paradigm. As this takes place, the overall energy, the overall consciousness and overall vibration of this world—–meaning Gaia and all of humanity and all of life with her—–are shifting, you see. These shifts are beginning to have a greater impact on the whole, and this is the way the transformation will take place. There will be wave after wave, momentum after momentum and there will be more and more lifestreams coming into this awareness. In this analogy, they will be moving from one side of the balanced scale to the other.

So you stand here today, in this analogy, you and perhaps several hundred thousand others on the planet, and you see what you perceive are the other seven billion of you there on the other side of the scale who are still choosing a lower vibrational experience. This is one reason why so many of you often feel overwhelmed by the task at hand. It is all of you working alongside the Company of Heaven who are holding the balance for all of life here and clearing the path ahead for others. These tidal waves of momentum will begin gaining speed, and you will see waves of individuals stepping firmly into their new 5D experience. In this analogy, they will be stepping onto the scale with you, those of you who understand your true nature as creator beings and are doing your part to call in and anchor these new energies of love and light. Before too long we will see the scales firmly shifting in our favor.

As we near the completion of the project, there will still be some who, for one reason or another, will appear to be stuck. They will not know how to move themselves out of their current paradigm and into the new experience that is on offer for them. Then, there will be those also with full awareness who will make the conscious choice not to participate and there will be various reasons for that also. So at some point in time, at what I anticipate may be between four to six generations out, we will near the full completion of this project. That is, we will come closer to the time of the actual shift; and when this happens, it will not be greatly noticeable to most of you. The reason is, as I've just described, that more and more of you are coming into the fold of a new collective consciousness;

and you will see New Earth being created before your very eyes. So again, it is not going to happen in a flash. It is a process. As waves of individuals allow themselves to move into higher vibration, you will begin to see larger groups and communities around the planet living a higher vibration of love and peace. The outer appearances, circumstances and events of your world will begin to shift simply because of the momentum of the new choice paradigm that you all will be living.

Outer reality is the emanation of the energies and the intentions of those of you who are stepping into your divinity and co-creating a new experience and a new world. This is how it's going to happen. You all will be the creators of the New Earth. Outer circumstances will begin to change and mold themselves to reflect your higher levels of expectancy. These will be your intentional co-creations, such as, for example, "Peace on Earth and goodwill toward men" or "It shall be on Earth as it is in Heaven," you see. This is all very real. As more and more of you step into your divinity and become aware of your divine birthright to manifest and co-create your experience, this is exactly what you will do. As more waves of individuals join you, the momentum will build, and outer circumstances will continue to change to reflect that which you all are desiring and intending. As each of you moves naturally into higher awareness, you will automatically be in alignment with all that we have discussed and all that you know to exist in a 5D or higher vibration. This is how it will happen.

As waves of individuals choose this experience there will be milestones along the way; and as these milestones are met, there are a number of events in the project plan that will be taking place. Some events will have a greater impact on the whole than others.

Some of them will be the bringing forth of new technologies that we have discussed, those of healing and health, new energy sources, new ways of growing food, technology to heal Gaia, new modes of transportation and so on. You will see the shift taking place, and it will be taking place at an accelerated rate. We see now these transitions taking place over the next 150 to 200 years. Please keep my previous statement regarding predictions in mind. Everything is in flux and you all are creating your experience in every moment. I am attempting to provide you with a framework based on how we see things today. The process is well underway already, so I am not suggesting that you will need to wait fifty years before you begin to see change in your world. That is not the case at all. My point is, as more and more individuals allow for their natural expansion, the scales will become not only balanced, but also fully swayed in favor of New Earth and the next Golden Age to come. As new energies flood the planet, so do the number of lifestreams who are moving into the new paradigm. Consider the intention and co-creation ability that is inherent within each of you and look out to the shifts that might take place in the world around you. Can you imagine what things would be like if there were a billion of you awakened and standing together in harmony, acceptance and love? And now, what if there were two or three billion who have elevated themselves firmly into vibrations of unity consciousness, Christ Light and the Divine Feminine energies? What do you think the outer experience taking place in your world will look like at that time? It will happen holistically. All of the pieces are tied together. There are checks and balances and there are milestones.

So yes, I tell you, there will be some large scale events that are to come and they will assist in various ways. These events will be noticeable by all, but as for the big shift you are wanting to know about, the final transition will be relatively seamless. To really sum up the answer to your question, what will happen is waves and waves of individuals will choose and allow themselves to come into a new paradigm and experience. As we near the end of the final transition we will likely have a number of individuals who do not wish to participate in the experience of the New Earth and it is their choice to make. At that point there will be the intervention of Creator; and those who choose not to participate will be given opportunities elsewhere such that they may make their transitions and continue to have their own experiences as per their soul's choosing. They will be allowed to transition to other worlds and other planets where they may continue on their path. This will be a transition for them just as it will be for each of you, and they will be allowed then to go on to other realms and worlds to continue their experience of lower vibration and density.

There are obviously many details which are not being discussed here; but generally speaking, at that time you will have completed the transition and you will be living on the New Earth. There will be a 5D level of awareness and consciousness existing everywhere on the planet at that time. We are discussing the completion of this great shift. At that point you will truly be experiencing a new Golden Age. We are to have our Heaven on Earth. Humanity will be fully, actively and consciously communing with us in Telos and other cities of the Agartha Network, angels, Ascended Masters and your many star nation neighbors. Mother Gaia, at that time, will be fully rejuvenated, healed and revitalized. Some things will look the same and some things will be very different.

But in all honesty, you have pondered this and you have thought perhaps of a situation where some kind of 5D hologram Earth will actually split off from the density of the 3D Earth such that you will have two separate Earths with one existing in 5D and a separate one in 3D; and I say to you, friend, it's just not going to happen that way. You are on the New Earth right now and that's why you are all here is to bring about the conditions of the New Earth environment and to begin your journey moving boldly and confidently with faith, trust and the awareness of all the beauty and joy that await you in this new paradigm.

It is our intention and endeavor, as much as possible, to allow for and guide a graceful transition but there is real work to be done, and change is not always easy. We are on an accelerated timeline. There will be major events taking place that will quicken the awakening and activity in one way or another and you will see many of them taking place in your lifetime. There is also a stepping up approach such that these new energies start gradually and gain speed and momentum, which results in more shifting. By the time we move into the completion of the project, most of those here at that time simply will not experience any huge event. It will not necessarily even be in the forefront of their awareness. It will be a requirement that those who have chosen not to participate will be given the opportunity to go elsewhere and live as their choice. For those who choose to go with Gaia, there will be certain levels of protection placed around your world. As each one is able to embrace their own divinity and divine sovereignty, you will be the creators of your New Earth. We have a plan and we will be assisting you step by step through this accelerated process. Humanity will be responsible for co-creating their new Golden Age and that is the Heaven on Earth you desire. You will know yourselves to be co-creators with Creator and with the Company of Heaven. We will be here by your side each step of the way and, I assure you, humanity will be given the assistance needed to move forward with confidence and success.

It is an exciting time to be present and participating in this grand, cosmic scale event. Those of you reading this book are on the forefront of this movement. You are the wayshowers, lightworkers, spiritual warriors, visionaries, paradigm busters and masters who have come back at this most auspicious time in the history of your planet to do exactly the work that each of you is doing now. We are in great gratitude for your courage, your love and your service to the light.

Bryan - *Well that's not nearly as dramatic as I thought it might be, Master Adama.*

Adama - Yes, I know. In terms of some of the scenarios that you and others may concoct for yourselves, the final shift itself is not expected to be nearly as exciting or perhaps as tumultuous as you might think it to be. Now, as I said in our earlier conversation, as this momentum is building, essentially what is happening is that all of humanity are being guided to make a choice. As we move forward it will become more and more difficult to simply opt out of your awareness of all that is taking place in the world around you. Many today, whether consciously or unconsciously, have chosen to simply opt out. They do not wish to participate. They do not wish to consider new possibilities and they are simply choosing to stay where they are and attempt to go about their daily life as they know it to be. Yet as the new energies are coming onto the planet, they are causing people to wake up, and it is coming into their awareness at some level that they are being guided by their Higher Selves. They will be guided to look around and take an accounting as to what is taking place around them to the best of their ability and then make a conscious choice as to what they would like to do going forward. Do they wish to embrace a completely new paradigm and way of being and living or do they wish to simply, as best they can, attempt to shut all of that out and remain there in the old paradigm? This is the choice that each one is being led to, and the momentum of having to make this choice will accelerate as waves and waves come into the fold so to speak. Due to the nature of the expanding collective consciousness, it will become more and more difficult for those who choose to simply barricade themselves in their current paradigm.

What most humans are living today will become the old paradigm, and as we move forward the pressures will be mounting. Still, there will be those who choose intentionally to stay in the lower vibrations of what they may falsely assume to be a "safe zone" of no change. It is what they know. Perhaps fear will not allow them to make the transition but it will become increasingly difficult for them to remain in the lower vibrations; for you see they will be living the old paradigm. The momentum of the mass consciousness is now such that the great majority of lifestreams will soon be functioning with higher levels of awareness. This is what is going to change the world. This is how you are going to create your collective future experience.

## Follow up discussion about Gaia

Bryan - *Master Adama, can we go back and clarify some points in our discussion of the transition of Gaia?*

Adama - Yes, I was aware of your thought process and questions last night. When you spoke to me and placed your attention on me you have, in essence "rung my doorbell." When you did this, I was with you and aware of the questions you had. I am happy to spend a few minutes with you on this topic. I wish also for you to make note of what I have just said. Whenever you place your attention on us, any of us across the veil who are your Family of Light, you have activated an energy connection via your own attention and intention. We easily receive your vibrations of energy which have been directed toward us; and in that very instant, we are with you, standing alongside you and fully aware of the details of your engagement. It is just that easy.

Bryan - *The first question is in regards to a book I'm reading where the author states something to the effect of, by the year 2032 all of humanity here with Gaia will be operating at a minimum of a lower 5D vibrational awareness. That seems like a very short period of time to me. I've read elsewhere about the Earth somehow splitting off into two separate planets, and I just want to make sure I understand it. This seems contradictory to the discussion you and I had, and I'm asking for additional clarification. We discussed that while there is great hesitation in making time predictions, it could be 150-200 years or let's just say 4-6 generations before we are living fully in the New Earth. One of my questions is to clarify what happens in sixteen years vs. the conversation you and I are having about the possibility of four to six generations before the transition to New Earth is complete. I have taken from you that there would not be a splitting off of two Earths but rather the Earth that we are living on now will transition from 3D to 5D, that we will transform this Earth into a New Earth of 5D. At that time of which you refer to as the "choice point", all of those who have chosen not to move into New Earth would have the opportunity to have their experience elsewhere. What will happen to those who have consciously chosen not to participate in the 5D New Earth? Will they transition by way of their natural deaths?*

Adama - I understand these are questions that you and others may have; so we will address them here today. This first topic you're inquiring about is the timeline in which all of humanity will be reaching a 5D level of consciousness. This is one of the great milestones in our project plans. It will be a big achievement and certainly the accomplishment of a major milestone when the majority of humanity have reached a lower 5D or higher level of consciousness. Certainly, this will come about much more quickly than what we have described as the completion of overall project plan. This is a milestone. I do not know that the actual date has been set at 2032, but I would agree that with the waves of momentum and accelerated timelines, a majority of humanity may very well have achieved a 5D level of awareness within the next fifteen to twenty years. This is possible. This would not include all lifestreams on the planet; for as we have discussed, there will be those who choose for one reason or another, not to move into higher awareness at this time. It is their path and their choice. So yes, I stand behind my original statements. I have taken your question to mean "When will New Earth resemble life as I understand it to be in Telos," and this would be the completion of the project.

So we need to make a distinction here. On one hand, we are discussing a major milestone whereby a great majority of humanity will be experiencing 5D consciousness. On the other, we are discussing the completion of the project when Gaia, all of humanity and all life here are living fully in the Golden Age and all that it entails. This is the Heaven on Earth environment that you all are creating now. Let us say within fifteen to twenty years the majority of humanity have moved into a 5D level of consciousness. There is still a great amount of work that must be done; this is all well and good, for all of you to have moved into this new level of unity consciousness. At this time, however, the real work will begin. In fact, it has already begun. There is actual real work that is going to need to take place to transform your planet into the New Earth. This includes the full rejuvenation of Gaia and her body. It includes the restructuring of your economic systems, political systems and social structures. It includes, perhaps, the rearranging of nations, governments and power centers such that a great balancing will take place. We have discussed such things as humanity and the animal kingdoms over time will no longer have a need for proteins and they will naturally move away from a predatory response and into unity consciousness.

My point is there are a great number of additional milestones that will need to be met before you are fully living in the New Earth, the completed project. That is not to say that you will not observe great change taking place through the remainder of your lifetime, for you will. There will be a number of major milestones being met along the way, so you will begin to see change very quickly and it will just continue on. Certainly then, let us say you will see great change taking place in your world over the next fifteen to twenty years; however, this will just be the accomplishment of some of the many milestones that must be completed before you are fully settled in your New Earth experience. In these two statements, I do not believe there is any conflict. We are simply discussing one as a milestone and one is what we might refer to as the successful completion of this grand project.

So now, in terms of how the actual transition will take place, this is a complex subject as you might imagine. In our last discussion on this topic, I have spent a good deal of time giving examples and analogies. One example was that you may have someone on the mountain with you who is not yet working at a 5D level of awareness as perhaps you are. In this example, as we come out of the mountain to greet you, one is aware of our presence and one is not. So we are already existing here alongside you; and because this is what you might refer to as an etheric city where everything is vibrating at the level of the fifth dimension and higher, most of you are simply not aware of us. That doesn't mean that we are not here or that Telos doesn't exist. You all will essentially be in what I would say is the same space or the same container of Gaia. We are dealing with some of the finer points, and let me remind you that this is a new event that has never taken place in the cosmos before. This is one of the reasons why there is so much attention being placed here at this time. So what will happen is, if we think of Earth as a container, we will not have two containers. We will not add on a full new container. There will be no replica of Gaia. Gaia is Gaia and there is only one Gaia and Gaia is transitioning into a new, higher vibration. She is making her ascension, you see. She is leading the way for all life forms present. She is shifting out of the levels of density and duality and moving into a higher vibrational body. She is making her ascension, and she will bring the fullness of her being with her into her new ascended 5D body. Now, as this happens, there will be many of you here within the container of this space of Gaia who will be having a 5D experience and all that it entails. Also, within the same container, there will be the remnants and falling away of the 3D aspects of her being. They will both exist simultaneously for some period of time. This is the transition.

You are creating in the space of this container, and you are evolving all that is there into a higher level of consciousness. Gaia is leading the way. This is all happening within the container of Gaia and everything in the container is evolving. It is being stepped up. We might view this in terms of percentage of completion, as a simple example. We might look at any point in time at Gaia and all of humanity and all life forms at the highest level of the project, and we might say we are 50% of the way there. Half of humanity and half of the animal kingdoms, half the elementals and so on...we are halfway there. We have discussed that this is similar to the process that each individual is going through also. As the transition takes place, all of you who are resonating with a 5D experience will be living it. This is the new reality that you all will be in and your daily experience will reflect the beauty of it. Simultaneously, while this is happening, there will be a period of overlap and this is part of the natural transition. There will be those who choose not to go forward and move into the higher levels and that is okay. While they are here, they will continue to experience all that they create for themselves. For all of those who have chosen to remain in lower vibrations of duality and contrast, then that is the experience they will be living. This will be their reality and both of these concurrent realities will exist within the same container for some period of time. The momentum will grow and grow until, let us say, some time has passed when we check in again at the highest levels of the project plan. We see now that Gaia and humanity and all life are now 75% of the way to their collective ascension.

Obviously this is a tremendously oversimplified example of how things will take place, but I want to explain it in a way that makes sense. So okay, we are now 75% of the way through the project and 75% of Gaia and all life there are now aligned with a 5D or higher level of consciousness. For those of you who are in the 75%, who are now fully integrated and aligned to your new vibration, you all will truly be experiencing your beautiful new realities.

Those who are stuck in the old paradigm will be experiencing their same old realities. Old and new realities will exist together simultaneously and, for the most part, as we get farther along, one will not be greatly influenced by the other. For those choosing to stay in the lower vibrations, the many opportunities and experiences that are available to all will simply pass them by because they have not chosen it.

This is the reason why I have given the analogy of Telos. You know that we are here in Telos and we are already occupying the same space or container as you, yet one is not aware of the other. There is no issue. Once we arrive at the final choice point, we will have brought along as many of you who have chosen and desired to move into New Earth and you will already be there. Then, there will be those in the 3D/4D paradigm who wish not to move forward. At that time what will happen is, yes, they will be phased out so to speak. Those who remain will still have a very natural experience in their chosen paradigm and they will just transition out naturally. Their lifestream experience will come to an end, and they will return home across the veil. If they wish to continue with a new lifestream experience elsewhere in the lower densities, they will have many choices and options to do that according to their soul's desire. It will be a very natural process for them. As the later stages of the project near completion, the "choice point" will be one of the final milestones. Generally speaking, you simply will not be aware of each other at that time. Most of you will be living in the New Earth and there occupying the same space will be the last remnants of Gaia who are still holding onto some piece of the old paradigm. The lower vibrational paradigm will be allowed to remain for a period of time to support life that has chosen not to come forward. In a very short period, those lifestreams who remain will naturally fall away.

Presently, there are no new lifesteams coming to the planet with blueprints of choosing a lower vibrational experience. Already those souls who choose to have those experiences are being given other options. There are many opportunities for those souls to have their chosen experience elsewhere. As we near the end of the project, all that is remaining in a 3D vibration will simply fall away naturally. By then, we will have passed the final choice point and we will move the remainder of what is left into balance in the New Earth environment. The grand project plan will have been completed. Gaia will be fully whole in her new, fully rejuvenated body and her New Earth experience. So, we are not splitting off into two worlds. This is Gaia. It is her body. She is making the transition fully in her body just the same as each of you is in your bodies. You are not splitting off into two bodies; you are transforming the one body, the one container that you have here. This is a greatly oversimplified summary of how things will take place, but I believe it has provided the understanding you were asking for. We are on an accelerated timeline and things are moving quickly. Timing and events will be dictated to a large extent by the free will choice of the individual and the collective results of those choices. This is not well understood at this time. It is all of you together who are creating your experience. This is a process and we have been discussing what I am referring to in these works as the final choice point. I cannot say when this event will take place. There is great change ahead of us and much work to do along the way. Do not feel that you need wait for anything or anyone. The door is open to each of you and the choice point is now.

# Chapter 6

## Balancing the Masculine/Feminine Energies
## Our bodies are changing
## Coming back into balance

Adama - Tell me, how many do you see sitting at the table.

Bryan - *I see ten of us with myself included. You on one end, I on the other and four on each side.*

Adama - That is correct.

{Bryan - *I am being asked to speak the conversation I'm having with Master Adama in the Great Hall. I looked to see, of the eight council members present, how many male and how many females sit at the table. I see five males and three females. I asked a question about why the council isn't equally balanced between the masculine and feminine.*

Adama - That is an old paradigm way of thinking. That kind of balance is not necessary for us in Telos and elsewhere. As you reach higher levels of awareness, you will learn to balance the masculine and feminine energies and aspects within yourselves. This also will be a natural component of the shift we are discussing. We do not experience the polarity that you experience in a 3rd / 4th dimensional reality. We have much more equilibrium and balance in all aspects of life including that within ourselves, which might be viewed as a masculine and/or a feminine aspect or way of perceiving life around us and the situations that come forth. This balance is a component of your self-mastery. This is a part of the path that is necessary for each of you as you move into your 5th dimensional realities. As this takes place, it will be a requirement of all individuals, to some extent or another, to balance the masculine and feminine energies within themselves. In this way, you are able to choose whether to exhibit a masculine based action/reaction or a feminine based action/reaction. This has to do with the way you perceive any situation or circumstance and the way that you choose to respond to it. This is a vital component of your current evolution, and gaining some mastery of this is beneficial for yourself and others.

There is an increase of the Divine Feminine energies coming onto the planet at this time, and all of creation is receiving this information. Everyone will process in a different way and in a way that is natural and unique for them. However, the net result will be such that we will begin to balance and harmonize the collective energies of humanity, Mother Gaia and all life on the planet. We are moving away from the Piscean age, which has been dominated by the masculine energies for so long; and this polarity is partly responsible for having kept humanity in bondage for such a great period of time. The chains of bondage are breaking free. At this time, Creator and the Company of Heaven are directing new, increased levels of Divine Feminine energies to the planet and to your consciousness and awareness.

Allow me to provide you with a few examples. When two individuals, regardless of their chosen embodiment within the masculine or feminine, come together and are balanced internally and energetically between the masculine and feminine energies, the nature of the relationship changes for the better. I reference a romantic relationship in this example; however, these principles will apply to all areas of your daily life, relationships and interactions. As you come into balance in this way, the communication, behaviors and responses move away from the old programming of duality and into a higher vibrational awareness. You may find, for example, that some of the limiting or lower vibrational thoughts and perspectives you held onto previously about your partner have changed or fallen away completely. You may observe that you are becoming more accepting and allowing. Perhaps you begin to see that you are responsible for yourself only, and you may no longer feel inclined to place conditions on your love to fit the circumstances of your desire.

The way you communicate will become elevated to higher levels of balance and awareness and display qualities of love and acceptance. You may experience certain emotions more deeply. This comes about because there has been a balancing of the masculine and feminine energies. In another example, let us say the autopilot response to a given situation may have been one of an unbalanced masculine, an overly authoritative or aggressive approach. There are many labels that apply to this type of response; but I believe you understand my meaning. As the energies are balanced in this same hypothetical scenario, what once may have been an unconscious reaction within a strong or unbalanced masculine energy is now transformed through your increased awareness and through the balancing of the energies such that your response will be different. With higher awareness comes a better opportunity to view the situation externally, meaning outside the point of ego. With this higher level of awareness as to what is taking place in any situation, number one, you are not so quick to react unconsciously or allow the old programs to run. The old program response to a situation now becomes one of more awareness with higher vibrations of love and understanding. Secondly, from this place of internal balance you may choose consciously to move into that conversation or situation with acceptance, cooperation, feeling and understanding, or perhaps you choose to have a more masculine approach of strong will, focus, logic and boldness.

A blending will take place in this process; and once the new energies have been integrated, this will all feel very natural to you. This balancing and harmonizing effect of the Divine Feminine energies will benefit you regardless of your current orientation in this embodiment. Just because one chooses to experience this human embodiment in female form, for example, does not mean she is living, acting and expressing in a way that is balanced and harmonized with the Divine Feminine energies. This discussion applies equally regardless of your current orientation. It may be some time yet before the majority have this concept in their awareness and have achieved some level of attainment in this regard. Those of you on the forefront of the shift, will begin to experience this internal balancing more rapidly than others. Some of you have already experienced or are beginning to experience this shift internally for yourselves, and you understand the conversation. Not to say there is not more work that can and will be done, but to say you have seen a glimpse of this activity and have achieved some level of integration in this balancing. The concept of this activity is in your awareness and you are using it in a conscious way. These new energies will guide each of you naturally toward this internal harmonizing of duality, yes, but you will benefit also by being aware of the shifts as they take place. This idea and these energies will continue to expand out, and you will begin to see more of the lightworker community having these conversations. Many, in fact, are already aware within themselves of these changes taking place and they are making their own observations as such.

Over time the collective consciousness of humanity will shift. It is taking place now, and this is what is necessary to bring you all fully grounded into your 5$^{th}$ dimensional experience; for you cannot gain your ascension without fully expressing the qualities and virtues of the Divine Feminine. There is no greater force in the universe than love. What do we think about when we think about love? What are the emotions we feel around this word "love" and the labels of those emotions that spring forth. Do we feel wholeness, purity and goodness? Are we reminded of our family and friends or maybe our loyal and always loving animal companions? How about those we see around us who give of themselves freely in service to their brothers and sisters without much reward or recognition? Perhaps we think of things like generosity, compassion, acceptance and forgiveness. Kindness, softness and nurturing are beautiful expressions of the love vibration. So is laughter. Love is a vibration and these are just labels or examples of what you may experience in your emotions of Divine Love and the Divine Feminine energies. Just examples. Perhaps you're watching a movie and a touching scene is playing out in front of you. Where there may have been little or no emotional response before, perhaps you now find yourself experiencing a surprising influx of emotion. This is the heart space opening and it is your very nature. This is one of the most important shifts taking place as we move into this new age.

As new levels of Divine Feminine energies expand globally, you will see the expansion of the collective consciousness of all your brothers and sisters on planet today. Souls coming into embodiment now are already aligned with a greater balance between the two polarities, you see. They are not as polarized as many of you who have been on the planet for some time were, when you came into your bodies. As the collective consciousness on the planet reaches the tipping point, we will see great change in all aspects of your current structures: social, political and economic. We will see changes in relationships and the way marriage is approached, for example. In another, we will see changes in the way decisions are made around childbirth and how those children will be guided to relate to the world around them. This is all coming my friends, and you will see positive change taking place on multiple fronts.

## Later follow up with Master Adama

Bryan - *Master Adama, as I was reviewing one of the previous books, I ran across a section where you and Aurelia are discussing the Telos High Council of Light. You say the council has been intentionally designed to have six males and six females with you as the 13th member and final decision maker. This seems to be in conflict with the discussion contained in this chapter. Would you mind speaking on this?*

Adama - Bryan, you have asked me for clarification regarding our councils and also the members making up these councils.

I appreciate your raising these questions. To begin with, in our previous works, Aurelia has referred to the Telos High Council of Light, and there we have said this council is comprised of six males and six females. I am the 13th member. This is true but we have more than one council in Telos. You joined members of the High Council of Telos. This is a different council altogether. The objectives and purpose of these councils are different and so let us speak on this for just a moment.

Regarding our previous works and the messages contained therein regarding the Telos High Council of Light, indeed there are thirteen members including six females and six males. The question you initially raised when you saw five males and three females, was, why did we not have a balance represented among the council. I have said to you it was not necessary and that this is an old paradigm way of thinking. And so, what I will say now is both are true. Allow me to explain. Our Telos High Council of Light is a council that oversees the spiritual plan for our community. This is an absolute foundational component of our society. In the Telos High Council of Light, our members are attuned to higher levels of consciousness and in communication with higher sources of light and Creator will, wisdom and love. This council is responsible for the spiritual direction of our community. It oversees all activities taking place within our spiritual temples here in Telos, as well as a number of activities such as counseling, education and community events. This council also oversees relevant communication between our extended family and homeland civilizations in other areas of the cosmos. Due to the solely spiritual nature of this council then, it was chosen that we do have an equal balance of the Divine Feminine and Divine Masculine energies, and this is in alignment with our Creator and our universe. This aligns with the nature of our Father/Mother God and the Alpha and Omega. This is why we have designed our council this way.

On the other hand, we also have the High Council of Telos. This is not the Telos High Council of Light. Both of these councils are involved with our project plan. This is the grand project I refer to here; and as it rolls down to our level in the Agartha Network, we have a number of activities that are and will be taking place. These activities at some time or another, will involve certainly most of the inhabitants here in Telos and also those in other cities of the Agartha Network. So you might view this council as a working council. They oversee the day-to-day function and long range planning of our city and the interactions, therefore, with our neighbors in the Agartha Network and elsewhere. You can see that both councils will be involved in our grand project plan. This council, let us say, is not a spiritual council but more of a working council. In these cases it is not necessary, whatsoever, for us to have this balance that you have asked about. For we are all balanced internally and therefore we do not need the outward balance. When you asked the question, what you were asking was "Wouldn't you want to ensure that both sides or perspectives, meaning those of the females and the males in Telos, would both have an equal say in the decisions being made?" Is this correct?

Bryan - *Yes sir, that is correct. I was projecting my current view to your experience in Telos and thinking about how things often take place here on the surface.*

Adama - Yes, and so I believe I have answered your question accordingly. It is an important point to note and I am glad we have had the opportunity to address it here today.

## Our bodies are changing

Adama - Look around this Great Hall and tell me what you see.

Bryan - *The hall has a hue of golden light that permeates the room. It's like a beautiful sunlight yet it has more shades of gold than yellow. It is more of an illumination and an energy than a light. I see the floor has a crystalline type of appearance. It is not completely clear like a quartz crystal; yet it is not a solid color such as stone either. It appears to be substance that looks to be a cross between perhaps a slate or granite, a hard stone substance yet with an infusion of crystalline properties that allow light and energy to pass through. The floor feels very solid and stable, a strong foundation; yet it allows light energy to transmit and radiate through.*

Adama - Yes, that is correct. I have helped you to place your attention here momentarily. Before we continue, please allow me to make note. You will see that we enjoy using analogies. For we find that in the use of analogies, we may speak conversationally with you and those who will receive our messages. We endeavor to bring about important information in a way that it may be understood and applied in your daily lives.

The human form and construct have similar properties to the floor of our Great Hall, which you have just described. The nature of the human embodiment is one of coming into the lower forms of density. Of course this is not new information, but each of you comes into this lifestream experience such that you do not fully see or remember that which you truly are. You don't remember the realms from which you came, the light and truth of who you are and all that you know. You enter into this dimension of density, matter and polarity. In our analogy, if one were just to view the human experience in passing, what we may see is a hard substance of slate or granite. We may not see light passing through. We may not see the crystalline features within the slab of stone that does allow the light to shine through, to shine within and without. These crystalline substances are there to receive light and to transmit light. That is, to receive the information that is the light. And if one so chooses, one may expand the crystalline grids in this stone structure in our analogy. For the structure is not made exclusively of slate or granite. There are porous materials within the stone itself. There are crystalline substance, molecules, fractures and lines within the stone that make up the stone. Upon observing this with the naked eye, it may not always be seen; yet it is there. It remains there. Those who choose to look upon it and ponder their own light within will see the equivalent of their crystalline substrates and fractures, for this is the light within. At first glance, it may appear to be overcome in matter and density or even something dark and heavy. Yet you know that the spark of divinity, the spark of Father/Mother God resides fully present in the secret chamber of your hearts. You would not remain in your embodiments if it were otherwise. As we move forward in this time, each of you will observe your own construct and the makeup of your systems, functions and bodies. With the influx of new energies, the body itself is evolving from a carbon-based structure to a crystalline-based structure.

Back to the analogy, what you see then, when you look at the floor of this Great Hall, is a foundation that is strong, secure and stable. It has those properties and we appreciate them, for it gives us a foundation on which we could build this hall. Yet, you also see in this substrate, that as strong and supportive and sound as this foundation is, you can see there are crystalline grids contained within the structure such that light passes freely throughout all parts of the structure. This is the change that is taking place within the human body at this time. The carbon based structures of density in a 3D human experience are evolving and changing. The light permeates first one or two small locations; and as this happens, the crystalline grids within begin to activate and pretty soon another grid comes online and pretty soon the grid beside that one comes online. As you do the work and continue bringing in more love and light, pretty soon the next grid beside it comes online such that through time what you will find is a balancing. This is another oversimplified explanation of the process but it will do. This balancing of substance, light and energy will be necessary to sustain the new human living in the New Earth. You will function in a world that is very similar, in some ways, as you perceive it to be now—–however, with a great shift toward light and consciousness and love.

We pick up now where we left off in conversation about balancing the masculine and feminine energies. As we move into New Earth, each of you is balancing your energies and bodily systems. The matter and physicality of it are also changing such that, as you all move into your New Earth with feet firmly planted on the ground, you will be, at that point in time, an evolved physical structure. You will not be the same as you were ten years ago, and you will not be the same as you are today. Yes, perhaps these evolutions, upgrades or enhancements, whatever you choose to call them, may not come quickly enough for your liking. There are limits. It must be a gradual process. If we were to download you too quickly with light and information, your circuits would overload. We feel safe in saying you would not be pleased with the outcome of this kind of approach. Each of you and indeed all of humanity, have an individual plan in terms of your forward momentum and progress relating to the changes taking place within your physical constructs of matter. Your bodies are moving from the world of matter into the world of light. We know that some of you may not understand fully what this means or what it will entail and that is all right.

Again to our analogy, as you stand on this floor here in the Great Hall, you feel absolutely secure and stable in your environment. At no time have you questioned whether or not the floor has the strength and solidity of form and matter to support your weight or this table or any of us. You have not doubted whether this foundation is strong enough to support the walls, yet you also see the golden radiance that emanates outwardly from the walls and floor. How is this possible? How is it this strong structure of form, matter and density can allow such great and beautiful light to pass through freely? Do you see the balance? In this analogy, we are attempting to convey the balance between the world of density and light. This is where all of you are going in the New Earth. It will be an experience unlike any before. This is a new experiment in the realms of the cosmos. Every one of you has chosen to be here and each of you has a role to play. Each of you got a golden ticket to ride. It is our endeavor that through this process and the information we will share with you that more and more of your brothers and sisters will begin to grasp the great change that is upon us and the magnificence of this time.

For you see, once you have arrived on New Earth, you will still recognize yourselves. You will remember your past and you will remember your trials and tribulations, joys and sorrows. You will remember what it was like to be in a body more based in carbon than of light and crystalline substance. However, you will be experiencing life in drastically different ways. The way you live, the way you think and process, the interactions of the ego or lower self, the enhancements that you will have received in your body and function, the abilities and gifts that will become your new normal—–these will all be new to you. Your new gifts will include self-healing, telepathy and a higher ability to manifest your desires more quickly, to name but a few. You will be utilizing many new technologies that you are not yet aware of. As you come to this place, new and wondrous things will come into your experience, perhaps things you cannot even imagine at this time.

The reason we have this discussion with you today and ask you to ponder this analogy is to actually think about your body, the makeup, the chemistry, the matter and all that is a part of your physical body. Each of the four lower bodies (physical, mental, emotional and spiritual) are connected and playing their roles, as are other influences that are moving in and out of your body; but for this discussion let us stay on the subject of the physical body. You see the floor, which is still quite strong and stable, yet a soft emanation of golden light just continues to outflow through the substance such that you might say it is both. It is both matter and density yet it is also light. You might also say it is crystalline light information. Can you see the balance? It is not fully one or the other. It is not fully matter and density and it is not fully light. It is not without form. It is not without structure. It is not without substance. So the two forms have combined and balanced to work together, and the result is one of great strength, beauty and light. We understand this is a simple analogy. We ask that you contemplate this within your own body structure and consider that the body, the form, the matter and density of it to which you have become accustomed is indeed shifting and changing in all manner of ways. It behooves you to be aware of the changes. We know this information has come forth already through a number of forms and avenues; yet we also feel that great numbers of humanity are having some difficulty really contemplating this or integrating it within themselves. Look deeply. Go into meditation and look at your chakras and energy systems. Look at your light emanations, your auras and your current levels of density and light. Look at the vibrations within you that are being transmitted out to the universe. Having this kind of awareness and looking at it intentionally is going to be of great benefit to you in the days ahead.

We ask you not to fear the changes that are taking place. This is all according to the plan of Creator. We are discussing the evolution of humanity, and you all sit now on the doorstep of this great change. And so, as you move into New Earth, you will become a combination of what you are now and that which is yet to come; and we say to you, that which is yet to come is most magnificent, radiant and beautiful. We also know that many of your brothers and sisters will have great fear of this change. They may not be ready to have the conversation. They may not be ready for new awareness to come in and that is okay. Each individual is on their own path in accordance with their highest good. We ask you to embrace the change. We encourage you to move beyond a point of thinking old programmed thoughts such as "This is the way it has always been and there's nothing I can do about it." or "It's too late for me to pursue my dreams. I might fail." etc. We understand that after years and years or even lifetimes and lifetimes of living in this particular environment this is all you have known. This may be your truth today; but what I say to you is, your truth is being expanded into something new and radiant.

As you continue to expand your light, knowledge and awareness, more gifts will come to you as you open to allow and receive. We ask you to embrace this change with great love, excitement and anticipation, not with fear, worry or doubt. This is the time to let your light shine through. This is the time to remember your divinity and where you came from. This is the time to remember your power and your light; and as you continue to move forward in this process, you will begin to experience these gifts of which we speak, these enhancements, these remembrances, these evolutions. I use the term "gifts" because it is a word this channel likes to use; however, I would clarify that it is not we or anyone else bestowing any particular "gift" upon you, for that is not the case. These "gifts" come through your expanded awareness into enlightenment, truth and remembrance. You are moving back into your authentic selves, that which has seemingly been long forgotten. Your memories are being restored as these changes take place and as your bodies and physicality are evolving. As more crystalline substance replaces carbon substance, as previously dormant DNA begins to awaken, as more light comes in where density used to be, so come the information, the authenticity and the remembrance. This is light and light is information. As you bring in more light, you bring in more information, and this propels you to higher levels of functioning and ability.

With the coming and expansion of these new gifts (they are not new but they will appear new), you will be required to maintain your balance, harmony and alignment within that light that is now coming to and through you in greater amounts. With greater amounts of light (understanding, awareness, remembrance, gifts) comes a greater responsibility to the light. That is why we encourage you day-to-day, moment by moment to be in your awareness with each thought, word and emotion. We encourage you to have an awareness of each thought and to see its point of origination. Does it resonate with beauty, light, love and grace; or does it resonate with fear, lack, control and resistance? For as you move forward on this path, the laws of physics are being modified, so to speak; and this is taking place within each of you. As you come more fully into the Realms of Light, it will be a requirement that you increase your levels of responsibility to the light. This is the way of things. It is universal law. I do not say this to alarm you; it just is. We will stay with you and we will assist you along the way. There will be times when you will fall back into density, emotion and ego and this is a natural part of the process. We encourage you, when this happens and if it is in your awareness, not to be too hard on yourselves but to allow yourselves the same levels of love, support and forgiveness that you would offer a dear friend. This is all a part of the process. There are hills and valleys. There are accomplishments and there are setbacks. Just know that each day that passes you will move closer and closer to your goal. This is for each and every one of you. The Company of Heaven stands beside you.

You have dispensations now from Creator that have never been granted before. You are receiving special assistance in the clearing of karma both individually and collectively, and you have an increase in the divine energy of the World Mother. There is greater opportunity existing in your world today than has ever been given before since the time of our last Golden Age. One of our primary reasons for this work is to share information that will help you to find your own truth and to choose, if you so desire, to step fully onto the Path of Light. This path will bring you to your own evolution with feet firmly planted on New Earth. It is our great desire to bring along just as many of humanity as possible. Gaia shares this desire with us, as do all realms within the Company of Heaven. Similar messages are coming forth in many ways and through many messengers now, all according to plan. We give individuals many choices as to how they may find, process and receive similar information and in a way that is as natural for that individual as possible.

The animal kingdoms, the plant and crystal kingdoms and elemental kingdoms are all going through a similar process that we have just described for humanity. The details of the process differ according to the makeup of each level of creation. The crystalline and mineral kingdoms are also going through their evolution, but they are going through their transformation with Gaia. They are linked to her grids of light and energy and she is assisting them. These are vibrational changes that will be necessary for them to move together as a single unit into the New Earth. Then, if we look at the plant kingdoms and animal kingdoms, we see that all species are undergoing their own evolutions simultaneously at this time. There are specialized teams within the Company of Heaven, and we mean all of those of the higher light who are here participating and working with the plans already in place for Mother Gaia and all life present. There are specialized teams working with each level of creation on the planet. A specialized team comprised of Gaia, Elohim, Devic angels, Archangels and others are working with the elemental kingdoms to assist them in their transformation, as one example. There are teams dedicated to the assistance of all of the animal and plant kingdoms, each one at its own level of consciousness, each one with its own vibration and each one with its own makeup of chemistry and matter. Perhaps you are beginning to see why we use the analogy of a grand, cosmic scale project. It's one of the largest projects of its kind to have ever taken place in the cosmos.

Now, I say again for the record, although we hesitate to make predictions within certain time frames of your linear time construct, it is true that we can see the final outcome. The book has already been written so to speak. However, as you have come to understand the question regarding fate and free will, this also applies to humanity at large in regards to the shifts taking place now. To simplify, we might say all of humanity are currently residing in Orlando, Florida and each and every one of you is being guided in a natural yet firm way to make the journey to New York City. Some of you will choose to fly first class. Some of you will choose to take the train. Others may take the bus. Some may hitchhike or walk. Horse and buggy…we do not know. We do not know how the individual choices adding up to the collective will come about moment-to-moment, and of course this collective consciousness is what is bringing about the events and manifestations happening in your world today. Therefore, much of this, meaning how you choose to travel from Orlando to New York, is up to the collective consciousness of humanity. Part of our endeavor is to bring each and every one into a higher level of awareness such that if they had thought before that they may have to walk from Orlando to New York without any food, clothing or comfort, perhaps with new information and understanding they may make the choice for themselves to take a different mode of transportation. Perhaps instead, they prefer to rent a convertible and enjoy the drive. Again, we use analogies because we feel it is an easy and conversational way to grasp the concepts at hand. We know that each of you is capable of higher levels of understanding; but we feel you may appreciate our conversational approach and hope that to be the case.

We know that eventually most everyone will end up in New York. There may be some who choose intentionally not to travel there. They do not want to go. They will not go. They are happy living in Orlando and they simply refuse to go. It is their choice to make. So those who choose not to leave Orlando will be allowed to stay there for the time being. From the very highest levels of view, I can tell you at some time as humans move along their soul's great journey, the time will come when they will make their own choice to travel on to "New York". That is to step onto the Path of Light and to gain the fulfillment of their own ascension. There is no judgment passed on those who choose to stay behind at this time. So you see humanity is evolving very quickly now and the time of the next great shift is upon us. It is not to be feared but to be embraced. One of our endeavors here is to assist you at this time to come to some level of understanding such that each one may have a smooth and graceful journey from Orlando to New York. We would much prefer to see each one take the appropriate transportation of their choosing, not what they perceived they were stuck with, not the so called cards they were dealt, but actually making the choice that brings them the most joy along the way: "You know, I think I would like to take the train. I would like to take a relaxed and leisurely trip to New York where I need not worry about driving or direction. I need not worry about traffic or road signs. I'll relax in the dining car and enjoy a nice cup of tea while the countryside rolls by". This is our hope for humanity and this is the work we are doing.

## Returning to balance

Bryan – *Note: this section stems from what turned out to be mostly a personal coaching session from Master Adama. After having spent the morning in First/Blue ray (Will of God) work, I was feeling heavy and downtrodden. Master Adama understands well the struggle that many of us go through from time to time, and we believe there may be some benefit to the reader through this example.*

Adama - I would like to comment Bryan, and say your auric field is looking a bit more balanced now. You have had some assistance from your family members this afternoon and you have seen for yourself the effectiveness of the violet flame. Also, as you have noted, sitting here peacefully in the portal has helped you to rebalance your energies. We understand why they have been set off balance today, and we thank you for this work you are doing on behalf of Gaia and your brothers and sisters. I am pleased to see that you have been able to balance your energies and that you are feeling better, lighter and more joyful. This is your self-mastery in action. This is why you and many of your brothers and sisters are being called to higher levels of service now. As we progress through the remainder of your time in embodiment, this trend will continue. Each of you is growing stronger by the day. When I say stronger, I mean to say that you are expanding in various areas, all toward the light of course. Your levels of clear knowing, seeing and hearing are increasing. Innate levels of understanding that come forth now––both from your Akash and the connection that is increasing daily to your Higher Self and your families in the light–will continue to expand. Your individual self-mastery, which allows you to have an awareness of what is taking place in your aura fields and the vibrations that you are carrying in your body by your thoughts and feelings, is also expanding. It is within these higher levels of attainment that each of you will be called to do higher levels of work than you have done previously or at least what you may recall in this lifestream experience.

I know that you have had a heavy heart this day, which stems from the great outpouring of love and compassion that you have for your brothers and sisters. As you have looked around the world today, energetically speaking, you have felt within your heart the burden of humanity and also your love and compassion for humanity. You have seen all that is taking place and all that is conspiring against the individual and collective victory in the light. You see the obstacles that are facing each of you in the current environment; and this has left you feeling downtrodden, heavy and sorrowful. I come to you today to let you know these are high levels of work that you and many others are doing and that you do not stand alone in this work, for indeed you have the Company of Heaven standing by your side and at your full support. We understand the heaviness in your heart and the concern for your brothers' and sisters' freedom. I would let you know that those of us who are here participating in the project–– and I do not mean just the Leumurian project, but those who are participating in the next great shift, those of the ascended master realms, the angelic realms, your star nation families––all of us know the burdens that each of you carry. We often feel this burden ourselves. I know there are things that you do not yet understand. Things that have confused you about how this current situation has come about. How could it have been allowed to be this way and how shall we ever break free of it? I will not go into the details. I would not attempt to provide a play by play of cosmic history as it relates to the current situation on Earth, for there would be volumes of information and still much of it may be confusing to you at this particular time. Know that all is acting within and accordance to Creator Law and the Logos.

So very many of you have a great empathy and compassion for your brothers and sisters, Mother Gaia and the many wonderful life forms that share your world. What I wish to tell you or request of you, is never to underestimate the effect that one person, one human with a pure heart, one who is stepping into his or her divinity and consciously co-creating with Creator can have in their manifestations such as that of peace on Earth. You have looked around energetically to your brothers and sisters and you have felt into their condition and all that is causing them to feel trapped and downtrodden, all that is keeping them from embodying the light of their own divinity; and you have wondered, "How is it that anyone ever made it out of here?" meaning out of the rounds of karma and reincarnation and that of earning their ascension in the light. I come here today with a message of upliftment and hope and to let you know that one person working with a pure heart can literally shift the consciousness of all of humanity. One person, just one person with the fires burning, those who have a passion for freedom, truth, light, love, peace; those that come with a pure heart through their prayers, calls, invocations, declarations and commands can shift the energy of the entire planet.

Do not think for one moment that the work you do is not having an impact. If you could only see the great army of light that you and all of your brothers and sisters bring with you when you make these calls. If you could only see the change, the shift in consciousness, the bringing about of more light and more truth for the benefit of the greater good. If you could see what one person can do, I promise you, my friend, you would be reassured in your work. You would be revitalized and energized and even more passionate about your work. You have read a message from Master Hilarion wherein he stated that it takes only two to three percent of a population to shift the collective and this is so. This is true. There are more and more who are being led by their Higher Selves and through the experiences they are given to come into new levels of awareness and who are stepping now consciously into the light and asking what they can do to participate in the lightworker community.

There is a tidal wave of light flooding the planet. You are not able to perceive this as those of us working at inner levels are. We can see the tidal wave. We can see the lights turning on. We can see the consciousness shifting. We can see that as the light comes in where darkness was before, darkness is being expelled and extinguished by the light.

So I come today to encourage you. Also, your interpretation in regards to different teams all working in the light, all working on the same grand project but that each of you is drawn to different areas of focus and to those activities which are aligned to your nature is accurate. Certainly you can see that not all individuals would be well suited to perform the kinds of work you are being led to do; nor would you be suited to do the kinds of work that others are doing. It would not feel natural to you; so just as those of the darkness have employed all manner of tactics, we are also employing all manner of tactics. The lightworkers who are embodied today are being called now to come into their remembrance and their awareness and to begin actively participating. Your brothers and sisters––especially those who came here to be wayshowers for those around them––are turning on left and right; and there are a variety of frameworks available to each one so that they may find their way into the work that is natural for them. This will be the work they came here to do. Some will be drawn to do this work and some drawn to do that work and that is fine because we are all working on the same project. There are a great many jobs and tasks that are to be done for the successful completion of our project; and every job is important, regardless of how large or small that job may appear to be.

So I encourage you in these times when you just simply feel overwhelmed or when your soul feels tired, I bid you take heart.

The tides are turning, my friend, and they are turning in our favor. The momentum is as a tidal wave sweeping the land. It is true that those of the lightworker community, all of the masters who have chosen to come back at this time—and there are many of you—it is up to you to carry the load for the time being. You all are being asked to hold the space, hold the light, and to do the work on behalf of your brothers and sisters who are not yet able to do it for themselves. This is the work that those of us on the inner planes have been doing for eons. So when I say to you, we understand your heart and your burdens, indeed we do. Call on us for your solace and your peace in these times. We will lift those burdens from you and we will shield you when you need to be shielded. We will give you peace when you need peace and we will help you rest when you need rest. We will help you find courage when you need courage. We will help you find joy and upliftment in your heart on those days when your heart is heavy. The blessed Mother Mary has spoken about this in our meeting just two days ago.

I say this again as a reminder. As you move into higher levels of awareness and work, it will be, if not necessary, at least to your great benefit to call on us regularly. We know your troubles and we know your hearts. You all—the masters who have come back to lead humanity into this next great shift—you are our front lines. You are the warriors of the light there in the thick of it, in the 3D construct bringing in the light for all to see. It is of utmost importance that you all remain grounded, healthy and balanced as you move forward, and we are here to assist you in every way that the Law allows. We will do so. It is our great joy to do so. The tides are turning my friend. I know that is difficult for you to see it from the higher-level perspective as we do. I come to assure you the work being done by all of you who are standing in the awareness of your own bright light is taking hold. The light is rushing in now and you are in good company. Also, and you have heard this before, indeed many of you who are the masters who have chosen to come back at this time to re-embody as bringers of the light, indeed many of you may feel inside you that your journey has been long and you are tired. I tell you this is so. It is true. For many of you, your journeys have been long. For eons of time you have taken embodiments here on Earth, and your preparation prior to your first embodiment may have begun even long before you first came here. And so many of you are feeling this. You are just feeling tired and we know. Believe me when I say we understand.

I ask you also to believe me now when I tell you that all of you who are here working with the light, you would not have missed this opportunity for the world. We are at the dawn of a new age and this is the most critical time. This is the tipping point of the great shift, and none of you would have missed the opportunity. It is what you have worked so long and so hard to bring about. It has been your work, your focus, your passion and your mission for many of you over eons of time, and we stand now at the doorway of the next Golden Age, which we refer to as New Earth. You have come on your own accord. You would not have missed it. You would not have been happy to sit on the sidelines and watch others come and participate; and this is why you, the workers and warriors of the light, are here. I say again take heart. Take heart. You are in the very best of company and you are doing the work that you came to do. We are all deeply honored to be working with so many masters and so many warriors of the light who have come back now, brave and courageous souls who have chosen to come again to bring the light that is dispelling the darkness day by day. The light builds its momentum as the darkness recedes from the planet. You all have come to bring your great light, to lead the way and to make your calls for freedom, to teach your brothers and sisters to be wayshowers and to set the example for others. We know you better than you know yourselves. We know the mighty warriors that you are. We know the mighty containers of love and compassion that you are. We know the mighty fires of healing and love that you bring with you. We know the sense of justice and equality that you bring to the world. This is why you have come, and those of us on the inner planes are honored to be working beside you. You are our family and we are yours. Take heart this day my dear friend. Our victory in the light is assured. All is well.

This is not the discussion that I had planned for today, but given our circumstances I felt it appropriate and beneficial to have this talk with you. It is my sincere hope that the message I bring you today will bring upliftment and a momentum to continue forward. Push forward on those days that you can push. Rest and take care of yourself on those days when that is what you need. Call on Father/Mother God and open your heart to receive. Call on us. Tell us your burdens and allow us to lift them from you. Know that we stand beside you at every turn. You are not alone, none of you are. You are all deeply loved.

# Chapter 7

## First meeting with Trindletothton
## Master Adama and the Mighty Blue Dragons of Venus
## Master Adama, Trindy and Anthuras
## Follow up with Master Adama

### First meeting with Trindletothton

Bryan - *This section introduces Trindletothton. These are personal notes taken directly following my experience on July 14, 2015. At that time, I was not aware that I would be invited to Mt. Shasta for this work or that my personal notes would ever be made public. The jumping off point for this journey was my personal pyramid in the 5$^{th}$ dimension. Archangel Michael had told me sometime before, that he had the most wondrous things to show me.*

Tonight, I traveled to the pyramid where I found Archangel Michael and two angel brothers already waiting. Archangel Michael told me to come with him and that he had something to show me. I traveled with him in his energy field. His presence was strong but it was difficult to interpret the speed and distance of travel. I perceive that Archangel Michael simply directs his attention to a location and we are there. In an instant we stopped, and it felt as if we had traveled to the edge of the galaxy. There, we were looking out at the Milky Way from the perspective of Space. It was beyond beautiful, beyond description. He asked if I was ready to go again and with a flash of light and in an instant we were there. I found myself in a field of tall grass staring up at a very large, white unicorn. He was standing very close to me with several others behind him. My mouth was hanging open and I did not know what to say. They communicate telepathically and I perceived them as very wise and kind beings. The first thing he said to me was "What, you didn't think we were real?" There were quite a few of them, perhaps six or seven, but one who was very close. He lowered his head so I could touch his face, and he appeared to me to be very similar to many of the images we see in our mythology. They are quite large, however, and I perceived the tops of their heads to be nine or ten feet tall with strong and muscular bodies. We were in the Fields of Telos. I could sense their great love and wisdom and it felt wonderful to be in their presence. He said they were coming back again to help us. He bid me a good day and said we would meet again.

Soon they left and we were looking out into the field when a great, blue dragon flew down and landed in front of us. I almost couldn't believe my eyes, but there he was in front of me. I was not afraid in the least. He put his head down on the ground in front of me, which I interpreted as a welcoming posture. His kind eyes also helped me to feel comfortable. Archangel Michael asked me if I wanted to take the ride of my life and I said, "Sure, Yes, Of Course". There was a strange looking saddle on him. The shape was odd and the seat was covered with a soft velvet-like material. The dragon told me telepathically the easiest way up. He put his head flat against the ground, and I climbed up first on his front leg and then just on the front side of his wing. His scales are very large and it was easy to get a foothold and handhold, so I climbed up into the saddle. I asked him for his name. It took several minutes and multiple attempts before I got it right, but his name is Trindletothton and he said I could call him Trindy for short. I asked him how I was to keep from falling off, and he explained to me that as his rider, he had attached himself to me energetically sort of like a magnet and that it was impossible for me to fall. He stood up; and with a few powerful flaps of his wings, we were off.

He flew over the city of Telos where I could see the people and the city skyline. Some of them were waving to him in a fun and friendly way; then we moved out and up at what I can only imagine is faster than the speed of light. I could sense movement but it was not the same kind of movement we understand. It was like being in the eye of a hurricane. It felt still but at the same time there was a sense of movement. He stopped, and again I found myself looking out at the stars from the viewpoint of the heavens. It was beautiful beyond description. I could see the Earth too, mostly dark on our side but I could see the light of the sun off in the distance.

He took off again in a flash and we traveled straight towards the sun. He let me know that we were going to Venus. I was aware of higher-level beings from Venus, but I didn't know anything about them. He flew me over a city and told me I might expect this to be a hot and intolerable climate but that was not the case. They have built cities, dwelling spaces and environments that are wonderful to behold. They also have inner planetary cities of crystal much like Telos. I could not make out a lot of it, but what I saw was a city made of crystals with soft colored lights emanating out in all directions. He landed in a small square where a number of beings were gathered. I perceived them to be very tall (12'or13') and more of light than of matter. They did not appear to have the physicality of humans or Lemurians; yet there was form. Their light was so bright that I struggled against it to see. I could not sense gender. Of the fifteen or so who were present, there were three that came forward to greet me and I knew they were the young ones. I do not know what young is in their years but I perceived the energy to be that of sweet and curious children. I had dismounted and was standing there to interact with them. Our communication was very basic, and I do not remember an exchange of words so much as the tremendous waves of love and light radiating from them. This was an experience of the heart rather than the intellect. They were letting me know they were inviting me to visit again and that their presence will become known to us in a greater and more profound way. I perceived they might be the Holy Kumaras of Venus. We said our very pleasant goodbyes; then Trindy and I returned to Telos.

As I climbed down, Archangel Michael was smiling and I was laughing. "This is unbelievable!" I said. He said that I am coming to understand more fully who I really am and that my primary ray / activity here is the blue ray. I asked Trindletothton if the legends about dragons breathing fire were true. He gave me a quizzical look and immediately let loose a bright blue flame that traveled hundreds of feet into the air. The flame had a bright neon glow about it and looked more like magic or energy than an actual flame. Trindy said that I could find him here. He said if I come to the Fields of Telos and call his name, he would hear me. I asked Archangel Michael about it, and he said that I should request an escort to this place either by him or one of my Lemurian friends until such time as I may be allowed to visit here on my own. There is so much more to see here in this place. This is just the beginning.

## Master Adama and the Mighty Blue Dragons of Venus

Bryan - *Note: Fast forward now. A year has passed. I'm in Shasta now making regular trips to the portal on the mountain. This section and the next include dictations that took place over the course of three visits.*

Bryan - *Master Adama, can you tell me if Trindletothton comes from Venus? Is that where the blue dragons are from?*

Adama - Yes, it is and your friend Trindletothton will be happy to speak with you on such matters in your future meetings together. Your old friend does come from Venus, and there is a great family and lineage of these advanced beings of light there on Venus yet today. It is with great love that your friend returns at this time to work with you and address those who would listen; for they, meaning Trindletothton and many of his family, were with you leading up to and in your last embodiment as a Lemurian. More of you are becoming aware of some of the events and history that have taken place. As is the case with many advanced beings of light that have been here at one time or another, the time came when they left or were forced to leave. Dragons understand the hearts of men.

Dragons are most wise and noble beings with a great capacity for love and service. You may ask him yourself; but we believe, it is with great joy and anticipation that Trindletothton makes his return to work with you and address your brothers and sisters. Their existence is beginning to come back into your awareness now, and many of you reading these words have had similar training in your past embodiments as Lemurians and Atlanteans. There is much more to come as your awareness expands and as you further expand in your roles here. Make no mistake, each of you is being guided now internally through your own inner awareness and Higher Selves and externally via your Families of Light. You are individually and collectively being encouraged to come into your full awareness and to begin using it for your greatest good and for the greatest good of all.

For the most part, this knowledge was withdrawn from your world during the time of the last great shift and in your last embodiments as Lemurians. By this time, most of the beings that you refer to as dragons had returned home. Several of them stayed; and your friend Trindletothton was one who stayed to what we would say was the very last moment in which he was working with you and all members of our family in those very difficult and challenging times. He has been a most dear friend to all of us and we enjoy his visits to our city very much. He visits with us often. So you see, after these many thousands of years he has returned with great joy in his heart. He has come in the anticipation of connecting with you all again but more specifically to work with you and others to help you to remember that which you have already known. It is time for some of the lost knowledge to come back to the forefront and indeed to be set in application. These remembrances or teachings that are forthcoming will be applicable in your personal experiences but also applicable to the great shift that we are all entering into now.

## Adama continues

Adama - Bryan, you have noticed the stillness on the mountain this day. Your weather is overcast and cloudy with a slight drizzle of rain from time to time. There is a special stillness about the mountain this day that you can sense. You are perceiving that your sense of stillness is due to your experience of the weather and in part it is. It is also an opportunity for rest for the mountain and all life upon it this day. This is a rest day, just as you and many others have experienced a recent need for increased amounts of rest to help you integrate the higher energies and light that are flooding the planet at this time. I will share with you that Mother Gaia and all creatures great and small are also integrating these new levels of energy; and they too, as much as can be afforded, benefit by periods of rest, peace and non-activity. So while you do often experience the peace and joy of the mountain on your visits here, I will just confirm your suspicion—that this is a day of rest and integration for the mountain. You are all connected; so doesn't it make sense in one way or another that the shifts humans are going through would also be necessary for all forms and levels of life here on the planet as well?

We have told you that your friend Trindy comes from a large family and long lineage of advanced beings of light, many of which currently inhabit what you know to be their homeland planet of Venus. This relates again to the message we delivered several days ago regarding the history of Lemuria when the dragon tribes were once there in great assistance to us, and we have reminded you that they left. The higher beings of light known as dragons left our planet. They have been waiting for the collective consciousness of humanity to reach a point where they may make their return and assist humanity in what we are calling the next great shift. We told you that your friend Trindy is now ready to come back; and through this joint project, he will be delivering new information from the dragon tribes. We understand there is a level of discomfort and reluctance on your part to go out among your peers and begin speaking of dragons. There are some who are ready to embrace and receive this information and the truth that it is; yet there are many who are not ready to receive it at this time. Other messengers are also assisting in drawing the dragon tribes back to your awareness. Do not be concerned. It will sort itself out in due time. These higher beings of light have been great friends to humanity and they come back now; should we say they are beginning to make themselves known again as we step into the doorway of this next great shift. They have so much to offer us. They are bringing forth what we might call the vibration of their collective, and this is a most beautiful and loving vibration of light and wisdom. They will bring forth dragon wisdom and dragon medicine at various levels such that many of your brothers and sisters will find great benefit and use in all they bring forward for you. We are just now stepping through the doorway in this regard. We will take you out and give you a vision of what will come to pass in this new Golden Age at some point in your dreams, visions and prayers of the New Earth.

Our friends from Venus, the dragon collective and dragon tribes, will be fully present and participating for at least some period of time. It will come to pass that the old ways of men are no longer. It will come to pass that the record shall be set straight; and this not only applies to these beings of light, the dragons, but to many more also. There are remnants in your current mythology and fairy tales that have been passed down through the ages in which great truth resides yet remains hidden. In many cases, the truth has been intentionally manipulated in such a way as to present information that is less than truthful. In your mythology today, dragons are beings most often portrayed as those to be feared, as those wanting to come and control mankind or hoard gold or however the stories may go. In the minds of most of your brothers and sisters, at least in your culture (this is not true in all cultures), most of you still have the idea that they are just creations of mythology, storybooks and Hollywood movies. You have come to see for yourself. You have been shown the truth of the matter by your dear friend Archangel Michael, who has arranged and accompanied you on your first meeting. Trindletothton is a blue dragon being, and he will be speaking more to you about this, for we know it is a subject of great interest to you and others.

There are many tribes or families of these great beings. Just as is the case with humanity, there are different colors, attributes, traits and configurations among you. You may refer to them as tribes, families or collectives (however this feels for you is okay). Many of the dragon tribes will be present and working with us as we move forward into the next Golden Age. In fact, they are working with us now. Their presence is already here among you. They bless us all by bringing forth great light, truth, wisdom, love and Creator Will.

The distinction that we make goes back to our reference a moment ago, that at some point, when we show you the vision of the future state, what you will see is a great many beings of light now on the New Earth visiting and living among you. This will be a time of great enlightenment and understanding—we are taking you out quite a ways, you understand. It will be a time when the collective consciousness of humanity has shifted and all have moved firmly with feet planted on New Earth. Everything on Earth will be moving, acting, vibrating and embodying higher levels of consciousness and awareness. At that time, humanity will walk among their brothers and sisters of light and all manner of beings. The day will come when humankind will walk side by side with dragons, Lemurians, angels, Ascended Masters, Pleiadians, Arcturians, Sirians and many more. You will take your place among your brothers and sisters of light around the cosmos. What a wondrous day this will be! This is the work we are doing now. Great change is ahead of us and we have much work to do, but what an exciting time for all of us to witness this. The time is coming when humanity will take their place at the table and sit among your greater Families of Light; and what a glorious day this will be for all.

## Master Adama, Trindy and Anthuras

Bryan - *Master Adama, I would like to confirm that Trindy and Anthuras were visiting with me here in the meadow today. Did I perceive that accurately?*

Adama - I have been sitting patiently waiting for this question. I have energetically helped you get there. You observed first the small tree that reminded you of a dragon; then you felt the presence of both of them in the meadow with you through your heart space. You were accurate in that perception. Your friends Anthuras and Trindy were there to greet you this afternoon before our work began. They simply wanted to make you aware of their presence. You have not formally met Anthuras yet, but you will. As you can see plainly, both of them are working together and come from the same family. Their work is very similar and each of them does spend considerable time visiting with us and many other beings in Telos. They are welcome to come and go as they please. They are known to all here and friends to all here. We welcome their visits always. Anthuras was a mentor in past embodiments both human and Lemurian to your predecessor Aurelia. They continue their work together to this day. In your time as Lemurians, when things were good, so to speak, there were many beings of the dragon tribes there working with us. You and your family, and this includes Aurelia, were working primarily with the family of beings that you recognize now as the blue dragons. Anthuras and Aurelia will be participating in our project, and they may independently or together pop in from time to time to lend their guidance, instruction or encouragement. They wish to have active participation in this project as we move forward and I trust that your heart is open to receive their friendship and guidance in this way.

Bryan - *Yes, of course.*

Adama - Aurelia has had the opportunity now to spend time with her friend Anthuras and his family, which of course includes your friend Trindy. She has traveled to Venus, the Pleiades and other locations for higher levels of study. Upon crossing the veil and after a settling in period, she has now set a course for her future path as it were, to include areas of interest and things she has a passion for. As you might imagine, she has a great passion for our project and the work we will do together. She will be assisting us from the higher realms. As she participates in our project, she is also pursuing her own endeavors. Growth and expansion never stop, and she has chosen to spend time with the dragon tribes. She is learning even higher levels of attainment than have been accessible to her in her previous embodiments. As you would imagine, she is in a place now where she has a much greater understanding of all that is. The veils of forgetfulness and illusion have been lifted, and she now stands in the full light of her divinity. She gets to choose from a huge array of wonderful opportunities and experiences, one of which is to continue her work with her friend Anthuras.

Again, although your meeting was not formal, Anthuras has come to you today with Trindy to extend his greetings and to let you know he will be participating in our project. Our friends from the dragon families are here in service to Creator and the Elohim. They are here offering their love and great assistance to all humanity, Mother Gaia and all life on the planet. They are also here to assist us in making a wrong right again. Some of the high level magic being used and deployed even today by those of the dark forces, those who have chosen to move away from the light and work in separation, much of the magic that is in use today was brought to us by the dragon families in the last Golden Age and golden ages before. This would not be your last embodiment but going back further to a time when we were all truly living in harmony and light. This was the time of Mu.

There was no discord at that time. It was a time of strong community and an age of miracles and light. At that time, our friends in the dragon tribes were teaching those who they felt worthy, high levels of magic. You know this already. What you don't know is, unfortunately, through the course of events these new levels of ability and higher levels of magic were intentionally sought out and destroyed within the Realms of Light in the earth plane. The knowledge was intentionally extinguished from those standing in the light who may have used the knowledge to combat that of equal force which had been taken and misqualified by those working in separation from their Creator. This advanced knowledge was intended to be used only in the light. Yes, it was misqualified by some of those you know as the Atlanteans but also with great sway and influence from others in the galaxy. Again, I will stop us from going into the depths of this topic. We may discuss it more in the future, but for purpose of this conversation what you need to know is these higher levels of magic were intentionally extinguished in those of the light who would most certainly have used it in the light. Those beings, groups of Atlanteans and others, who chose intentionally to hold and use this magic against the light and all life here, retained this knowledge. Some used it for their own selfish desire and they still do so today. This misuse of power is all coming to an end. Much of the information that was lost is coming forth now for those who would have eyes to see it and ears to hear it.

New information will be coming to your awareness from a variety of sources, bi-products of the shift we are discussing. Your previously dormant DNA is being roused. Memories from previous lives and embodiments elsewhere are becoming easier to access. Your four lower bodies are doing their best to integrate and keep pace with accelerated levels of light and information and your consciousness is rising. Your connection to your Higher Self and higher aspects is becoming easier and more recognizable. The angels and your Families of Light are supporting you in many ways also to come into alignment with harmony and grace. You are calling forth in this lifetime all of this knowledge, remembrance and gifts that are inherently yours. You have earned them yourselves through your own service to the light and through your own participation. Are you with me so far?

Bryan - *Yes sir, I am.*

Adama - So what we have is a situation where select groups of humanity, through their own inheritance, their own free will choice and other manner of ways, have retained this knowledge which of course was always intended to be used in service to the light. Those standing in separation have practiced this knowledge, and it has been one of many causes of all manner of suffering for humanity. What I say simply is, the dragon tribes have come back now to assist all of us in the light, in the balancing of the scales and of setting things right. They work from the highest levels of attainment of consciousness, love and light. The blue dragons of Venus are highly advanced beings with great wisdom, understanding and abilities far beyond your current comprehension. They are here to play an active role in the creation of New Earth.

The offer is extended to each of you today through me: as you go about your light work you may invoke the presence of both Anthuras and Trindletothton. They graciously offer their friendship and assistance should any of you choose it. You are divine, sovereign beings of light and it is important for you to maintain your awareness as such. It is always your choice. I bring this to your awareness today to let you know that a higher/stronger connection with your Families of Light is not only possible, but is available and on offer for you.

You, Bryan, have been shown a vision this afternoon in the meadow to allow you to have some sense of their power at all levels, physically, energetically and with high light and great authority. Anthuras showed you a vision when he stamped his front foot on the Earth, and you have seen and felt in your vision the Earth tremble and shake under his feet. He has shown you this in a way that was not intended to bring fear but to let you know what powerful allies they can be for you. As you saw this in your mind, you made the statement without any fear or concern "Whoa, I feel sorry for anyone who stands in your way". (Authors note: Other things were said.) All this to say simply: should you, the reader, choose to be in service in this way (planetary work / first ray) that you and all of us may benefit by allowing these two beings to join with you. According to Creator Law, your Families of Light cannot impose upon your free will and therefore require your invitation in order to assist you. I have gotten myself sidetracked but one point of note is, they have come here not only in service of the light but to reclaim that which was stolen from them. You could say it is also personal for them. I believe I can say this to you without creating confusion or misunderstanding within you.

Bryan - *Yes sir I understand.*

Adama - Also, I wish to say, please do not make the mistake of thinking that you need invoke the assistance of Anthuras and Trindletothton only in those times when you are actively working with the blue flame. You may also rely on them as a trusted friends and advisors. They are quite wise in all the ways of the world. This is an important note. They here to assist each of you with all that relates to the fullness and joy of your being.

Bryan - Note: *Allow me to provide some background regarding Master Adama's statement of* "I believe I can say that to you without creating confusion or misunderstanding within you". *He is addressing a thought I had and reminding me that the blue dragons of Venus are here in service to the first ray. As such, they embody divine neutrality at all times. The reclaiming and fulfillment of our collective freedom and ascension is personal for them, but these feelings stem from their great love for humanity and Gaia, not from a place of lower vibration.*

*It can be challenging not to have judgment, be angry or hold animosity against those who may have acted against us. By embracing these energies we only harm ourselves. This has to do with balance and alignment. As an example of blue ray work, perhaps we make a call such as, "In the name of God and my own beloved I AM Presence, I command God Freedom for all sentient beings. We are the sons and daughters of God and we stand in the Light of God that never fails. Our victory is assured. May it be on Earth as it is in Heaven. Thy Will Be Done." Many of you are doing this kind of work each day. Thank you.*

*Archangel Michael has spoken with me about striving to remain in a place of divine neutrality at all times really, but especially in this work. That is not to allow myself to move into the lower vibrations of all that we see going on in the world. In my words and to put it bluntly, he let me know that we and those who I refer to as the Angels of the Sword of Blue Flame and others are indeed fully in the midst of casting out the darkness of this world, but it is by and through the Will of Creator rather than our own. The angels also require our prayers to Father/Mother God and/or our direct calls for assistance if they are to act in our world with full authority and presence.*

Archangel Michael's Message - We're talking about divine neutrality. This means to keep the negative emotion out of it. Command from a place of power that is God's Will acting through you. This power is Divine love and light. It can be nothing else. Make your commands with the authority of the Light but do not allow yourself to come out of balance or into a lower vibration during your prayer process. It is just a matter-of-fact kind of approach in regards to the kind of work being referenced here: calls for God Freedom and the full removal of all dark forces acting in this world. First ray Angels are the embodiment of God's Will being done. This authority comes from Father/Mother God who is also love. Love is the highest power of the All That Is.

## Follow up with Master Adama

Bryan - *Master Adama, as I was going back through the last Telos series I see that Aurelia tells us Anthuras comes from the Pleiades. I have made note that the tribe of blue dragons, which I am familiar with, come from Venus. Has there been some misunderstanding on my part?*

Adama - What we have here is another situation where really both are true. Neither of these pieces of information is inaccurate. We have made the statement that your friends, the mighty blue dragons come from Venus, and this is one of their current (what you might call) homeland civilizations. This is the way you have referenced it in all of your materials and this is accurate. Just as we have discussed––and we will use ourselves as an example––in our Lemurian community here in Telos, there is a great variety of options and opportunities available for us to travel, live, learn and explore a great many other locations and star nations. For those who desire to have the experience of travel, adventure or higher learning, there is truly an endless variety of opportunity available for any who choose to do so. Many of our citizens in Telos will take assignments in other areas of the cosmos, generally for higher learning but also for the experience itself. It is not uncommon for one or some of us to go off even perhaps for thousands of years to live among other civilizations. We may enjoy those places and those cultures or those opportunities that are available to us there. As you know, the Pleiadians are one of your primary starseed parents. Indeed, many of you will trace your origins back to your Pleiadian brothers and sisters.

Many of you also have Pleiadian aspects that exist somewhere now, either in their homeland of the Pleiades or elsewhere. Many of you on the planet today in one way or another, regardless of your specific origins, will have ties back to the Pleiadians. It just so happens that Aurelia's friend Anthuras has, over millennia, come to form great ties and relationships with his Pleiadian brothers and sisters. While it is true that the majority of what we will call the homeland civilization of the tribe of blue dragons is residing at this time on the planet Venus, they do have other areas, groups and civilizations in which they enjoy spending their time. We have made note here that Anthuras and Trindy and some of the others, enjoy visiting Telos quite often. So while they are not taking up residence here in Telos, they come to visit us quite often and this is for our mutual benefit and enjoyment. That is to say, these brothers from the dragon kingdom enjoy our city and our citizens very much. They have a great many friends here and many of us have a great love and respect for them also. We enjoy spending time with them very much.

What we have here is a situation where Anthuras has made what we might call a long term yet temporary home there with his brethren in the Pleiades. This is just his choice or preference at this time, but again let me make a note here as we are talking about this. You are still framing it up from a perspective of a third dimensional paradigm. I would like to remind you that the limitations you experience and know there do not exist here in the higher dimensions. Time and space and other points of perception as you know them do not work the same. These beings, the dragons, are a highly expanded level of being. The framework in which they operate is not anything that you are familiar with, and frankly I am having some difficulty explaining this in a way that makes some sense for you. But yes, both statements are true.

Anthuras does spend a great deal of time there in the Pleiades and he has made that his home for the time being. He has made the decision to be there at this time for a couple of reasons. One is his great love for his Pleiadian family, but also because he is playing an integral role in this grand project. He was the first dragon in our works to be introduced through Aurelia. The Pleiadians are playing a major and important role in the project plan. They are firmly established as some of the leaders from the other star nations who are assisting us and participating in this grand project. It has been enjoyable and beneficial then for Anthuras to spend time with them there. He comes from the Pleiades but he also comes from Venus. It is just a matter of which eon or eons you want to select as your time frame reference. Again, it has been told to you that the mighty dragons were some of the very first beings present in this universe, even at the time of its creation; so essentially they are truly some of the oldest and wisest of beings in the cosmos. So really, they make their home wherever they choose.

Anthuras is in constant communication with his family on Venus, and they all see each other quite regularly in one location or another. You see there is no limitation here in terms of their ability to commune or travel about. At the time Aurelia brought this information about, he was and still is choosing to remain in the Pleiades. That is where he is now. That does not mean this is where he will be 25,000 or 100,000 years from now. Perhaps he will choose to make somewhere else his home, you see. Just keep in mind these great beings of light that you know as the blue dragons do not have just one home world. They are infinite beings of light, so we are really using this as a reference point. It is true that a great many of them have chosen to make their homes in the planet Venus but just keep in mind this is simply a reference point, you might say. They are much more expansive than that. I hope this makes some sense for you.

Bryan - *Yes sir, Master Adama, it does.*

# Chapter 8
# Message from Trindletothton

Bryan – Note: *As I was sitting in the meadow relaxing and moving into the vibration of the portal prior to our session, the clouds were dancing over the mountain. I sat and watched them take the shape of a dragon several times. I knew Trindletothton was delivering them to me as gifts of joy and to let me know he had come for a visit.*

Adama - Good afternoon Bryan. Welcome back to the Great Hall. We see that you have already observed the presence of your dear friend Trindletothton among us here in the Great Hall, and we see it has brought you great joy to see him. We feel comfortable in saying he feels a similar joy in having an opportunity to visit with you. In our recent discussions of Trindletothton and his family from Venus, he has been aware of what is taking place at multiple levels in this regard, and he has come this day to visit with us and with you.

Trindletothton - Good afternoon my old friend. It is good to see you again. It is good to see you here on the mountain. Many changes and much growth have taken place within you since our last meeting, and my family and I are so very pleased to see that you have followed your soul's calling to the mountain. We are pleased to see that you are here doing your work with our dear friends in Telos. Isn't it exciting to be on the forefront of these wondrous truths that you are coming to be shown now?

Bryan - *Yes sir, indeed it is. I am deeply honored to be able to work with you in this way and to share the truth of you and your family.*

Trindletothton – Yes, dear one, we thank you for that and we appreciate the opportunity to bring forth our messages for humanity through this project. We have much to share. You would like to know if we prefer to be referenced as dragons or if we go by another name. My answer is "yes" to both. Although there are misunderstandings currently present in your culture and others about the mythology of our race, we would say this is perfectly acceptable to us for the time being. In other realms of the cosmos, we are known by a different names. This is not so important. Many things like geographic locations, families of beings and even individual beings such as many of the Ascended Masters may also be known by several different identities. It depends on who is perceiving them––the level of being and embodiment of those who know the being. We are the race of beings you know as dragons. What we hope for and endeavor to do is to make ourselves known to humanity again in the way that you have known us before. That is, as great friends and allies, for indeed we are those things. It is our service to the light to assist you––humanity, Gaia and all life here––and others like you in your evolution, in finding your way home. In those days in which you and I and others worked together, we brought you information having to do with what you might refer to as high magic of the light. We were assisting you in bringing forth all that is your divine birthright. As the Light of Creator shines within each and every one of you, you hold within the palms of your hands a great power and authority which has long since been forgotten. We too have been forgotten. Now is the time of the great awakening and now is the time of our return. We endeavor to make it known, as time and consciousness allow, as collective growth and evolution allow, that we are here again.

We've come to pick up where we left off in assisting you and all of humanity in the raising of consciousness and in the return to the next great Golden Age of peace and light. We understand that there are few, relatively few on the planet at this time, who may be ready to accept our truth and message. Indeed, we understand there are few who are willing, perhaps, even to accept that we exist, due in great part to all of the knowledge and historical data that was lost since the time of Lemuria. Other information was intentionally locked away for use at a future date. You understand a part of our history as it relates to yours, and you know the time came when we were forced to leave. However, that was not before we took appropriate action such that most, should we say at least some of the information, the great teachings and many artifacts had been safely transferred to their current locations around the world. One obvious example is your family here in the mountain, who chose this place as their primary refuge. There were other groups who went out to other geographic locations, and many of them are still connected and in communication with each other. The time came when we were forced to leave and "leave you all with it" so to speak and allow you to sort things out in your own way. This became a requirement as your world fell further into density and darkness; we had no choice.

Our hearts are full of joy this day, that the time has come again when the doors have opened and we see more and more of you embracing your own divinity, embracing the light and truth of Creator and stepping into that truth and knowledge in a way that has been long forgotten in your world. And so, it is with great joy in our hearts that we tell you we have come again to assist all of you in making your transition into a new paradigm, a new way of living and a new way of being. Mine is a family of teachers and wayshowers. We are a family of Ascended Masters and this is one of the primary roles of service we play. It is our honor to be here assisting you. We have a great love for humanity. We have a great respect for and we honor the story of humanity. We honor the brave souls that each and every one of you is. For when the call was made, each of you came forth to volunteer for this grand adventure and what a grand adventure it has been.

Believe me, dear friend, we understand very well the trials and tribulations that each one has experienced on this journey through rounds of embodiment, rounds of learning, karma, expansion and growth. While this process may be somewhat confusing to you at times or perhaps you wonder why any of you would have signed up for such a role as this, we ask that you hear our truth and be assured in the knowledge that each and every one of you will––at some point, upon your own choosing and according to the path of your own soul––make your ascension in the light. You will return home again and when you do, your victory will be celebrated around the cosmos. Each of you will return with a specialized set of advanced knowledge. This is not the knowledge that may be imparted as what you might refer to as book study or classroom study, for it must be experienced fully and wholly by the soul itself. With this experience comes true knowledge, growth, learning and understanding. When you return home, each of you will have within you a specialized set of experience and knowledge that will make you extremely valuable within the Company of Heaven. You see, relatively speaking, there are very few among us who hold the information set and wisdom that each of you will have upon your return home. This information set will be most valuable, useful and applicable to many, many other locations and all manner of beings around the cosmos. Once you return home you will be great teachers; and with this advanced and unique set of information having been earned, each of you will have many opportunities available to you. I will give you a few examples. You may choose to join a collective in which new worlds are created and formed. You may choose to work with a collective to take on different embodiments and actually dwell upon other civilizations as master teachers much in the same way that many of the Ascended Masters you work with now have also come and walked the Earth as great teachers and bringers of light. Each of you, upon your graduation, will have the opportunity of service that is not unlike those of your Ascended Masters. Perhaps you may choose, with your advanced degrees, to assist other councils and boards, ruling councils who are assisting many civilizations from our side of the veil. There will be much more that is available to you, but I trust these few examples give you some idea of my meaning.

So my friend, as you and other bringers of light like you move back into your mastery at this time, we come to work with you. You are the Ascended Masters of the future. You are the teachers and wayshowers both in your present state and in that which you will become in the future. Now, I am speaking in linear time fashion. We need not go into that discussion. You understand my meaning. I offer this information to you as a sign of hope despite what you see taking place at, should we say, the street level view of your current experience on the planet and within humanity that so many of you are sending your light and prayers to. You are calling for the end of suffering for humanity. You are bringing great light, love and compassion to your world. We ask you not to allow yourself to become overly dismayed by all you see going on around you; for, in fact, these are signs of growth, change and progress, as painful as they may be. I bring you this message today to lift your hearts in joy and in anticipation of all that is coming for each of you. In your time as a Lemurian, you and others, some of whom will find their way to these works, were capable of great magic and great achievement, great levels of thought and possibility that you may hardly fathom at this particular time. You have known these things and they are still within you. They are there in your Akash and DNA. More and more remembrance is coming to each of you and there is more to come that will help you on your paths both individually and collectively. Many of you are being brought back together with your teams at this time and you have team members on both sides of the veil. As we move ever closer to the tipping point of the collective consciousness, many teams have chosen to come and participate in this most critical time. You bring with you your great light to help lift up, educate and enlighten your brothers and sisters along the way. I say to you, we have come back to assist your world in this endeavor.

Our race of dragons is one of the most ancient of presence, of beings here in your universe. We have worked and continue to work closely with the Elohim; and we have performed many tasks, many missions here within your universe. This has been our station of service and we have been here longer than your mind can contemplate. This is not meant to be in any way a derogatory comment. It is truth and simply an attempt to express my point. We were one of the first to reside here in the creation of this galaxy. We have seen all of the comings and goings within this realm of the cosmos since the time of its inception. We have worked with all manner of beings. As is quite obvious to you, I am a blue dragon. It just so happens that my tribe and I are in service to the blue ray of Creator. That is not to say that we are required to serve a particular ray nor is it to say that our color or form designates the ray on which we serve. However, in my case, it happens to be true.

I answer this as a question that has just come to you. Doesn't it make sense, as one serving primarily on the blue ray, that you and others like you would have a great kinship and relationship with me just as you do with Archangel Michael, Master El Morya, the Elohim Hercules and Amazonia, Astrea and Purity and others who you know to be in service to the blue ray? Master Adama is also a blue ray master. Our study in the times of Mu was centered on teaching you and many others high levels of light and magic. This includes many of you who are primarily in service to the blue ray. It is who you are in your origins, so this feels most natural to you. It is what you are drawn to. But in that time you used high magic to express service to the blue ray of Creator; and one of the aspects of service was for protection, protection of the light. You and others expressed your service to the light by the holding of the light, the grounding and earthing of the light, and ensuring the Logos and laws of Creator were acting and fully present in your world. You are aware of the fact that many made the deliberate choice to turn away from Creator law and light. One of the roles that you and many others played in our last Golden Age was for the protection of your cities and those who lived there.

Indeed, there are great things to come. I come today to invite each of you to call on me at any time that I may be of assistance to you. I come simply to offer my greetings, to say hello and to let you know that we are moving into a wondrous time. It is with great anticipation and joy that I find myself having this conversation with you and which I know you will deliver out to those who would find it. Some of you who will read these words know me well. So, it is with great joy that we embark again on this joint project. I am here to be at your service. I am looking forward to our time together and I come with a message of love and hope from the many tribes of dragon consciousness. You are loved, each of you, all of humanity, most dearly loved. We are here in your service and support. We are here in the service of our Creator. We are here by authority and in cooperation with the Mighty Elohim. We are here in service alongside your Ascended Masters and the realms of Heaven and light to assist Gaia and all of humanity in this great shift. We have much to share. We will speak again.

# Chapter 9

## The Seven Rays
## Follow up on the five secret rays
## Master Saint Germain on
## Sunrise and Sunset
## Author's notes on use of the violet flame

### The Seven Rays

Adama - We encourage you to set your awareness and intention on the city for just a moment and to consider the temples you have visited here. Think about the beautiful energy and activity, the beautiful beings, rays and colored flames of each of these temples. You have seen light radiations that go out into the world at large as they emanate from the temples, seven of which hold the eternal flames of the seven rays. These flames are attended to around the clock by Lemurians, angels, or perhaps Ascended Masters and their chelas. We hold these flames and maintain them. We tend to them such that they are never extinguished. This activity also takes place in other great temples around your world, most of which are located in the 5th dimension, some even higher. Many of you are aware of some of these halls and retreats. In these sacred places, the flames of Creator are tended to, and this is what holds the balance for Mother Gaia and all life here. For had these flames not been tended to down through the ages by those who were willing to step in and be of service in this way, I say to you I cannot be sure we would be having this conversation today. It will not be long before the truth of this comes into the awareness of more and more of your brothers and sisters. The time will come when humanity will reach a level of consciousness such that these truths are in the full awareness in the hearts and minds of all men, women and children; and when this happens, the responsibilities of tending to the Creator flames will be transferred back to the ownership of humanity whose responsibility it once was to maintain them.

This shift of responsibility has to do with what we have referred to as the last great shift at the end of the last Golden Age. At the time of the great shift, for a number of reasons, the seven rays/Creator flames were no longer able to be fully tended. Many simply chose not to do it any longer. They chose a different path, believing it was no longer necessary. In fact, it has been an absolute necessity that these flames be tended to, for had they been allowed to die out completely, this world would have been utterly consumed in darkness. It is only through the tending of these flames that there has been brought forth a balance, a balance between light and dark. We are in great gratitude for all the beings who have continued to tend to these flames.

The flames we are discussing are not fire as you know it to be in your 3D experience. They have the appearance to your eye to be of fire, yet the flames do not create such a great heat. In fact, many are quite cool to the touch. The flames carry an innate consciousness and intelligence. It is an activity, you see. They are not some inanimate substance or process. They are the fires from the Heart of Creator bringing forth the primary aspects or radiation of our Creator for this world––and we specify for this world. If we consider the many realms of the cosmos and all that exists, it seems reasonable that each system or universe would be a unique expression of creation, each with its own set of Creator Law and design. In this plane there are seven primary rays or emanations from the Heart of Creator. There are more, many more; and this knowledge will be expanded when the time is right.

It is a requirement for each one on the Path of Light to come to some level of mastery and understanding of the seven rays and the attributes, virtues and activity of those rays. The more you work with them and invite them to come into your four lower bodies to express their activity and divinity within you, and the more you receive their light and vibration, the more you will integrate their activity and blessings. This is part of the self-mastery that each of you is learning. Each of you comes into this embodiment with a primary and secondary ray orientation which aligns with your divine blueprint and the work you are to do here. As you become more familiar with the rays and their qualities, you will see that you are naturally and particularly drawn to one or two of them. Many are expressing their ray orientations through their careers and hobbies. Before a person may be firmly planted in a 5D consciousness and experience, each one must have some level of attainment within the seven rays. We would say there is nothing difficult about it. Simply allow yourself to become familiar with the characteristics associated with each ray. Those of you with good hearts who are living well balanced and harmonious lives are already embodying and expressing many of the qualities or natures of the rays.

This channel Bryan sometimes references the material that was given by us previously through our dear channel Aurelia, to whom we have explained that each day of the week has a predominate ray of light (Telos Volume 3, 142-144). You may refer to them as light, flames or rays. Each day brings one ray that is sent with a stronger level of radiation. It has a stronger field about it on that particular day so it is the dominant ray for that day. The rays cycle so that each day a new ray is dominant. The information which we have brought forth offers a very simple way to allow the rays to come into your awareness and experience. For simply beginning your day with the contemplation of that ray and the characteristics of that ray, number one you bring the energy of that ray into your being such that you receive the blessing and activity of that ray. Secondly, in so doing, you honor those aspects of Creator; and as you go through this process, most of you will have a recognition and gratitude for the gifts that each ray brings forth to the planet. You will receive great benefit even if you were to spend just one or two minutes each day contemplating a ray. It need not be the ray that is dominant on that particular day.

There are many ways in which you may familiarize yourself with the rays and primary aspects of Creator that are being directed to the planet. They are intended to be dominant tools of assistance. They bring forward light, understanding and truth. They bring forward the very essence of Creator. We spoke to you recently about the Divine Feminine energies coming onto the planet. We said to you, this is one of several avenues in which greater light and information are coming onto the planet now and into all levels of your being and awareness. New dispensations and increase of Christ Light and Christ Consciousness are one such avenue. The seven rays are another. They all work together, you see.

We return now to the benefit of even just a short time contemplating and thinking about the rays. In so doing, you add your own momentum to that ray; and by embracing that ray you allow it to come into your bodily systems and awareness, allowing it to radiate within and without. This is a great benefit to all. Once you have begun to step into your divinity and recognize your power and that which you are capable of, you begin to see that you have it within you to use the rays. You may call the flames about you for your great benefit. You may work with either the light or the flame of a ray depending on which one you are more comfortable with. Many of you have this process in your awareness already, and we know that you are intentionally using those rays to which you are most drawn on any particular day or time. You may bring the flames (or light) into your four lower bodies by your thought and intention, which command great power. Perhaps you are choosing to be a conduit for that flame/ray and expanding it out through the core of your heart center still point, allowing it to radiate out to the world at large. This is high-level work. For those who participate in this kind of process with a pure heart, we can assure you that the assistance you receive from what this channel refers to as the Company of Heaven, is beyond your comprehension. For when you intend global good and service, standing in the light and for the greatest good of all, we tell you the impact is great. If only even a tiny fraction of those of you on planet today would work in such a way, we would see great change in the twinkling of an eye.

We began this discussion a few minutes ago by asking you to think about the combined light, radiation and vibration that come from our city. You may also think of it as the collective consciousness of Telos, and we invite you now to feel into this energy and consider these great temples and halls. Consider the great flames being tended to by angels, masters and Lemurians. This care reflects the consciousness of all the citizens here who are all living in and working in 5D and higher vibrations. Consider all of these energies and light being collected and combined to a greater expansion of light, a blending of the energies, will and activity. We invite you now to feel into this collective energy of light and love.

The light of the individual colors of the rays forms collectively the beauty and grandeur of a rainbow. This was written in your Bible as a great sign and a promise. It is a sign to all of humanity of Father/Mother God's never-ending love. You will see that there is great synchronicity in the seven rays as they are the colors of the rainbow and also relate to your seven chakra energy centers. As you become more aware of the individual characteristics and attributes of each of the rays, a similar kind of process happens with you, within your body and within your consciousness. Once you become familiar with each ray and its attributes at some level and with some training––which is nothing more than simply repeating an exercise for some time until it is set firmly in your awareness––you allow and open to receive the blessings of the activity of each of the rays within your four (physical, emotional, mental and spiritual) bodily systems. These primary emanations from the very Heart of Creator, which are sent for the full blessing and experience here on Earth, now come into your body through your own intention, and they begin to blend in the most beautiful and radiant way. Imagine the aura and light radiating out from your body is one of a magnificent rainbow full of color, vibrancy and high vibration of only the highest light and purity. And this, my friends, is exactly what happens. This is the beauty that begins to come about from just a small amount of effort on the part of those who would choose it.

So, we encourage you to familiarize yourself with the rays. As you take a moment to contemplate a ray each day, we encourage you to open your hearts to invite the flames of that ray into your four lower bodies. Ask that it would bless you with its activity. In a short period of time, you will have a beautiful blending of the rays within and without. In so doing, you will bring great benefit not only to yourself but also to the world at large.

We encourage you also to be mindful as you contemplate each ray to consider for a moment the point of origination of these rays. That is, consider that these are great gifts of light, truth, illumination, healing, abundance, intuition and Divine love (to name but a few) from our Father/Mother God. As you receive the blessings of these rays we encourage you to radiate the rays and those energies back to the Heart of Creator from which it has come. In so doing, you may radiate the beauty, the light, the love and activity of those rays out to the world at large but also back to the Heart of your Creator.

This is exactly what is taking place as we were discussing the flames here in the temples of Telos. It is a requirement that they be tended at all times such that they not be allowed to simply die out. When we say "tended to", the process we are referring to is that of standing in acknowledgement and awareness, great appreciation and gratitude of these gifts from Creator that must be maintained and with a portion being returned back to the Heart of Creator from which they were gifted. You will reach a point of understanding that the tending of the flame comes not as a requirement but from such a high level of gratitude and service, love and blessings that it is truly your heart's desire to radiate back to our Father/Mother God these most beautiful blessings of love that have been bestowed upon you to hold this world in balance until such time as all were ready to move into the next Golden Age and take your place again in the Cosmos.

We are all connected. We are all a part of this grand plan. This is why we have tended the flames for so long on your behalf. We have patiently awaited this time which we are now coming into.

## Follow up on the five secret rays

Bryan - *Master Adama, would you like to say something about the five secret rays?*

Adama - We are discussing here today, in this chapter, the seven primary Creator rays for this solar system. There are five additional rays that have been termed "secret" rays. They are not necessarily a secret. They are galactic rays and when combined with the seven primary rays, they make up the twelve primary rays for our galaxy. There are many of you today who may already be working with them. There are an almost infinite number of rays; and this has to do with the blending of light and color.

We have discussed that light is not just light. Light, or a ray in this case, is an activity with its own intelligence. It is an energy with its own intelligence. It is its own activity. What we have with the five additional rays are specific combinations or a blending of color; and when we say blending of color, we are really discussing a blending of Creator attributes and qualities. As you are able to advance in the work, and after you have become somewhat proficient with the use and application of the seven primary rays, then the next levels of achievement in this area of focus would be to begin working with the five additional rays.

In the working of the five additional rays, there are new levels of understanding and application that come as a requirement for the use of those five rays. We are not discussing them here in this chapter. Perhaps this is a topic we will discuss as an independent course of study in one of our future works, but for today I am primarily interested in the discussion of the seven primary rays. There is all manner of achievement, progress and opportunity awaiting those who would choose to begin simply to become familiar, and to begin working in some way, with these seven primary Creator rays. Most on the planet today, even if they have some awareness or they have heard of them at some time, are not working intentionally with the seven rays. My endeavor today is to invite those of you who are reading this book to begin some kind of a regular practice, or at least to become familiar with the rays, such that you may begin to apply them in some way for the benefit of your own lives and for the benefit of others. Then, of course as I have said, these are just the primary rays for this solar system. We have these five additional rays, which are combination rays, and then we have truly an infinite number of rays and combinations thereof, that are present in other areas of the cosmos. Truly, you could make a life study out of the rays. There is an astounding wealth of knowledge and attainment that comes with further study and application of the rays.

## Master Saint Germain, Sunrise and Sunset

Adama - Bryan, would you like to include in our book the epiphany that was given to you last night by Master Saint Germain? I do believe it was his intention that we include it here. It is not a coincidence that you were given the message last night while you were transcribing our discussion from the previous day.

Bryan – *Sure, Master Adama. I really appreciate the beauty of this truth being brought to my awareness and I'm hopeful that others will also.*

Adama - We were discussing the balancing of world karma and we mentioned several times the importance and blessing of the activity of the violet flame. Master Saint Germain gave you last night the knowledge that your world is being bathed twice a day in both the pink ray and the violet ray. All of the seven Creator rays are coming onto the planet and into your world each day. This is the full spectrum of color, the full spectrum of the rainbow; and so your world is being flooded at all times with light, and in light are the seven primary colors or rays. They make up the purity of light, so the activity of the seven rays is there. There are many combinations of rays, so it is not only the seven that are being sent to Gaia and humanity; there are other variations, and the intensity of those applications will come to and fro according to the will of Creator. But the seven primary rays are always active and present in our world. There has been much discussion about the seven Creator rays. We have spoken about it in our Telos books and Archangel Michael and his dear channel Ronna Herman have also provided you with a thorough understanding and view of the rays.

In our last discussion, we spoke of the great value and benefit of the activity of the violet ray. Particularly at this time of your planet's evolution, the violet flame is one of your most valuable tools. Each day, life force energy from the Godhead and the Great Central Sun flood our planet. It is a gift from our Father/Mother God that is sent out to the universe and comes forth to bless all life everywhere. This is life force energy. Also contained within this life force energy are the predominant aspects, the seven rays of

Creator for this solar system. With each sunrise and sunset, there is an added dispensation of love and light flooding the planet. This has not been in your awareness before, but you have always had a great appreciation for the beauty of a sunrise and sunset; and of course this is not uncommon. Most of you have an earnest appreciation for this natural beauty. Often in the early morning and late evening as the sun is just beginning to rise or to sink low on the horizon, you begin to see a beautiful matrix of color filling the sky.

Your science has an explanation for this and that is the refraction of light against the gasses and dust of the atmosphere and so forth, and indeed it may be explained that way. But to tell you truthfully, each of you experiences your days and nights, and each of you experiences each day a sunrise and a sunset. What is happening is that all of life is being bathed; you are basking in and marinating in the beauty and activity of various rays but predominantly those of the violet ray and pink ray. You have learned recently through the teachings of Archangel Michael that according to each one's free will, you may send out to others only the violet light of transmutation or the pink light of divine love. You may actively send these two rays to your brothers and sisters without having any interference with their free will choice. The other color rays may still be used for yourself and the betterment of your world; however, according to Archangel Michael, they are not to be sent directly to your brothers and sisters, for this may interfere with each ones free will. Through this teaching however, you can see there is great value and benefit for all life just from these two particular rays.

As we have said, there is an extra dispensation of love and transformation that is given to your world two times each day. It is an extra dispensation of divine love of the pink ray and of the transforming and transmuting energies of the violet ray. You have come to know in your heart, in the moment of this epiphany, what a beautiful gift this really is for truly it is the pure love of Creator. It is a blessing from the heart of our Father/Mother God that is bestowed upon all life, and all life here is bathed in this beautiful light twice each day.

There is much more we could say about this. Think about the dispensation of these special energies that are coming to you. They provide you with an opportunity to connect specifically with these rays as you both begin your day and end your day with blessings of divine love and the activity of transmuting any misqualified energies that have come about throughout the day. Each day you have a new opportunity to balance your misqualified energies and come further into alignment. Each day you may start anew. Today is a brand new day, and as the sun comes up, your world is bathed in the beautiful colors and energies of the violet light of transmutation and the pink light of divine love. As you end your day, these same blessings come to you again allowing you to transmute any misqualified energies. If there are things you have done, seen, observed and participated in throughout your day that have, in your perception, created some imbalance or disharmony within you or others, the violet flame is a most efficient and beautiful tool for helping you to simply release those energies. Release them from your mind and your four lower bodies and transmute them back into pure white light substance. The harmony and grace of divine love come forth through the pink ray.

The next time you view a beautiful sunset and see these colors being radiated out into the world, I encourage you to feel into the energy and activity of those energies/rays/colors/vibrations that are coming to you. You observe them with your human eyes. You see the colors. I invite you to sit quietly for a moment and feel into the energy and the blessing that is inherent within that color spectrum and ray. Feel into the energy of it and see if this does not resonate with you. See then, if you do not feel sincere and deep gratitude for the gift that it is. They are sent for the love and blessing of all, all life everywhere.

## Author's notes on use of the violet flame

Bryan - Note: Some of you may not be familiar with the idea of using Creator rays/flames as a part of your spiritual practice. Please allow me to share some information about the violet flame and describe some of the benefits I've observed in my own experience. The violet flame is made up of energies and intelligence that are also contained inherently in the blue flame and the pink flame. In using the flame, I am consciously surrounding myself with God's protection and God's love. We simply draw the flames around us through our focused intention. It is not an imaginary exercise. It may feel that way at first; but with some practice, it begins to feel quite real and even natural. I believe the real world benefits become clear for anyone who will take the time to apply it with sincerity. God's Love and Protection!

The violet flame is one of our greatest gifts from Creator. It was well known and used in our time of Lemuria. This knowledge was passed down through some of the ancient mystery schools, but eventually it became all but lost to the world. The Master Saint Germain has brought the violet flame forth for us again. This was an act of great love and service to our world as we step through the doorway of this next great age. He has said, "The use of the violet consuming flame is more valuable to you and all mankind than all the wealth, all the gold, and all the jewels of this planet."

The mystery schools of Egypt taught that, at the time of death, the soul would be taken to the scales of Osiris. The heart of the soul would be placed on the scales and weighed against the white feather of the Goddess of Ma'at. She represented balance, truth, justice and harmony. If the heart was lighter than the feather, the soul would be allowed to continue on in a blissful state in the Field of Reeds. They are describing the process of the ascension. Our human experience is transitory. We are divine beings of light having a human experience. Do we wish to continue our soul's journey in an environment of duality and contrast like the one we're experiencing now, or do we wish to elevate ourselves out of this lower vibrational experience and the ongoing rounds of re-embodiment that accompany it? We graduate this Earth plane and return to the Heart of God, back to love and light, beauty and grace, by earning our victory in the light. This is our ascension.

The violet flame transmutes all negative energies, even those that are created by our own thoughts. I view it as a karma cleaner that runs continuously in the background. This is very high frequency light energy that literally transmutes all lower frequency energies. If I have a negative thought about someone, it may not seem of much consequence in the overall big picture of my cosmic bank account (karma). However, our causal body, residing in higher realms, contains the records of every thought and deed of a lifetime. This is what I refer to as our cosmic bank account. I do my best to keep any withdrawals as small as possible. I much prefer to add to the account as I continue to balance my debt to life. I endeavor to make my ascension in this lifetime; and outside of prayer and God's grace, the violet flame is the most effective tool I am aware of to assist me in achieving this goal.

We also have our aura energy fields, which can pick up and hold all kinds of energies. Think about all the people and things you might come into contact with in a given day. Think of the people and their moods and attitudes. We have our news, internet and a variety of inputs "good" and "bad" coming in each day. Perhaps we've taken in lower vibrational or unhealthy foods. All of those things are energy. Perhaps we've had a disagreement with someone and we've allowed ourselves to carry that vibration around all day. Perhaps a friend confided in us about some of the difficulties they're going through and we've inadvertently taken on those feelings and moods also. These are subtle energies, but they are absolutely having an effect on the way we feel and experience life because we carry them with us in our energy field. Even a short time in meditation with intentional use of the violet flame really does have the ability to help us release lower vibrational energies, the stuff that doesn't feel good. New energies of harmony and balance come in and we feel better as a result.

# Chapter 10

## Lemurian DNA activation
## How Lemurians live so long

### Lemurian DNA activation

Adama - You have been guided to read a work from Kryon in which he has discussed the 12 strand DNA; and you will remember that three of them relate to your Lemurian embodiments and lineage. Those attributes, qualities and gifts that are associated with your Lemurian embodiments or higher aspects are a natural component of your DNA. Lemurian DNA is present in all of humanity and has laid dormant alongside the other sleeping strands for thousands of years. All strands of your DNA are being activated at this time; however, due to the work that you and others are doing with us, the strands of DNA relating to your Lemurian qualities will begin to accelerate at a faster rate of speed than others. This is due in part because we will be assisting you in the modification of your bodies and your awareness. We are happy to support you in the further awakening of your Lemurian DNA. If this is something you desire, simply ask for our assistance. We will work with you mostly in your dreamtime when the body is at rest. We will assist you to gently awaken those particular strands of DNA that will improve the overall health and function of your four lower bodies and help you connect more fully and easily to your Lemurian family here in the mountain.

In a previous discussion, we made note that, over time, each of you will begin to see your bodies change in numerous ways, and this is one of them. As strands of your Lemurian DNA are allowed to awaken and as their activity is allowed to take place within the bodily systems and the four lower bodies, you will begin to experience these enhancements. For those of you who request our assistance, we will step up the activity in a way that is graceful and easy for each of you. In these activations, we ask that you not expect to undergo a full regenesis of your DNA and four lower bodies over the course of days or weeks. It is not likely to happen that way. However, we do not wish for you to become discouraged. In a relatively short period of time, this expansion will most certainly come into your awareness and use. For many of you, the time has come with the passing of your initiations when you step onto a new course or onto a new rung of the ladder. The time has come when we are able to work with you in new ways that were not available to us before. We feel certain you will enjoy and appreciate the new levels of awareness that are due to come for those of you who choose it. The changes will be slightly different for each one as relates to your particular path and makeup as well as your ability to receive and integrate the new energies. Suffice it to say, over a relatively short period of time, with your intention and endeavor, you will see these changes fully blossom within you.

If the Lemurian DNA activations are something you wish to have for yourself, there is nothing in particular that is required other than to make the request of us from time to time as it comes to your awareness. The call for these activations is in no way a requirement. It is simply an offer of support. We encourage each of you, as always, to feel into and use your discernment as to what is right for you in all situations. The awakening of your dormant DNA is already taking place in a more or less natural way. This activity is taking place at all levels of life on the planet as the new energies come in. We remind you again in case you have forgotten, we are your family and you are ours. We stress this to you because it is our desire that each of you will come into the full awareness of this truth in your hearts and at the core of your being. You are dearly loved, so, we want similar kinds of things for you that you might want for yourselves, your family and your own loved ones.

## How Lemurians live so long

Adama - What shall we discuss today?

Bryan - *I don't know, Master Adama. Whatever you wish.*

Adama - Would you like to know how it is that we may live for hundreds, indeed even for thousands of years in our current embodiments?

Bryan - *Yes sir, I would.*

Adama - Okay, let us discuss this for a bit. First, I will simply remind you that none of us on this side of the veil interpret time the way you do in your 3rd dimensional reality. We understand that time is very real in your experience but know it is an illusion that has been placed about the 3rd dimension. As you move into 5D and beyond, time as you know it does not exist. This is a subject that we may discuss in more detail at a later date. You have heard that time in our experience is one of a looping pattern or a spiraling staircase and so it is not a straight line, linear construct as it is in your 3D reality. I understand this is a complex subject; and as your awareness expands, you will also come to have additional clarity in regards to this and other matters that are truly complex.

We, here in Telos and in our other cities of the Agartha Network, may easily live for thousands and thousands of years in your time. I have been in my same body form for over 26,000 years now. Many of you have known me in this bodily form even during the time of your past embodiments in Lemuria. As you can see, Bryan, I do not appear in any way to have aged during the course of these years. We are able to maintain our bodies and our body appearance in a variety of ways. We may change our appearance to look older or younger as we choose; and I choose this appearance, which to you might resemble someone of an age of 35-40 years old. Would you agree with this, Bryan?

Bryan – *Yes sir, Master Adama. I'm not real good at guessing age with humans so I wouldn't expect to have much success with Lemurians, but I agree with you. You look even younger to me than I do.*

Adama - You have heard stories of Ascended Masters, those who once walked the Earth in their human embodiments, who were able to directly transition into one of relative immortality while still maintaining a strong presence even in the 3rd dimensional reality. Master Babaji has shown the way for this. Your dear friend Master Saint Germain has demonstrated this as the "Wonderman of Europe", where he lived for several hundred years. There have been others, quite a few actually. Most of them have been forgotten over time, and some of their memories have been intentionally erased from the record. For when your feet are firmly planted in the 5D New Earth reality, humanity also will experience lifetimes that may well run into the hundreds of years. This is New Earth.

There are a number of factors that contribute to our extended lifetimes. First and foremost is that in the higher levels we are not residing in bodily forms that are as dense in matter and makeup as your current carbon based body structures. We are in our light bodies, you see. Our body structure is not nearly as dense as yours; and because of this we are able to bring in, absorb and put to our use and benefit the light––the light that you may refer to as life force energy, Prana, or Chi ––that emanates from the heart of Father/Mother God in the Great Central Sun. We have a great reverence for the life force energy that comes to us each day from the Heart of Creator. We have reverence for all life. We have reverence for our own lives and reverence for the glory of our Creator. We have a great appreciation of this life force energy which pours forth each day, that we may receive it with our own blessings; and through this kind of a process we are able to take in, hold, contain and emanate a much higher level light quotient than most of you at this particular time.

This process is somewhat similar to those whereby you actively and intentionally work to bring in as much light and life force as you can contain while speaking your intention to your body. The light of divinity, of your own beloved I AM Presence, is present in every cell and particle of your being. If God is everywhere then there is nowhere she is not. As you consciously connect with those God particles that are within your own being at every level and as you consciously and intentionally "turn on that light", all grace flows from there. You may use this light in a number of ways. You are allowed, through your own free will to qualify or misqualify the life force energy that flows to you each day in any way that you choose. You, Bryan,, are choosing to take a portion of that light and apply it to the health, vitality, purity, joy and radiance of your being and four lower bodies. This is a beautiful activity and one that we would encourage each of you to do as you are guided. Suffice it to say, all of us here in Telos work with this kind of application daily. We spend time in our many temples including those of the seven Creator rays and receive great benefit as a result. It is our natural way of being and doing. Also, because we live in a 5D awareness and experience, we do not create so many of the self-imposed obstacles and roadblocks that humans often create for themselves. We are fully in control of our thought processes and therefore of all that we are manifesting moment by moment. Because our thought processes and emotions are more conscious and more favorable, we do not allow unwanted outcomes to come into our experience.

Our bodies are light bodies, yet we do have physicality. You can reach out and touch us. We have a makeup of matter and physicality. You can hold our hands. However, our bodies feel much lighter than yours do. Our bodies feel more free and vibrant. They express more of the joyful radiance of light and energy coming to us. We are able to receive it in a more pure fashion and we are able to express it out in a way that feels good. We feel good in our bodies.

Also, because we are living in 5D and above, we have created about us a world that does not allow for many of the influences that humanity currently has acting upon them, such as any number of diseases and physical / mental body afflictions that are a component of your current earthly experience. I will tell you that much of this, if we were to go back and recount the steps of history, in many cases the root cause of the diseases present in your world now are a direct result of dark influence. Many of the ailments, afflictions and diseases taking place now have been intentionally designed and propagated among you for their benefit. This is something humanity has been straddled with for a long period of time now, and most are not able to understand why such things are taking place. Much of this condition relates to a direct influence that has come about by those acting in separation but also through the ignorance of man and what I will call the dark creation of man. This is not meant to be derogatory. It is simply truth. We are coming to a time now when all such influence, which has resulted in so much suffering among humanity, is now coming to an end. The dark days are numbered.

What this means then, in terms of your various diseases, ailments and imbalance, is these will also be coming to an end. There are two things that will bring this change about. One is the raising of consciousness of humanity. All must move into their own sovereign divinity, understanding and application that you indeed do have influence over your own bodies and health. You get to make the choice and create your own realities moment by moment. Once the collective has this idea firmly ingrained and it is being applied with success, it will be a huge step in the right direction. Secondly, there will be technologies that are allowed to come forth now which will eliminate many forms of human suffering, which will disappear practically overnight. You already know that mankind holds the cure for cancer. This has been given to humanity and it is known. Those working in separation and darkness have intentionally locked it away, but this situation is changing. This is just one of many examples we could use. Information will be made readily available to the world soon. We need for the collective to continue to expand. The more quickly you expand into unity consciousness, the sooner we can begin offering additional assistance in these ways. Again, there are milestones and accomplishments that must be met at each step along the way, but this is forthcoming to you. You see, these kinds of diseases and suffering regarding your health simply do not exist here in our experience nor will they exist on your New Earth.

Lastly, we have technology available to us such that we are able to supply energy and power sources of all kinds, provide food sources, transportation and more without the need for a resulting contamination or pollution. You can plainly see the results of fossil fuels, nuclear power, chemically laden foods and agriculture, manufacturing pollution and waste, mining of precious metals and minerals, mining trees for construction-development, and on it goes. There are contaminants in many of your medicines and food supplies. As an aware society, we simply do not participate in these kinds of activities that would result in any kind of contamination or pollution for ourselves, our bodies, our communities or our world at large. As we move forward and as consciousness is allowed to rise, we will be coming forward (we meaning we here in Telos and many of your star nation brothers and sisters) at that time to teach you how to go about the same objectives but without any negative consequence to your bodies, to Mother Gaia or to all life on the planet. We are going to help you find ways of achieving those things that are necessary but without the negative consequence that you have today.

You are wanting to know if we eat and drink liquids and solid foods. Yes, we do. Our experience of eating and drinking is not the same as yours; but yes, we most certainly do. Our sensory perceptions are more expanded than yours, so enjoying nutritional and tasty foods is a delightful activity for us also. We rely on various forms of nourishment to assist us in balancing our bodies with light and intention. We supplement our physicality through proper nourishment, which of course is a vegetarian diet. We have food supplies that are similar to your fruits and vegetables. We take great delight in the many wonderful food sources that we make available for ourselves, just as you might enjoy a fresh strawberry. In a moment of stillness and appreciation you might gaze upon a big, fresh strawberry that has just come from your garden. As you gaze upon it you may find reverence for the life that it is and then, with intention, you may bless that life to the life that is your body. As you take a bite you really settle into the taste, texture, flavor and joy of the experience. This is something we also enjoy very much. So yes, we do eat and drink here. We have pure water supplies and the most wonderful liquid elixirs. Just as you might go to the market and enjoy a fruit smoothie and get to choose your ingredients, we have a great variety to choose from. We have physical ingredients such as your oranges and cherries, but we might also add what I will call elixirs of light to these concoctions. We may infuse a beverage with a pleasing mixture of qualities of light, and these are enhancements for our bodies.

Our experience is different than yours but it is something we enjoy very much. I hope this addresses your question. We are keenly aware, in my description of how we might enjoy a strawberry, that this is another form of life force. We take in life force through direct light channels but also through the enjoyment of our food supplies. We recognize in gratitude that we are taking in more life force energy this way. The strawberry, in this example, also contains its own life force. It contains Creator light and life force energy. How else would it have known to be a strawberry? As we bring it into our bodies, we are adding to our overall light quotient, our overall health and vitality and our overall levels of life force energy. It is by these factors that we are able to live extended lifetimes.

I will say lastly on this subject as I have noted it in your awareness. You are thinking, "*Oh Boy, I don't want to live 200-300 years. No Thank You*". I understand this sentiment as you are expressing it; but let me say again, in our experience we are already living what you might view as Heaven on Earth. We are already home. There is nowhere we wish to go; and if we do, we can easily make arrangements for that. We have opportunities available to us for further experience and expansion just as you do. It never stops, not at any level of being. One may go as far as one's soul chooses to go out into experience, adventure, learning and service, always in service. There are many opportunities for us. We are not trapped here. We are here by choice and our experience here is a wonderful and joyful experience. We are not subject to the duality that all of you experience at this time. I just want to say this to you. We enjoy our experience. We are all feeling good in our healthy bodies. We are fulfilled individually and collectively in service to ourselves, our communities, all of life and Creator. We are blessed. We are living blessed lives and this recognition is in the forefront of every individual here in Telos. Each one that you talked to would give you a similar answer and this would be recognized as truth emanating from their own hearts, you see.

Bryan - *Master Adama, will we evolve to the point where we are living extended lifetimes?*

Adama - Yes, you will. It will take some time yet. I would say that you will observe great gains being made over the course of the next several generations, which is a very small amount of time if we look at the bigger picture of your linear time construct. I suspect that by the time we get through the next several generations, many of you will be living in your new 5D experience and light bodies. You need not think you must wait that long, however, before you see positive change. While this global transformation of evolving into your light bodies is underway, new technologies will come forth to extend your lives and bring great benefit to all. Truly, humanity will be living in a different paradigm. New Earth will provide a completely different experience; and at that time, for all the reasons I have stated as to how we live so long in our bodies, the same will be true for you. I am not saying you will live as long as we do, but humanity will come to extend its life easily to a doubling, tripling or greater effect as we move into this new age and New Earth. When that day comes, it will be everyone's desire to be in their good-feeling, healthy bodies. You will be in a different paradigm. You will be watching this transition all the way through either from your side or ours, and you will not miss anything my friends. None of you will. You will see soon enough that there has been a full evolution of life as you know it to exist today. It will not be the same. This is the new age that we are telling you about and it's why we are so excited to be here and participating now at this momentous time and occasion. This is why so many of your star nation family are coming to assist you now. It is most exciting. Can you feel the truth of this?

Bryan - *Yes sir, Master Adama, I can. I am also excited to be here at this time and playing my role. I look forward to the day this all comes about, and it can't happen soon enough in my mind.*

Adama - Yes. While we are on this subject I will add that as you move fully into your New Earth and a 5D consciousness, your bodies will be much different. They will not be as dense. They will be more similar to our bodies. You are moving into your new light bodies, and the process is already well underway. As humanity come to take their place at the table among your brothers and sisters of the cosmos, the restrictions and limitation that you currently experience within your bodies will naturally fall away. You will not be constricted by your bodily form; nor will you be constricted by your geographical location. We are able, here in our current embodiment, to travel through space and time. We are able to do this ourselves or with our merkaba light vehicles or ships, and we are able to go and visit with any number of star nation beings around the galaxy. I assure you, no one is sitting here in Telos wondering what they might do to live a life of adventure and service if that is what they choose. There are a tremendous variety of opportunities available to us in Telos, other cities of Middle Earth and many other planets, all with a great variety of interactions with other beings of light.

Bryan – *I can't wait. I have expressed an interest to Commander Ashtar. I have wanted to visit the Pleiadian ship, New Jerusalem, in hopes that I might get to visit our Pleiadian family and others, such as Mother Mary, who I'm told frequent that ship. I am looking forward to the time when I can interact directly with you and my friends in Telos as well as my extended Heaven Family.*

Adama - Yes, Bryan, we are well aware of this and it is a quality within you that endears you to us all that much more. You are an explorer, indeed. We sense this always in your energy and we enjoy and appreciate it. Do not worry my friend. You are going to have wondrous experiences beyond your imagining that are yet to come. Trust me, you are not going to miss the party. None of you will. We have had another good discussion today and this is a good stopping point. We will look forward to your next visit to the mountain.

# Chapter 11

## Coming into balance

Bryan - Note: *This chapter illustrates another coaching session whereby Master Adama offers me his wisdom and encouragement. He has asked me to include this section because all of humanity will be experiencing similar challenges as we move forward. We are all moving through this experience together.*

*After completing the draft of this chapter, Master Adama gave me the following:*

Adama - The process of clearing and cleaning will happen for all in a natural way even if you are not actively aware of it or seeking it out. The collective consciousness is rising and we must make room for this new light, information and consciousness. This is how it will happen. Here, we offer one example to the reader. There is a wide range and spectrum of experience that is unique and specific to each of you according to your path, life choices and higher guidance. Every experience will be different but each of you will benefit by learning to bring yourselves into balance.

Adama - Welcome Bryan. It is good to see you today. I know that you had hoped you were through your clearing and cleaning processes, and indeed the bulk of the work has already been accomplished. However, there will always be further refinements to be made while you are in your human form and otherwise. You are at a stage now where we might say you are making finite adjustments. These are relatively small attunements for additional clearing. All of humanity is experiencing this clearing, cleaning and releasing process now to one degree or another. You made note yesterday that you were receiving our activations. By activations, we mean you have requested our assistance in the bringing forth of more light (enlightenment) and simultaneously releasing from your field all energies and limitation that no longer serve you. You were sensing in your energy field some work that was taking place yesterday. However, the majority of the releasing was done in your dreamtime last night. You have awoken this morning with some residue remaining from this clearing and activation. You may not always have an appreciation for the immediate results that come from these activations because they often include more clearing and releasing of heavy emotions and feelings that may have risen to the surface. While you may not always enjoy the experience in the moment, I can assure you that within a small amount of time, another round of releasing, clearing and integrating will have taken place and you will be all the better for it. You will recognize the benefit of it in your experience. I can assure you of this.

It will be of great benefit for you. This is true for all of you. The energies being released now are energies that are deeply embedded within you––and that is to say all aspects of you, all past, present and future experience and timelines, the totality of your being. So

I share with you that some of the releasing you are experiencing today—–I suspect you would label this something other than releasing *(Master Adama is laughing a bit because I am just really feeling frustrated and irritated today)*—–is a result of multi-dimensional clearing. It comes from deeper levels. Up until this point you have, for the most part, been concerned with clearing and cleaning all that is within your four lower bodies. This is your cellular memory, your Akash and all that you brought with you into this lifestream experience as well as all that you have experienced and come to believe about yourself throughout your current embodiment. This clearing is the major building block on your Path of Light and a process that each one will be going through.

A strong foundation has already been laid in the work that has been done previously and you are now moving into a new level of clearing that is multidimensional. On this day, you have attempted to locate the source point of the frustration that has bubbled up within you. I would say it may be extremely difficult to do this and, in all honesty, not worthy of your effort. It would serve no purpose for you to dwell on this situation or to go poking around looking for the origin point. That is an old paradigm way of teaching and thinking. The path of least resistance, in this case, is simply to acknowledge all that is coming forth, bless it and allow it to release. As old and perhaps uncomfortable energies bubble up to your awareness for release, my encouragement is that you do not allow your emotions to take hold of it. You are consciously or unconsciously choosing emotions that are aligned with love, grace and harmony; or you may be choosing, for example, emotions of frustration, anxiety, impatience and lack of trust. These are just labels. I am not spelling them out for you but just giving examples. As the ego and emotional bodies are allowed to attach to these kinds of emotions that may be bubbling up from who knows where, as you tighten your grip on them you are holding them inside of you. As you allow yourself, in this example, to experience frustration around the energy that is bubbling forth and if that frustration is allowed to grow and expand within you, you will be holding those energies and keeping them bound in shackles such that you may enjoy them again and again at a later time (Master Adama laughs lightly again). I suspect it is not your intention to hold onto these kinds of emotions.

My suggestion is to use the skills of mastery that you have within you to bring yourself back into balance. It would not be our suggestion to think, act and move in ways that will hold those uncomfortable vibrations within you. It would be of no benefit to you. It is not a requirement that you understand the origins of these energies as they are being released. Simply honor them and the contributions they have made to your beingness and ask that they be released. Simply open yourself to allow them to move out with grace and ease. You, Bryan, are utilizing the violet flame and this is a most wonderful tool for this kind of application and work. Also, simply slow down. When you find yourself getting worked up, so to speak, take a minute or two to stop, be still, and come into your still point and breathe...just breathe. The breath is the key to many aspects of your work. Proper breathing can be most valuable in a situation like this where you have energies that are trying to release. It may appear to you that they have become stuck somewhere along the way. When they do, you may use the breath to assist those energies in fully releasing from the body. Breathe in light and love. Breathe out all that no longer serves you, all energies that are not in grace, harmony and alignment with your highest desires and of the highest light; simply within the breath allow them to release.

Breathe deeply, in a slow and gentle way from the belly. Let go and allow the violet flame and breath to move them out. Call on your Heaven Family to assist you in releasing lower vibrational energies and returning to balance. Within a short period of time, with your intention being applied in this manner, you will release that which you feel may be stuck in your solar plexus or elsewhere in your body. You may literally feel the release and you will feel lighter as you move yourself back into alignment.

I encourage you also, in these kinds of situations, to remember self-love. You, like so many of your brothers and sisters, are often much too hard on yourselves. We would ask that you allow yourself the same leeway, the same forgiveness, the same grace and understanding that we know you would show to one of your dear friends. We know your nature is often one of a strong willed approach. This refers back to our previous discussion when we talked about the balancing of the masculine and feminine energies. In these types of situations, what we might refer to as your default programs more often than not lead you to a very masculine approach to viewing and solving the "problem" at hand. This kind of approach can be most valuable in a variety of circumstances and situations. It is the strong will. It is the determined attitude. It is the pushing forward to complete the task at hand. These are the kinds of energies that you might experience when you are working in the masculine aspect of being, and I suggest to you today that there will be different occasions and situations that may be better served by a different approach.

The residual clearing and cleaning that you are experiencing today may be better served by your choosing a feminine approach; that is to say, one of acceptance, understanding, patience, self-love, self-care, and non-judgment. It is simply a soft and caring approach, a compassionate approach. We see that often you afford yourself very little compassion, for this is your nature and this again is true for many of your brothers and sisters. I am encouraging you today, when these kinds of situations arise for you, to look at the situation differently and then make the choice as to how you would like to respond to it. What I suggest to you today is that you may benefit in this experience by moving yourself into and holding the vibration of the feminine qualities we listed a moment ago. Simply have compassion for all that is coming up today. Do not have judgment about it or try to whip it into shape or put shackles on it and lock it down. Don't try to kick it out with your cowboy boot but rather use a soft approach. Just acknowledge the feelings, "*Oh I see I am feeling this and this in this now moment.*" Sure you may contemplate for a moment, "*I wonder where these feelings are coming from?*" "*Is there something I need to learn from this experience or is this simply residual releasing as a result of the activation and new light that I've brought in?*" I would encourage you not to go too far down the rabbit hole. Simply view it with discernment and see if there is something there for you that you feel needs to be addressed. If not, then simply remain in a place of non-judgment. Have compassion for yourself and the experience and then, as much as you can, allow yourself to move into the vibration of self-love, understanding and grace. Just allow yourself to move into a state of grace. Intend that you are moving now back to a state of trust and faith, trusting that all is happening in a divine way for your best benefit and according to the divine plan and divine timing. This is what we mean by coming back into alignment.

This attitude is often in conflict with what the ego and lower self want; and we hear you say to yourself often, as if you were instructing young people, that "*Life is full of disappointment and the sooner you learn to accept it the better.*" While we would say that view is more aligned with a masculine approach, we would say there is some truth in it. You know that life is not always going to go your way, and it doesn't take long in your human experience to begin learning the truth of this. But you sit here today as a master in training, and you are able to see beyond a given circumstance that others may simply take at face value. You are at a point where you are able to use your wisdom and discernment in guiding yourself, asking for help and guidance and relying on your own inner knowing in managing any events or situations that may arise from this point forward. You get to choose. You have struggled this morning in remembering that you get to choose.

The emotions you are struggling with in this now moment are based on the particular experience you are having this day, and yes, I am able to feel and see right into it; so I understand very well the energies and thought processes that are taking place. I would say that you may benefit greatly by connecting with the Divine Feminine energies in regards to managing your situation. Let me say here also that it makes no difference whether you are in a masculine or feminine embodiment at this time. We are discussing energies that are inherent and always in play within each and every one of you. Have patience and allow yourselves to have these feelings as they come up. You have not failed yourself or anyone else. You have not made any errors or mistakes that have led you to what you are perceiving as internal discourse. It is simply a new level of releasing that which no longer serves you, and it just so happens that you personally are now working in a multi-dimensional format that you don't have a lot of experience with up to this point. Acknowledge it, bless it and allow it to move freely out of your awareness and out of your emotional body. Take care of yourself in whatever way it means for you. This is a very good situational opportunity (ha-ha) for you to put into practice that which we have recently discussed in the balancing of the masculine and feminine energies. You have all this stuff going on inside you this morning, and you said it yourself that you were out of balance. Recognizing consciously that you are coming out of balance is the first step. These kinds of occurrences are a natural part of life and the human condition, yes, but they also represent a component of your masters training as each of you naturally moves to new levels of awareness and expansion. It is not necessarily a test or an initiation. It may be a result of specific work you were guided to do or a natural bi-product of the increased vibrational energies coming in now. You and everyone else will experience more of these kinds of energies coming forward as you continue along your path.

I know that life in the human experience is not always easy. You and your dear brothers and sisters are revered around the cosmos for your great courage in coming here. We are all aware of the many difficulties, trials and tribulations, the hazards, the roadblocks and pitfalls, the highs and the lows. This is one of the reasons we encourage you and your brothers and sisters to call on us. At every opportunity we lend you our support, love, guidance and momentum. The more you allow yourself to ask for our assistance and allow for it to come in, the more you are blessed. In this way, we are often able to assist you in moving past a particular roadblock with relative grace and ease. If you are someone who is still relatively closed off to our assistance and, let us say perhaps you are more firmly identified with the ego at this time, then this same obstacle might be blown into something much, much bigger. This small obstacle, rather than moving through with relative speed and grace, now has the potential to be magnified tenfold by that which the ego would do to it. Become more attuned to those negative energies and vibrations coming forward and allow them to release with grace such that the ego cannot latch onto them, become identified with them and hold onto them. That attachment is how, what may have been a relatively minor obstacle now becomes a giant mountain standing in the road before you. I think you understand my meaning in this analogy. Discernment is a skill that can be applied to many areas of your experience and certainly this might be one of those situations where discernment can play a big part in your experience, helping you choose to move through it with awareness. Let me remind you that the ego is not something to be shunned or shut down. It is an aspect of you. Simply use your discernment to recognize the role it wants to play. You may think of the small self/ego as a small child, which has good intentions for your well being but not always the wisdom of your highest good and best guidance. It wants to have its way. Do your best then to move forward in cooperation and alignment with all aspects of your being.

You are feeling better now?

Bryan - *"Yes sir, I am feeling more settled now than I was a while ago"*.

Adama - Yes, I will make note and say––this not to pat myself on the back but to state what is––as you came here to meet with me in the Great Hall, one of the first things we did here in this meeting is I held out my hands. You knew that I was offering for you to place your hands in mine. I have energetically assisted you to nullify the resistant energies that were stuck within you. As you know, a lower vibration cannot influence a higher vibration unless we allow it to. The higher vibration will always hold sway over a lower vibration; so all that we have done here is I have observed the vibration that you were in when we started and I noted the disturbance in your auric fields. I can see it energetically. I can see it and feel it. It expresses itself vibrationally with energy and color in your aura such that I was able to look at you and immediately see the discourse within you. I have simply offered you the benefit, which you have gladly accepted, and I have simply moved a higher vibrational energy into your aura field such that the lower vibrational energy was released. This is important and I would ask that you make note of how gently and easily we were able to release the discordant energies within you.

It is our joy to assist you in this way, and this kind of assistance is available to all of you. It is a very easy thing for us to come in with your request and allowing, that we may offer you our higher vibration. Again, I do not say this to boast but to state the obvious truth of the matter, and that is to say your Families of Light on our side of the veil are working at much higher vibrations than each of you are in most cases. As you were connecting with me today, it came into your awareness that the lower vibrational energies you were feeling simply did not exist here in this place. You knew this to be true. As you felt into me and the collective energy of Telos, what you received back was a resonance of grace, harmony, love, peace, stillness, and joy…just a gentle, relaxing kind of feeling. By being in the energy of the city and connecting with me in this way, we allowed your discord to quite easily dissipate and move out.

Make note, this will not be the last time you will experience such energies, and this is a wonderful process in helping you return to balance. When you have something that feels stuck, I would encourage you to work with whichever Master you feel drawn to on that particular subject and sit quietly, stop the mental activity, stop the ego from moving and acting and taking your further down the path of whatever energy that is that you choose not to experience. Breathe, bring the violet flame, call on those Ascended Masters or angels that you are drawn to and ask them to come help you move those energies and vibrations out of your field. As you continue on this path, each of you will become more adept at doing this work for yourself. You are all on the right path. Tap into your inner knowing and call forth your own divinity. You may quite easily learn to move out these discordant energies on your own, and we endeavor to help each of you reach this goal. This is a part of the process that all of you are going through now resulting from the accelerated timeline of the global expansion of consciousness and the transitioning into your light bodies. You are becoming even greater containers of love and light and so you must make room for it. Between here and there it is our joy to assist you in this way.

You are feeling better now.

Bryan - *Yes sir, I am. Thank you.*

Adama – As I said, when you came in I could see the disturbance in your energy field and chakras. They were not putting out the luminosity of color, and in your auric fields two to three feet beyond you I could see where the energy was stuck. We see this as a cloudy and milky substance and often in shades of off-green, brown or grey; so it is quite easy for us to observe these kinds of imbalances. You are looking much better now and hopefully feeling better as a result. Take care of yourself today.

# Chapter 12

## The Crystal Kingdoms

Bryan - *What should we talk about today, Master Adama?*

Adama - I thought we might have a discussion about the crystal and mineral families and how we work with them here in Telos. Some of this has been discussed in our previous messages and we will be discussing it again as we move along in our project.

Many of you are becoming increasingly aware of the beingness of the many crystals and minerals that are here present with us on Earth. You, Bryan, have been led, and you were correct in following our suggestion and your inner guidance in welcoming the crystals and minerals that you have brought with you to the mountain. For you to relay your blessings through energy vibration has been a most kind and appropriate thing to do. The energies of the mountain are assisting them in activating and attuning to the higher vibrations, which are quite prevalent here. They are thriving. I believe you have sensed this as you walked around your home and allowed yourself to connect with them and feel into them with intention. In checking to see if you would be able to sense a vibration returning to you, you have received a vibration that feels like joy, dancing and laughing…just joy. This was the vibration that was being sent for you to receive. You have interpreted accurately.

We understand these concepts may be challenging in much the same way as our discussion of the dragon tribes might be. Humans are coming into their awakening now and allowing their minds to expand beyond the old paradigm and that which they think or thought is or is not possible. Slowly but surely, all are beginning to open and receive higher illumination in their own way. There are many among you now who already know that crystals hold within them an innate intelligence and ability. This seems so foreign to your old paradigm way of thinking. If we were to apply labels, we might say that some of your brothers and sisters are fully asleep and others fully awake. There are many varieties of shades and colors of vibration of asleep and awake between the two points and there is never any judgment of it either way. As new energies and light come in, certain aspects within the human are being activated. This happens beyond your conscious awareness in most cases, and in your terminology you might say a fire is being lit in the belly of the human or that their love lights are turning on. Once you are activated so to speak, you are then set on a new path, a different course. Sometimes you may choose to go very slowly and at other times very quickly. Regardless, as the activations and light come forth they are naturally guiding each of you to step into new levels of awaking, understanding, allowing and acceptance. You are all––Gaia and all life here––evolving together. The shifts are happening holistically; it cannot be any other way.

So we have a similar case and activity with all of the beautiful crystal and mineral kingdoms on the planet and there are many. For you see, just as there are different families and cultures of human, there are different families within the crystal kingdom. We see all shapes and sizes, all variety of color, shade, density, luminosity, radiance and clarity; and they combine to make up a most beautiful family of the crystal kingdom. The crystal kingdoms carry their own level of consciousness. It is a collective consciousness but also a family consciousness within the collective. So we might say that aquamarine is within one crystalline family and amethyst in another. Master Saint Germain has shown you the Crystal Cavern, residing in the higher dimensions. It is a library of study in which all varieties and families of the crystal kingdom have been placed so it could serve as a place of higher learning and teaching. Within this great hall—which does not look like a cave but is most beautiful and rainbow luminescent—there are specimens from each of the families within the crystal kingdoms and each of these families holds an innate set of wisdom, knowledge and application. The crystal kingdoms add a most beautiful and important element to our collective experience here on Earth.

Located around the planet within the body of Gaia, there are very large pockets of various families of the crystalline collective. These crystal families serve Gaia in a number of different ways. There are energy grids located within Gaia that function similarly to the energy meridians within your body. They are natural paths by which energy flows. Gaia has crystalline grids and magnetic/electromagnetic grids within her body. The magnetic grids are facilitated mostly by the mineral kingdom. I am speaking of these two kingdoms together. They are separate families of the whole. Minerals such as iron, silicon and aluminium make up density and mass within the body of Gaia, and they assist with her magnetic grid systems and energy fields. They were placed there strategically at the time of her creation to assist her in maintaining her balance, and this is quite literally what we mean—–maintaining her balance. You can see how important this is for her own vitality and good health, but it is also of great importance to all of life that is here with Gaia now. It would not take much of what we will call a weeble-wobble effect and the world as you know it could literally be upside down in an instant. So the magnetic and electromagnetic grids are of vital importance. She has already made her ascension, yes, but she is not fully settled in the change nor will she be for some time. The rest of sentient life on the planet will need to catch up with her so to speak before you can all make your transition to New Earth. We have work ahead of us. Gaia has made great strides in recent history; but the clearing and cleaning process, the rejuvenation process are not complete. Things are still in play. With these shifts that are taking place globally, obviously they are affecting her, humanity and all life on the planet. The star nation of Sirius and others have come to assist us in the transition, and one of the key roles they play is assisting Gaia in maintaining harmony and balance within her grid systems. The mineral kingdoms also hold within them an innate wisdom and intelligence, you see. They too are being activated at this time; so very simply when we say the star nation of Sirius have come to assist Gaia in this way, they are in essence activating and communicating with the mineral and crystal kingdoms within Gaia that hold the electro-magnetic vibrations, which, in turn, assist her in maintaining a proper balance. This is taking place now.

The time will come when all of humanity will work in a cooperative manner with all that exists here—–Mother Gaia herself and all kingdoms present alongside you, including the crystal and mineral kingdoms. Returning to the discussion of families of crystals, we tell you there are greatly enhanced technologies to come forth with the use of and in cooperation with the crystalline kingdoms. We use crystals here in Telos for a number of things. We use crystals as a power and energy source. Some families have the ability not only to hold, but also to regenerate energy. You might look upon them as an engine in much the same way that a gasoline engine runs and produces power for some output. That engine requires that some fossil fuel be added to make it operate. In the days to come, fossil fuels will no longer be necessary to generate power; for you will come to know, understand and apply different forms of energy and technology. One of the primary forms of energy that you will utilize is within the crystal kingdoms. It may in fact be us who come to teach you of these things. I cannot say this with certainty, for I do not know if this has been fully established as a plan of record but certainly it is a possibility. We would be most pleased to work with you in this way.

We have shown you that the crystals here are a source of power generation and that they can be used as holding tanks of energy. The energy may be utilized at any time. The power generation comes from light and intention. We are at a point in our understanding where we are able to communicate with the crystalline kingdoms and that is not to say (joking) that we would sit down at the table and have dinner with our friends of the crystalline kingdom. It is to say they have a family consciousness, and there is activity that they are designed for or aligned with and we understand such things. Having that understanding, we are able to work with those crystalline families; and with their assistance, and through our intention we are able to utilize those gifts and attributes which they bring forth for these purposes. There is collective consciousness within these families. It is not the same kind of consciousness that you and I are experiencing in this moment, but there is a consciousness and an awareness there nonetheless. When you hold a crystal and send blessings of energy through your hands, at some level I can assure you the message is being received and most likely being appreciated and returned to you in kind. I understand these concepts may be a bit difficult for some to grasp and that is okay. We will continue and as time goes on we will circle back around.

I've shown you some of the ways we work with crystals. One is for energy production and use. We use them to propel our merkaba light vehicles. We use them to provide light and frequency vibration in which we grow many of our plants and food crops. We use them for the radiance of sunlight. Even though we are here in the mountain in what you might think of as an etheric 5D city in Middle Earth, we very much enjoy the rays, beauty and light coming from our sun. We have crystals that transmit and bring forth the rays of sunlight, and of course this is also energy which allows these crystals to regenerate and refuel themselves. We have other crystals that are record keepers able to hold and organize information in a way that is similar to your memory chips. There are liquid crystal displays and other components in your phones and laptop computers. Those components contain magnetic, electrical and crystalline substances, so humanity has already unlocked a small piece of this technology and understanding. There is much, much more to come, for you have not even begun to scratch the surface. I bring this up today so you may recognize that there are a great many natural elements––crystals and minerals, silicon, quartz, gold, silver, copper, lead, and so on––that are already in wide use throughout your technology. This knowledge will only continue to expand.

Some of our crystals here are record keepers. I have described, as one example, something similar to an encyclopedia. They are able to project holograms that we use for our educational purposes.

The young ones use them a lot in their training and study. We may choose a historical topic, for example; and through the crystals that hold the information we can, through our intention, call forth that record and access it in a number of ways. We may simply access the information telepathically, or perhaps we may choose to have the record show itself in a hologram type of way so we can have the enjoyment of watching the show so to speak.

These uses are possible and many more. We also construct the majority of our architecture with crystals. We can grow crystals rapidly. We can choose the variety/color, density, shape, luminosity and inherent properties of that crystal family that is most pleasing to us, and we can construct in any piece or in whole any architecture that we choose. Growing crystals is something that you are also already doing. Some of them are made into semiconductors and other components that have assisted you in bringing forward much of your current electronic technology. I said a moment ago that we refer to some our crystals as record keepers. You are using them for the same purpose in your memory chips: we're just going about it in different ways. So we are not talking necessarily about a quantum leap, but of further learning and understanding of the tools that are available to you. The crystalline kingdoms and mineral kingdoms are one of our most beautiful and useful of resources here on the planet. I say again, they do have their own level of consciousness, so we always approach our work with them as a cooperative. We work with them. We have a great reverence for all of the crystalline and mineral kingdoms and that which they share with us for our benefit.

While we are discussing this, I will take a few steps back. We spoke for a moment about the minerals within Gaia and some applications. I wish to speak now about the crystalline families that are with us and I will tell you that all of this is within your remembrance. This is ancient knowledge of which many of you have been aware, but you do not fully remember the use of the crystals during the time of your embodiments in Lemuria. There is great power contained inherently within some families of crystals, and within your remembrance you know which ones they are. In your times in Lemuria there were great, mighty crystals that were in use in many different geographic locations; of course, their proper use and application within the law was well understood at that time. I say "mighty" because many of them were physically very large in size. Some of them were huge with a mix of shape, color and quality. Imagine a clear quartz crystal as big as a city building or a large church, for example. These crystals were used with great intention and authority in the light and they were used for a number of things. Many of these large crystals were used to anchor and expand qualities of goodness from the light of the seven rays. Some were used for signaling: basically transmitters and receivers of light placed in special locations. They were used individually or together simultaneously to receive and transmit, for example, the light of the seven Creator rays or perhaps the golden light from the Heart of Creator. They might be used to receive and transmit communication signals from other parts of the galaxy for example. So crystals were used in all manner of ways and they were of great benefit to us all at that time. This information was primarily lost or destroyed in the time of the last great shift. Some of the most large and powerful crystals were either destroyed or hidden by us such that they would not be allowed to fall into the wrong hands. Had that happened at that particular time, we could have experienced even further devastation. The situation could have been much worse. This is how powerful some of these crystals are, so many were hidden or destroyed. We are coming into a time when we will be able to unearth the great crystals that have been hidden away until such time as mankind was ready to use them again within proper authority and alignment. We are approaching that time when we may find them and put them into service again. This will happen once we and others have made ourselves known to you again. You will need proper instruction for use of these tools; and of course this will not happen until we can be assured they will be used within the highest light and greatest good for all. We don't expect this to happen next week but I want you to have an idea of where we are headed.

As you are led to do so, I would encourage each of you to work with your crystals. Hold them and connect with them while you send your loving energy and intention. They will pick up on your communication through the vibration that you are sending. If you are touching or holding them simply think of transmitting the thought energetically through the hand. This is an easy thing to do and they will perceive it at some level. They will not receive it in the same way that I would receive your conversation, but they will understand the tone and meaning of the vibration. An example of what might be a good practice is from time to time hold your crystals, gaze upon them and be grateful for their beauty and the beauty they radiate out into the world. As you do this, allow the vibration to flow through your hand and flow freely into them. Then, as you become familiar with their innate qualities, you may also request assistance that you would like to receive. I would suggest a very simple statement and intention. The simpler, the better. You may also send them pictures of what you're asking for. It's all about feeling and vibration. This is so you may more successfully transmit the vibration of the request. You see, in this simple process now comes a new level of cooperation and connectedness and new levels of application and benefit for both of you. Also, keep in mind there is a school for this very subject matter. Master Saint Germain is the Headmaster of the school that you know as the Crystal Cavern. This knowledge is widely known and utilized in the higher dimensions. So I tell you my friend, you have not lost your mind when you feel compelled, as you were, to welcome those crystals to the mountain with a blessing. I can assure you the intention and blessings at some levels were understood and appreciated. Isn't this an interesting discussion? (We are laughing together.) Do not worry. Those who are ready for this information will receive it. You need not worry about it. It will sort itself out and in due time all will come to understand these truths.

# Chapter 13

## Body Elemental and Body Double

Bryan - *Good afternoon, Master Adama. I see there are two others here that I don't recognize. I see two small ones beside you. I believe you are telling me they are my body elemental and body double.*

Adama - Yes, Bryan that is correct. You are aware of your body elemental and you have heard the term body double, but you do not fully understand who this one is. As you are working now more and more with your body elemental, I thought the two of you might enjoy a face-to-face meeting as it were. (Note: *what I observed is the body elemental appears as a smaller version of me about 3.5 feet tall and looks much like I do today. The body double looks like a younger version of me.)*

Bryan - *Hello gentlemen, it's good to meet you both today. Master Adama, I have a limited understanding of these aspects. Would you share more information please?*

Adama - Yes, your body elemental and body double are from the elemental kingdoms. You recognize members of the elemental kingdoms as sylphs (air), undines (water), gnomes (earth), and salamanders (fire), who work closely with Gaia and the nature kingdoms to help keep them in balance. Also within the realms of the elementals are these beautiful beings of light who come to be in service alongside each and every one of you. All of humanity have a body elemental and a body double. The body elemental is primarily concerned with the overall health, wellbeing and functioning of the four lower bodies. He or she works with your innate body intelligence––that is your beloved I AM Presence, Higher Self and all of the components within your body that contain their own intelligence and activity such as the subconscious mind, DNA, cellular memory, the nervous system and chakra energy centers, etc. all functioning across the four lower bodies. There is inherent wisdom and intelligence contained there within your four lower bodies.

Your body elemental is here to be in service to you. Most on the planet today are not aware that they have a beautiful being from the elemental kingdoms who is attending to them daily and striving to assist them in maintaining health and balance. As people become aware of this truth they may begin, if they choose, to work consciously with their body elemental. Your interaction will likely not include a full two-way conversation such as the one that is taking place now; but I can assure you, whatever you are thinking, vibrating and sending out to the body and the world is also being received by your body elemental. Your body elemental looks like you only smaller and in what you might call an etheric or light body. This one for you is about 3.5 feet tall so just a bit over half your height and of similar proportion. Your body elemental will often take on the same challenges that the human has taken on, which may have been by choice, albeit perhaps not a conscious choice. Whatever you bring into your experience as it relates to the health and balance of your four lower bodies is also being experienced by your body elemental.

You are connected in a very real way. Your body elemental comes in with you at the beginning of your embodiment here and will remain with you until such time as you return home. This is a service to each person that is provided with great love and with great joy. They are in service to the light; and as masters, all of you have chosen to be here at this time. They have also agreed to come here and be with you at this time. Just as you are in service to the light––this is in your awareness and consciousness and it is what your soul desires––so too is their service to the light and it is what their soul desires. Their service to the light then provides them with an opportunity for further growth, expansion and new levels of achievement. This cycle is ongoing. This is the nature and expression of Creator.

Most are not aware that their body elemental even exists; so without any cooperation from the human, often the body elemental will become overwhelmed with a wide variety of negative frequencies and vibrations, which, for example, might be fearful or unproductive thought patterns, beliefs and influences coming in from each one's environment or even the collective consciousness of humanity. For you see, just as the elementals who are working with Gaia are significantly affected by the collective consciousness of humanity and all that is existing in this world, so then each of your own body elementals are also subject to picking up those vibrations and levels of consciousness that they are living in and experiencing alongside you.

The body elemental can be a most powerful ally in this lifestream experience. Although the body elemental does not have the same level of consciousness that would facilitate a two way conversation in your language, they have in other ways, much higher levels of understanding and the ability to apply that understanding more so than you do. For example, if you choose to actively bring light and life force into the body or golden liquid light or whatever it is you're working with, you are blessing the body through your intention. Perhaps you bless all aspects of your four lower bodies or some specific area you feel may require your attention at that time. You may choose an activity such as this, and you may be quite effective; however, your body elemental has within him or her higher levels of understanding as it relates to such activity that you may not be aware of yet. What I mean by that is that because they are from the elemental kingdoms, they are well equipped to work with light, sound, color and various forms of energy and matter.

So in this example, if you were to invite your body elemental to participate with you in the activity, you would find over time, as you come to trust the truth of this knowledge and begin to form a co-operative, collaborative relationship with your body elemental, what you will find is these kinds of endeavors will become much more successful and effective for you. The two of you together may accomplish significantly more than you are able to accomplish on your own. Generally this would be a true statement. The exception might be some of the higher level masters who are present on Earth now and working with higher levels of their own attainment. For most of humanity on the planet today, that would not apply; therefore, my statement stands in that you will accomplish much more in cooperation and collaboration as a team than you would individually. What you are doing in this work is simply acknowledging that your body elemental is always there with you and always working in service to you. They are most loving and kind beings that come here for the sole purpose of tending to your four lower bodies through your lifestream experience. Their purpose for being here is to love you and attend to you, so why not take advantage of this opportunity and the prospect of a beautiful friendship, for truly it can blossom.

The signals being sent to your conscious awareness by the body elemental are just that: they are signals. They are cues, nudges and feelings. Most of the time, they will not communicate to you with a conscious language. This is true in most cases; again there are exceptions. In most cases, what you will receive is a nudging or impulse. Try not to listen with the head but move into the heart space and FEEL what the body is trying to tell you. You have heard these phrases over and over again: "Feel into the body", "Listen to the body" and "Let the body tell you what it needs." These phrases are good advice indeed, for this would be the same as saying tap into the awareness of your body elemental and listen or feel into what they are trying to communicate to you. So on one hand, this is a very common, everyday kind of thing that you hear. You read about it and people talk about it. You hear this advice being given, "Listen to the body." This means you need to get out of the headspace, the ego, and the logical, cognitive left-brain approach. Move instead to a place of calm relaxation where the mind and chatter are allowed to still, settle yourself, quiet the mind and simply drop down into the body or heart space. You can drop down into the body and simply allow yourself to be patient and feel into what is coming forth for you. As you become aware of your body elemental, you may intentionally engage with him or her. Set your attention and intention to your body elemental and simply ask the question you want to know about. Be patient and still and see what comes. It is not difficult but it does take a bit of practice.

Those of you who are meditating and have other practices that help you come into stillness and peace will not have any difficulty. I would encourage you to speak to your body elemental often. Engage him or her and speak your intentions for yourself to your body elemental. Ask them directly to assist you in whatever it is you are endeavoring to achieve across any or all of your four lower bodies. Your body elemental is well versed and well equipped to work not only with your physical body but also to work with your mental, emotional and etheric/spiritual bodies. Anytime you recognize that one of them has come out of balance, you may engage your body elemental. Speak to them about what you believe the imbalance is and ask them to see to it that those imbalances are brought back to perfect harmony and health. You may assist your body elemental by intentionally drawing life force light and energy into the body using your breath and still point. Another process example would be to draw golden liquid light down through the crown chakra and allow it to flow into and through every particle of your four lower bodes and all the cells, organs and tissues of the physical body. Whatever it is that you are doing to sustain your good health and vitality, simply ask that your body elemental participate and cooperate with you in those endeavors. I can assure you that over time, once you have come to firmly accept this relationship and once you have begun to feel the two-way connection that exists, you will see results going forward.

So while your body elemental may not, at this time, have the level of consciousness that would facilitate a two-way conversation in your language, they are sending you clues and hints that your mind will readily pick up on if you are attuned to it. Because of their beautiful nature and level of being that they are, they have access to a great wealth of knowledge that your conscious mind does not have access to. They are able to enlist assistance from the Devic angel kingdoms and others. They also have within them innate levels of ability to use light, sound, tone, color and energy/prana for your benefit. They understand many aspects of creation that your intellectual mind, at this point in time, does not. The two of you working together become powerful allies for a common goal.

Now we will discuss your body double. This is another aspect of your being that most of humanity is not yet aware of and that is why we are speaking about it today. Your body double is also from the elemental kingdoms; however, their general makeup, their level of being and purpose is somewhat different. They work with you also in a cooperative manner. Your body double is here to serve as a master blueprint for your four lower bodies. The body double allows your Higher Self the opportunity to run an infinite number of simulations. Most humans do not consciously work with the body double, but your Higher Self, primarily in cooperation with your body elemental, utilizes them. We have been discussing the many changes taking place globally that have to do with the increase of light, sound and electromagnetic frequencies, Divine Feminine energies, and essentially more love and light coming onto the planet now. Throughout the process of day-to-day living, perhaps you are aware of these changes and perhaps you are not. All that requires releasing will begin making its way to the surface. You are making choices for yourself each day that have some impact on one or some of your four lower bodies. Sometimes those impacts will happen simultaneously and sometimes not. For example, let us say you have made the decision not to have a salad for lunch today but to opt instead for a banana split. As you are enjoying your delicious banana split and bringing it into the body, the body and body elemental, who are always working as a team, will help facilitate the intake of the banana split into the body and all that it means for the body. These would be your normal physical body processes such as digestion and elimination. The body will take nutrients from the banana and dispose of the sugar and so on. Now, let us say that as you were eating the banana split, you had a bad feeling about it. Perhaps you felt guilty that you have broken your diet plans and have opted instead for what you view as an unhealthy choice. So now this food choice also impacts your emotional body because you feel the guilt of having broken your own promise, or whatever the case may be, and now your emotional body has something to deal with. You placed it there by your attitudes, thoughts and beliefs and it is now theirs to deal with. This is all the fullness of your being, of course, but I'm breaking it down this way for understanding. Now your emotional body has something new to deal with. Perhaps your mental body has also become engaged as you ponder the steps you might put in place to prevent another backslide tomorrow. You get the idea. This is a very simple example but it will do.

We might run a simulation using your body double so we can see, in this example, what the effect would be on the four lower bodies if you choose to have a banana split for lunch today. We can run different scenarios even if it has not taken place yet in your physical experience. Let's say you have not yet made the decision to enjoy a delicious banana split and your Higher Self is wanting to see what the overall net result would be of your having had this experience. Your Higher Self may work in cooperation with your body double and body elemental to run a simulation to see what would happen, in your case, if you make the choice of having a banana split. Now this all sounds very simple and really it is, but I will give you a few more examples as to how your body double is in service to you. Again, your body double is also from the elemental kingdoms and has chosen by his or her own choice to come here in this lifestream experience to be with you and to be in service to you. This is also their service to the light. They both love you very much or they would not have agreed to come. They are your great advocates.

As another example, with higher levels of love, light and vibration coming to the planet now, your Higher Self or your family members across the veil, may want to see how a certain upgrade or activation will affect you. There are many among the lightworker community who are feeling within themselves a sense of urgency, and many of you are moving along now at a highly accelerated rate of speed in terms of the adjustments being made across your four lower bodies. This is the expanding of your awareness, your consciousness, opening the seals of light packets of wisdom, awakening dormant DNA, raising of the kundalini energy or activation of your body's energy centers and so on and so forth. You're all shifting from a carbon based body structure to a crystalline-based structure. There are a great many changes taking place within you now. Those of you who are doing this work are already aware of the shifts and changes taking place within you. Your Higher Self, body elemental and guardian angel will do their best to minimize the effects for you, but many of you have experienced multiple side effects resulting from your shifts. They are being referred to now as ascension symptoms and that is exactly what they are. Your bodies are changing now in big ways and there is only so much we can do to minimize the resulting symptoms. Many of you within the lightworker community have already moved past your greatest challenges in this regard, but there are many of your brothers and sisters coming right along behind you who will benefit by your example and understanding.

Many of you are endeavoring and setting your intention on increasing your levels of light, love and awareness. You are choosing to put yourselves on the fast track of gaining or moving toward your ascension. This is your soul's desire so this work feels very natural to you. It is highly beneficial for us to have the ability to run a simulation and to see, with one activation or another, what the net effect might be across your four lower bodies. With the assistance of your body double we can run a simulation and see the result. Has the net result been beneficial for you or has it inadvertently caused you to take two steps back? None of us want to see any of you taking two steps back when you have within you always the ability to take successfully one step (or as many as you choose) forward. So if your Higher Self, for example, is considering that it is time now for a particular initiation, upgrade or activation, they may run a simulation with the assistance of your body double and they can see what the effect will be. If the effect is deemed to be to your benefit and for your highest good, then the activation, in this example, would be given to you and you would experience that event. Additionally, we, the Company of Heaven, are able to run simulations at various scales with the assistance of body doubles. We can run simulations based on communities, nations or global levels. We can see what the overall effect on human populations would be if the light and energy frequencies on the planet increased from X to Y. With the cooperation of each of your body doubles, we can see holographically, you might say, what the net result would be for that scenario. This allows us to have information to make a better decision and to know if this is the appropriate choice for the greatest good of all. I know this will be new information for many of you, but I tell you this is truth and this is what is happening.

It is a beautiful friendship and awareness that you will come into once you allow yourself to accept these aspects of self and begin working with your body elemental and body double in your own way. For the most part, you will be engaging your body elemental. You may of course also speak to your body double at any time, and you may also ask them for assistance: however, your body double is primarily acting as an intermediary between your Families of Light and your body elemental and your four lower bodies. They are really acting as a gateway if you will. Your primary engagement and ally in these things that you want to accomplish (harmonious emotional states, more energy, a healthy and balanced digestive system, etc.) will be your body elemental.

I will not go too far into this today but I would be remiss to have this conversation without also mentioning the great benefit you will receive by actively engaging your Higher Self in these same activities. You are hearing me more and more discussing a holistic approach where we use a number of tools being applied to the same task or we use various pieces to make the puzzle. We are taking a holistic approach so anything that you want to do within your four lower bodies (healing, harmony, balance) will benefit most greatly by engaging both your body elemental and your Higher Self. Your intention, your spoken word, your divinity, your power, your authority to co-create and manifest, coupled with the cooperation of your body elemental and always with the guidance and supervision of your Higher Self––this is your dream team.

Of course there are other aspects that we would bring into this discussion. Prayer is always encouraged. There are a great many of us within the Company of Heaven––masters, Archangels and guides––whom you may choose to work with for all manner of subjects and topics; but today we are discussing the four lower bodies and bringing them into vitality and good health or restoring balance where needed. So, you may also be working with others and that is also to your benefit. The point I really want to make here in regards to your overall health and wellbeing, which is the fullness of your four lower bodies, is that you will receive the greatest level of result if you will actively engage the assistance of your Higher Self and your body elemental.

There are other things still that we could talk about. Your dear friend, Master Saint Germain, has brought forth, some time ago, the information he refers to as the mighty workers of the constructive process, and that is your beloved I AM Presence that is always present in all levels of your being. It is in every cell and particle of the fullness of your being. Your I AM Presence is the divinity, intelligence and activity of Creator residing within you and flowing through you at all times. So this is something else you may choose to work with and I would encourage it. Perhaps we will discuss this more in the future. As you intentionally bring light and Creator life force into the body with the intention of bringing in life, vitality, healing and perfection, you may set your intention such that golden liquid light, in this example, be received fully by your I AM Presence and the fullness of your being and body. This is just another opportunity to work with Creator and with all that has been given to you as your divine birthright. There are many, many processes and methods that may be used effectively to strengthen your overall health and vitality. I am bringing this forward today as what I consider to be an important, foundational piece of understanding for this kind of work.

What you would see then if you were able to view it from our perspective, as each human becomes aware and is able to feel into the truth of this information, as each one then actively acknowledges his or her body elemental and body double, what you would see is they are lighting up with joy. They are so pleased that you, the human, have come now, after all this time, to have them in your awareness and to acknowledge them as the friends and allies they are, to acknowledge that they have come here to be with you in the fullness of this experience with unwavering loyalty and service. When you come to the place where you are able to acknowledge them and engage them in a real and meaningful way, you bring them great joy and contentment. I would encourage you to show them your appreciation. Let them know how valued they are, and what you will see is that love and that acknowledgement being reflected back to you in the most wondrous of ways.

# Chapter 14

## Gaia

Adama – Hello, Bryan. Welcome again to the Great Hall. Perhaps you would like to have some discussion on the environment and Mother Gaia today?

Bryan - *Yes sir, that is a topic of great interest.*

Adama - Gaia is a celestial being with her own consciousness. We know there are many of you on planet today who have your own awareness of this already; and if not full awareness, you may have an inner feeling or sense that what you have been told in this regard is true. I say to you now it is true. The planetary bodies and solar sun bodies that you see with your telescopes out in our galaxy and beyond really are heavenly bodies. This term, "heavenly bodies" has been use for a great long time and you are all familiar with it. Does it occur to you why they have been referred to in this way for so long? Just as it may be difficult for some to accept that crystals and the crystalline kingdoms have their own levels of consciousness, so too does Gaia. She is an advanced level of being and she is ancient. She took this form and came into this embodiment eons ago.

Our universe was created from the Heart of God, the Alpha and Omega. Life and consciousness are always expanding; and our Creator is always expanding through light, love, consciousness, will, the Word and through his many creations. It is a never-ending cycle of expression and expansion that radiates out into the cosmos in which there are infinite numbers of ways the expression of Creator may manifest itself. Often this happens in ways that are difficult for you to perceive or understand at this time. When our universe and galaxy were being formed from the heart of creation, it was set down by the architect (Alpha) and then allowed to flow into the womb of creation (Omega). It was then expressed out of the womb and into the world of form and matter. The blueprint for our galaxy was set down by the architect, and this was the blueprint of all that you see taking place in our galaxy and in our world. At that time of creation, higher levels of being who had made the decision for themselves to choose the experience of a heavenly body, were brought forth and given the opportunity to participate here in this galaxy and our solar system at that time of its creation. Gaia was one of the advanced levels of being who chose this experience for herself. She came forward at that time and was elevated in form to that of a heavenly body, which you know as planet Earth, as Gaia. This is true also for the other heavenly bodies.

Expansion, expression, growth and higher levels of achievement never stop. This was an opportunity then for the soul of Gaia to have an experience that she had not had before. It was also an opportunity to provide a great service to the light and to Creator and therefore to all of life that she supports here, including of course all of humanity. This was to be your home and this was to be the home of an almost infinite number and variety of life forms and expression of life, expressions of Creator. There is life also on many of the other heavenly bodies occupying our galaxy. Your scientists may not have the technology available at this time to produce this as fact, but this information will come forth and make itself known at the appropriate time. You already know, for example, that there is a civilization of advanced beings there on the heavenly body you know as Venus. This is her common name just as Earth would be the common name for Gaia. And so it was with great love and light and enthusiasm that this solar system was created and that Gaia was allowed then to come forth as a heavenly body and the container of life that she is.

As we are having this discussion I can see you are wondering about how it is that an advanced being and advanced soul might be willing to volunteer for this role, knowing the length of time that would be required for this service and also knowing the challenges that would be faced in agreeing to be the home for humanity. I remind you to try to see the difference between a 3rd dimensional view of linear time, your earthly illusion of time, and that which we experience across the veil. It is much different. Once this creation/expression was sent forth by Creator, the Elohim, who are the builders of form, were next to take the blueprints. They worked closely with Creator in the birthing of this universe and our galaxy from the womb of Creator, that of the Omega. The Elohim then, were the builders of form such that they took the blueprints and holograms for this galaxy as provided to them through the womb of Creation and, all working together in unity consciousness, formed this galaxy. One aspect of the building of form of this galaxy and thus our solar system was the choosing and stepping forward of those advanced beings who had decided for themselves that this was an opportunity for expansion, growth and service that they wished to participate in. From this place, Gaia and others stepped forward. These heavenly bodies have been residing here for eons, and they are in full awareness of time as a linear construct. Gaia has agreed to be here and allow a 3rd dimensional construct and framework to be placed around her body such that it would facilitate life as you know it. She has agreed to do this, and yet she is also an advanced being, able to work and commune with all of us in ways that are not limited to a 3rd dimensional experience. She has agreed to hold the 3rd dimensional construct for all of this, yet she has also never been disconnected from Source.

As humans, you come into the world with a veil of illusion set about you such that when you come into this experience you have forgotten a great deal of what you have known and experienced as the higher level beings that you are. This has not been the case with Gaia. She has always maintained her higher levels of communion with Creator and the Company of Heaven. She is a multi-dimensional being. As a multi-dimensional being, she is able to travel and to experience other areas of the cosmos in ways that far surpass what most of you can imagine at this time. Her experience of time is much different than that of a 3rd dimensional construct.

What I am trying to say is, you have wondered and had compassion for Gaia for all of the time that she has been required to be here and serve in this capacity. What I would like to say to you is this has not been nearly the hardship or burden that you may perceive it to be. Her experience has been different. You might perceive that she has been here for billions of years patiently waiting for humanity to evolve, and she has. You may perceive her as having been agonizing for billions of years, and I tell you this is just not the case. However, she is indeed ready to move on at this time and she has made this known. This was incorporated into the blueprint some time ago and there have been events that have been leading up to her ascension and her next transition. And so, while yes, she has been here in service for a great long period of time according to a 3D linear construct of time, time for her passes differently than it does for you. Although she has allowed a 3rd dimensional framework to be placed around her to facilitate all that you are experiencing, she herself is experiencing higher dimensional realities alongside this one. She has agreed to allow her body to hold a construct of the 3rd dimension that facilitates all that you see now on the planet. It was not a requirement for her awareness and consciousness to move into and stay in a 3rd dimensional construct. In her awareness and consciousness, she has always been here with us at the higher levels such that the passing of time for her is not nearly as burdensome as you might think it to be. Now, that being said, she made her decision to ascend some time ago and this has been incorporated into the master project plan that we have discussed.

I have told you that the master blueprint and master plan will be published, but revisions are being made and adapted as events take place and as changes are required. Gaia decided some time ago that she was ready to make her ascension in the light such that she may continue her expansion. She is ready now to move into greater levels of light and service. What we have taking place is a series of events whereby all aspects of the master project plan are coming together to facilitate this desire that Gaia has to move into the next advanced levels of service, and it has been decided that you would all go together. Mother Gaia is a most radiant and loving being of light. She would not have agreed to be in service in this way if she were not. It is her desire to bring as many of you with her as possible. She wishes to bring ALL of life with her as she makes her ascension in her body. Her body is being allowed now to move into higher dimensions such that she will no longer be subject to a 3rd dimensional framework being placed around her.

As is obvious to anyone who looks, the activities that have been taking place on Earth since the time of the last Golden Age have created fields of imbalance and disturbance at all levels of her creation. Her physical body, the resources that she provides to sustain life, have been misused and unappreciated for the most part. They have been scavenged. In the days of the last Golden Age when you were there in your Lemurian embodiments, at that time you were working with, communing with and in cooperation with Gaia just as you were with the Company of Heaven and Creator. In this way there was great harmony. In those days it was common knowledge and accepted practice to actively engage Gaia and commune with Gaia. It was a two-way conversation and it was the same for those of us whom you refer to as the Company of Heaven. There was free and open communication between the realms of Heaven and Gaia, Heaven and Lemuria, Lemuria to Gaia and Gaia back to them. You get the idea. These levels of consciousness and awareness were all connected and working in communion. The great shift took place; and for the past twelve thousand years or so, this world has moved steadily into lower vibration, density and duality. Indeed, this has taken a great toll on Gaia and her physical and emotional bodies. She is sustaining all manner of assault on her physical body at this time. She has done her best, in working with the elemental kingdoms, to maintain a healthy body that would continue to support and sustain life. This has become increasingly more and more of a struggle as humanity continues to develop higher forms of technology that are capable of destruction at higher levels. This technology has the ability to create imbalance and destruction in expanded and more powerful ways such that the effects are not easily healed. This has been going on for some time and continues so today. All you need do is look around and you can see this.

Since the time of the last great shift and all that has resulted since that time, there has come about a layer of energy––the collective consciousness, the astral plane and lower vibrational energies––that has been trapped in her bodily fields now for a great period of time. This negative energy and consciousness have been allowed to expand and expand and expand such that the time has come when Creator has decided that change is needed. This is the activity we have been discussing. This activity includes such things as previously Ascended Masters coming back at this time to offer assistance and leadership, new levels of light and higher vibrational energies, increased levels of Divine Feminine energies and Christ Consciousness, and also special dispensations that have been brought forth from the Heart of Creator. These activities offer opportunities for humanity to advance, opportunities that have never been present in this world before. One such example is that of grace and a new, lessened requirement for the balancing of individual karma such that humans now may only be required to balance fifty-one percent of their karma to move forward. Through new levels of grace that are coming forth now, the Company of Heaven may assist them in releasing the remainder of their karma. This was a special dispensation sent forth by Creator with the specific intention of raising the collective consciousness of humanity and giving each of you an opportunity to achieve your ascension in the light.

There are several reasons for these gifts. Mother Gaia has made the request that all of you be allowed to transition with her as she makes her ascension and moves into the higher dimensions. This is the transition of humanity from a 3rd dimensional experience to a 5th dimensional experience, and indeed all life on the planet will be making this same transition. She has made pleas on behalf of humanity that come from her great love of humanity and indeed for all manner of life that she is supporting here. Secondly, the Ascended Masters and Ascended Master Councils have also made pleas on behalf of humanity such that dispensations may now be offered to assist each one in their own personal evolution to move confidently into a 5th dimensional experience of unity consciousness. This is also why those of us here in the Agartha Network have chosen to stay behind. We have continued to keep the flames burning on behalf of humanity, knowing this day would come; so we are here, as are many others from other star nations, working with the project teams to facilitate the ascension of Gaia, humanity and all life on the planet. We are using a holistic approach and you could say, in some regard, that Gaia has been the catalyst for all of this activity. It was not known at the time of the creation of this galaxy, at the time of the creation/transformation of Gaia into this heavenly body and that of the seeding of humanity, it was not known at that time exactly how things would play out. Universal law of course is always in effect. The Logos of Creator is always in effect, yet there were many variables that were unknown. They were not foreseeable at that time due primarily, to the nature of this environment and the free will choice of humanity.

To make a long story short, no one thought that we would still be having this conversation today. It was not expected that Gaia would be required to hold the 3rd dimensional construct for supporting life here for such a great period of time. And while it is true, she is not only experiencing her time in the 3rd dimension, she has decided to move on to greater levels of experience and expression and she is being supported in that decision. It is also the will of Creator that humanity now be given the assistance you need such that you may also make your ascension in the light. So here we are, standing in the doorway of the next great shift. I tell you we are all ready for this, not just Gaia but all of us here in the Agartha Network who have been waiting patiently, waiting for humanity to step forward and claim their own victory in the light and advance themselves beyond a third dimensional experience of duality. Those who you refer to as the Company of Heaven have also chosen to stand beside you and hold space and light and love for all of humanity and Gaia. They too are ready to see humanity reclaim your divinity and take your place among your brothers and sisters in the cosmos. You are to elevate yourselves, then, into a new 5$^{th}$ dimensional experience and that of unity consciousness, to move fully into the light. You are moving forward with your evolution.

Just as each of you is moving through various levels of clearing and cleaning––and this is happening individually and collectively as higher vibration and light flood the planet––this process is also happening for Mother Gaia and the elemental kingdoms. They are having to shake off the dust as it were. They are having to cleanse and purify their bodies and consciousness just as each of you is. This is very similar to old cellular memories, patterns, false beliefs, programs and such that often become stuck in the physical body. They must be released in order to facilitate the higher level functioning of the body and energy centers. This is the case with Gaia where much of what we will call the old paradigm, the 3$^{rd}$ dimensional matrix of duality, this lower energy and consciousness, have become lodged within her own body, and it must be released. Several things are happening when you see natural events or extreme weather conditions taking place around the world. Gaia and the elementals are releasing stuck energies and cleaning and clearing the old matrix. She is disconnecting from the old matrix.

Often there are events you see taking place on the surface that are not necessarily related just to cleaning and clearing but have been brought down through the project plan for other purposes. You have many examples of this kind of activity in your religious and spiritual traditions and often the conditions that groups, communities and nations may experience, such as tragic weather related events, often happen for a higher purpose that may be difficult for you to understand. Such events may, for example, have to do with the meeting of the law of cause and effect, or karma. This law applies not only to the individual but also to groups of collective consciousness. It may apply to communities or nations or peoples. You may witness an event that has created destruction and loss of life. Those who have participated in that event have done so by their own choice and with understanding of the higher purpose. Many of those events are brought about to expand levels of love and compassion in the world. Often times, it is through suffering and hardship that the heart space is allowed to open and expand in new ways and to allow in new levels of light and compassion that the collective may not have previously experienced. In this way, many hearts may be opened further to receive new levels of love, illumination and light.

You have asked for me to clarify the statements about timing. Your question has been: *How is it that Gaia has been here for billions of years and is just now becoming impatient in perhaps these last several thousand years?* You have wanted to know if it was just a timing issue or if it is related to the fact that technology of mankind has advanced such that she is being harmed now at a greater rate of speed than she is able to heal herself. I appreciate your raising this question and it is a good point of clarification.

It is not so much a timing issue. You are correct in that, from Gaia's perspective, having been here in her form for billions of years, certainly a few thousand years give or take is not going to disrupt her plans to a great extent. Gaia has requested some time ago that the transition of her ascension be started now. Another way to say this is, the request was made that we bring about added momentum (light and energy) so that she may begin the process of her ascension more fully and speed the timeline. The reason for this is that, particularly over the last hundred or so years, the technology being used on the planet today has become infinitely more destructive to her body. Placing additional burdens on her are the ever growing populations that she supports and the natural resources that are required to do so. She desires to remain in her most healthy and radiant state such that she may support all life that is here with her. With the increasing levels of destruction, she is finding it increasingly difficult to maintain a balance and harmony within her body that will continue to support herself and all of you. Similar tolls have been taken on the elemental kingdoms, which are here assisting Gaia in these ways. So again, this was Gaia's request yes, but it is evident for all of us to see that the time for change is here. The current path that Gaia and humanity are on now simply would not be able to sustain future life for any of you. The simple fact of the matter is that you are destroying yourselves through ignorance, through carelessness and some even by design.

As we looked out on the overall big picture timeline and as we looked into your third dimensional future as it were, we were able to have some sense of how things might progress and what outcomes were possible. If we were to step back fifty years of your time and look at the path that you all were on, we were not pleased with the range of possibilities and outcomes that we have seen and of course this is no surprise to any of us. It did not sneak up on us. But my point is, change is needed at this time. Let me also just say, we are speaking in this discussion primarily about Gaia and the nature of her being. It is true that she has decided for herself that it was time to begin the next great shift, but this decision was not made in a vacuum nor was it made without consideration of humanity and all life on the planet. While I have stated that Gaia's request was a catalyst for much of the movement we see taking place now, there were many other factors involved, most of which simply have to do with Divine Timing according to the Divine Blueprint and plan of Creator. There are many among you who are referred to as astronomers, astrologers and cosmologists. They are different arts; but they apply to the observation and attempted levels of understanding of, among other things, your origins, the creation and workings of the cosmos and the roles heavenly bodies play in your world. For indeed, there are often great changes and events taking place in your world that are connected with the cycles and events of heavenly bodies and with the divine cycles taking place naturally in our galaxy and the cosmos. There have been a variety of factors and events that have lead us to this now moment and all that is taking place.

In the case of the human body, if you ingest small amounts of substances that are known to be harmful to the body, such as caffeine or sugar, we know the body has within it the intelligence to compensate for those toxins and the body adjusts to it. The toxins are released, the body is healed and this is the way it works until such time as further toxins are ingested or not. However, if you were to eat a box or two of rat poison, there is a good chance that your body would not be able to heal itself because it has become overwhelmed by the amount of poison that has come into the body. It is not able to compensate.

This is a very simple example, but it is similar to what is happening with Gaia's body now. She is being assaulted on all fronts; and more than anything, what I wish to convey is just as we have discussed that Gaia is an advanced level of being with her own advanced levels of consciousness and awareness, so is the physical Earth her body. She has sensory perception of her body. She is aware of her body and how it feels. She is aware of how it is functioning, at various levels of health or decline. The different elements of her body also work together in a holistic way which are intended to maintain health and balance; as one or some of these individual systems come out of balance, they must be set back in balance to achieve proper functioning. So I give you some examples. The tree and plant kingdoms act as Gaia's lungs. They help her to breathe. Their root systems occupy considerably more space than the tree you observe on the surface. Many tree families utilize their root systems as underground networks to exchange energy, nutrients and consciousness. There is an exchange of energy and information taking place between the air and the earth. Gaia receives this information via her own direct connections and with the assistance of the elemental kingdoms and others. The tree and plant kingdoms bring forth important nutrients and minerals that are essential to many if not most forms of life. You know that trees provide life-sustaining oxygen for the planet. These kingdoms serve as natural air purifiers for Gaia and the life she supports.

Water is crucial to life on our planet. Most life forms require fresh water to live, and this is becoming a growing concern. It is a global concern. In addition to fresh water supplies, we have our oceans, which are a world of their own. They sustain a great wealth of life on the planet. Gaia's oceans and seas are teeming with an almost endless variety of life forms and natural beauty. She uses her waterways in ways that are similar in function to the human bloodstream, which carries nutrients, and food supplies to the cells. Water carries oxygen and removes waste and so on. It is the lifeline of the body. So too the ground waters, the rivers, streams and oceans serve in a similar capacity for Gaia's body. The petroleum in her body assists in lubricating her bones, her tectonic plates.

Gaia relies heavily on the plant kingdoms, her waterways and the elementals, the crystal and mineral kingdoms, etc. The rocks, the mountains, the forests and streams: these are the ways that Gaia receives and utilizes life force energy from Creator. I am describing her outer body. These resources and systems are required to function properly in order for her to be able to bring in the life force energy that she needs to sustain herself. With ever growing populations and the continued destruction of her natural environments, the pollutants that are being pumped enmass into the water supplies and into the earth, air and atmosphere add up to a situation that limit the amount of life force energy she is able to bring into her body. The atmosphere of her body contains both environmental pollution and also a layer of lower vibrational, dense and murky consciousness/energy that has accumulated over ages of time. So you see, we have stepped up the amount of light and the frequency of vibration that is coming to the planet now. We are taking a holistic approach such that all life on Gaia is being elevated together. It could not be any other way. We have already passed the apex of this new direction in which we are all headed. We have made the turn and we are all heading home. We are moving confidently now in the right direction to the overall raising of consciousness. This is good news for all of us.

There are many of you on the planet today who are well aware of the assaults taking place on Gaia and humanity, especially in regards to the environment and many of you are troubled by what you see. I'm not suggesting that you should not be troubled; however, I wish for you to know that in the coming days you will be receiving new technologies that will do a couple of things for you. One, you will no longer be required to rely on your current energy sources such as fossil fuels, nuclear power or any sources that have a bi-product of toxicity. You will be shown and provided new forms of technology for the power generation you need. Also, technology is forthcoming that will facilitate the healing and cleansing of Gaia. All that has been damaged will be healed. These events will be staggered over a period of time such that they can be brought into the awareness and use of humanity and applied with efficiency. These are large, global scale projects; and since there are over seven billion humans on planet at this time, it will not happen in a flash. But technologies are coming that will show you new forms of energy, help you to rebalance and, for lack of a better phrase, clean up the many messes you've made.

As you come into unity consciousness and as more individuals open their awareness to accept truths they may not have been open to hearing in the past, the technology will come forth to help you create balance in a whole new way that will benefit all. This relates to your transformation from a 3rd dimensional experience into a 5th dimensional experience, and this is the shift that is taking place.

We are still on the front end of the shift but it is well underway and the momentum is building like a wave sweeping the planet. So while I certainly encourage all to do their best in taking responsibility for the choices they make pertaining to the environment and overall health of Gaia, I bring today a message of hope and upliftment for those who find themselves to be deeply troubled by what they see taking place around them, especially those who love Gaia and the nature kingdoms. I bring you hope and I tell you this day that all will be healed and all will be made right again. The destruction that is taking place today and the rate at which it is increasing must indeed come to a halt, and it will. But also to let you know, despite the damage you see having been done, we have it within our technology to bring about purification and healing for Gaia. I can assure you, as she moves firmly into her 5th dimensional environment, she will have returned to her most radiant and healthy body.

At that time, all of humanity, having come into a 5th dimensional awareness and unity consciousness, will be working with her holistically. With new technologies that are becoming available, you will move forward in ways that are not yet fully conceivable. I would also like to add for your understanding, at the time of the last great shift, as we were coming out of the last Golden Age, the dispensation of light and energy coming onto the planet was intentionally reduced and withheld. As you have been told, in the time of the last Golden Age and golden ages before, there were much greater quantities of light, vibration, illumination and love coming to the planet. There was a two-way exchange between Creator, Company of Heaven, Gaia and all those present at that time. So you see in those times, Gaia and humanity were receiving higher levels of light that are required for the good and healthy functioning of Gaia. It became a requirement through the choice of free will acting, that the levels of light, vibration, life force, communion, illumination and so on––all that was being sent forth from the Godhead––were drastically reduced because these gifts and blessing were being used in ways that were not appropriate. There was no choice but to reduce these energies, which Gaia also required to sustain her healthy body.

If we go back to the issue of timing, you might ask, "Well, she has been here for billions of years and that was all fine so what is the problem now?" Part of the problem is the amount of life force, light and energy coming to her have been drastically reduced. She has essentially been left on a starvation diet for let us say these past twelve thousand years, and she has had some difficulty sustaining herself. She is not receiving the levels of prana, love and light that are required to fully maintain her body structures and all levels of her beingness. Add to that now these other factors that we are discussing and you can see, I believe, why it is that Gaia now has some sense of urgency around this next transition of moving into her ascension. She will bring all with her who will make the choice to come. We are moving into a new paradigm and experience such that the previous levels of love, light, energy and vibration may be turned on again so to speak. Her body will become fully replenished and fully rejuvenated.

# Chapter 15

# Gaia's Weather

Adama - Bryan, I thought we might discuss the wildfires that are taking place here in California and elsewhere in your United States and other areas of the planet. We know this is something that is of great concern to many. It is of particular concern to those of you who live in areas or regions where wildfires are taking place. From your perspective it is serious business, and I know it is quite saddening for many of you to see your forests being destroyed by fire. There is always the possibility of the loss of life of both humans and animals, and this has been the case with the fires this season. Just in your United States this year, there have been a number of individuals who were lost in wildfires and other weather related events. We often encourage you of the lightworker community to strive to maintain a vibration of balance and harmony within you, despite the events and circumstances taking place around you. Quite often there is a higher purpose when such circumstances or events take place that are not always known to you at the time.

Wildfires are natural phenomena that happen on your planet. They are typically created by lightning and thunderstorms; but now, with your ever-growing populations, wildfires are being created not in a natural way but more often than not by acts of humans. Sometimes these fires are accidents and sometimes they are set intentionally. On one hand, these wildfires are indeed a tragedy. We see there is often loss of life, sometimes that of humanity and the animal kingdoms, the birds, squirrels, deer and so many animals that make the forest their home. The tree and plant kingdoms may also succumb to the fire, so those animals that do survive have perhaps lost their homes.

We have discussed that Gaia is in the process of her transformation just as all of humanity and all life on the planet are. You are all making the transition together. Just as most of humanity will experience some ascension symptoms, so Mother Gaia does also. For humanity, the process includes the clearing away of lower vibrational frequencies, outdated beliefs, patterns and energies. They must be released from your body, from cellular memory and from the chakra energy centers. It is through this process, as you clean and clear the lower vibrational energies from your four lower bodies, that you are creating a space in which you may embody more light. We have discussed that many of the weather patterns and what you might call natural disasters, are often related to Gaia's necessary cleaning and clearing. Her body is undergoing a very similar transformation as that of humanity. She is clearing her energetic fields of the lower vibrational energies which exist in all aspects of her bodily form. She has her core, the great crystal core of Gaia that is her heart center. There are regions here in Inner Earth and there is the surface where you all make your homes. Lastly, there is the air and atmosphere that are her outer body or her protective shell. All of these aspects make up the fullness of the body of Gaia. She too, is going through her ascension process to make room for higher levels of light and vibration to come into her bodily forms and to be held there. She is rebalancing and recalibrating her body. She is moving toward the calm and peaceful state of the 5th dimensional environment of New Earth. New Earth will contain only those vibrations and frequencies that are aligned with a 5D or higher experience, and she is preparing herself now to support this transition for all of us.

I understand this is a complex if not confusing topic for many of you. I will try to explain. So you have events there on the surface that are weather related events such as tsunamis, hurricanes, flash floods, tornados, fires, avalanches, earthquakes and storms of various degree and type. These kinds of events have always taken place, but you have seen an increased activity taking place for some time now. This is not anything new and your charts and records have made note of all this. I would say that statistical records are not necessary for any of you who have been around for any length of time. You have seen it for yourselves. We feel that the great majority of her clearing and cleaning process is now complete. It is not over just yet. There is more to come, but we feel the bulk of it has passed. The collective consciousness of humanity will have a major influence on what lies ahead in this regard.

The case is similar for many of you. Many of you have been working tirelessly and diligently to intentionally clear yourselves and to raise your own vibration. You have been aware of the need to do this, and you have been guided to do the work. Because a great many of you have been working in a very intentional way, you have some understanding of the process. There will be many more of your brothers and sisters who are coming into this work now. In fact it has already begun. The process is similar for Gaia in that there are energies that you might say have been stuck or trapped within her bodily forms and she is releasing them. Many of these energies are stuck, particularly in some of the larger crystals buried below the surface. Throughout her body in various parts of the globe, there are energies that have been stuck and must now be released. This release happens with the assistance of our star nation families, the Elohim, realms of the Devic angel kingdoms, the elementals and through her own intention and effort. As she releases these stuck, compacted energies, they move up and out of her body. Once those energies have made their way to the surface, they are not allowed to stay there because they have only moved from what you might think of as the inner body to the outer body. They are still there and must be released completely from her bodily forms. This is often what is taking place when you see extreme weather patterns. The elemental kingdoms, water, fire, air and earth are primary elements of creation and they are the primary elements of Gaia. The elementals are here to assist her and many other levels or forms of life that are here with her. She is being assisted in coming back into a fully balanced and harmonic resonance of the higher vibrational frequencies. As this takes place, all that is vibrating at a lower than $5^{th}$ dimensional frequency must be released. Once these energies have made their way to the surface, how do you suppose then that they are released? They are released by way of the activity taking place with the assistance of the elementals; and these are the weather patterns that often have been extreme. This is the cleansing of Gaia's body.

There are a number of ways in which compacted energies may be removed from the surface. By wind they are swept away, by water they are washed away and by fire they are burned away. With earthquakes and shifts, openings and gaps are created in which compacted energies may have a route of escape. They can make their way fully to the surface where they may be carried away and cleansed. Lower energies are being transmuted and lifted out of the physical body and they are rising into her outer body, which is your atmosphere. From there, they are being burned off or fully released, if you will, through the Light of Creator and those of us in the Company of Heaven who are assisting Gaia. We make use of the various Creator flames; and again I will reference the violet flame as one of the primary tools of assistance. As these energies are lifted, they come into the atmosphere but they must still be transmuted for them to be allowed to move fully out of the body/atmosphere.

So through natural weather related events, the energies are being lifted away from the body of Gaia but they are still trapped in her field or her shell where they must be transmuted and lifted out completely of all levels of her being. This is why the violet flame is so very valuable at this time; for when you call Master Saint Germain and Archangel Zadkiel, and you invoke the activity of the violet flame, you are assisting all life on the planet. You are assisting Gaia, your brothers and sisters and all life in releasing all that has been accumulated over ages of time within all aspects of each of you. As these energies are allowed to rise up into the atmosphere, they must be transmuted by the violet flame; then they are released and returned to Creator as pure white light substance, as Source Light. The Company of Heaven, alongside many of you, are working diligently to help her clear these energies; and we can see the result. We have many ways of observing energies to see what is taking place: so when there has been a release of energy coming up into the atmosphere we are aware of it. We also go to work then in helping to transmute those energies.

So this is what is taking place. We know these extreme weather events often create a great deal of disharmony, destruction or even loss of life for those who are in the way of them. We encourage you not to become overly invested, even when you see situations that cause loss of life. Now, this does not mean that we would encourage you not to have a true and earnest compassion for your brothers and sisters, or that you shouldn't want to go and assist in some real way, or that you shouldn't want to send your love and light to all involved. We encourage each of you to do those things as you are led to do so. In these situations, what I would suggest is that you do your best to hold your vibration of love and light, compassion and harmony. As you are able to maintain this vibration for yourself and those around you, then you are in a real position to assist by sending love and light to your brothers and sisters who may be struggling. It is only from this place that you are able to offer real assistance. If you allow yourself to become overwhelmed by what you perceive is happening in these events and if you become overly dragged down by the weight of it or allow yourself to be overcome with grief, sadness, sorrow and lack of hope, then you yourself are not in the best position to offer assistance to your brothers and sisters. At that point you yourself require some assistance to move back into a balanced and harmonious state. It is from this balanced still point position that you are able to effect real change in the world and you may send your love, light and blessings to those who are in need. Call on our Father/Mother God. Call on the angels and the Ascended Masters. Spend time diligently and intentionally invoking the violet flame of transmutation or pink flame of divine love. This is how you may be of greatest assistance when you see these events taking place in other areas of the world.

If you are someone who is being directly impacted by such events then certainly we understand this is a more difficult situation for you. In these cases, real world action is required. If you are in a region where these events are occurring or have taken place, we encourage you to make the calls and do the best you can while you go about the business of helping yourselves, your neighbors and your community in whichever way you are led to do so. Also, what I wish to remind you is that each and every one of you has chosen to come into this lifestream experience, knowing what your divine blueprint was before you came. When you see the loss of life as a result of a natural disaster, those individuals have come in knowing that there was a higher purpose for their participation in this way. Again, there may be a behind-the-scenes reason or activity that is not always known. These lifestreams have come in with the full knowledge and understanding that this was to be their experience. They have chosen to come into this experience and this is their service to the light, their service to Gaia, and their service to each and every one of you. So would we say this is not tragic? No, we would not. All loss of life is tragic. We are always in full support of all life everywhere. Indeed, it is a tragedy when we have these kinds of events and lives are lost as a result. Please keep in mind, as painful and difficult as these events are to witness and even more so to participate in, we ask that you trust that each one of these lifestreams has come in with full knowledge and agreement, and not only agreement, but wanting to come and participate in this way. It is what they have chosen for themselves. It is the divine blueprint that was set about in cooperation with their Higher Self and others before these lifestreams came into this experience. Remember too that death is an illusion. There is no death, only transition back home from whence you have come. So you know this and we know this, but we also know that in the heat of battle it can be extremely challenging and difficult to find the higher levels of understanding. So yes, we understand this. We have great love and compassion for all life.

We are moving into the New Earth and all that has been lost shall be regained. Any and all levels of destruction and harm that have taken place on the body of Gaia, all will be healed. We have the technology available and I assure you, at some point in time, Gaia will be returned to her most radiant, beautiful, healthy and vibrant body. We have much work to do as we continue on our project. Gaia is leading the way for all life, for all of you. Her body is releasing all toxicity, all compacted and stuck lower vibrational energies; and as these are being released, her body is being rejuvenated. As technology is brought forth, I can assure you that in a relatively short period of time, Gaia will be fully rejuvenated in her good feeling and healthy body. We know dear ones that your hearts are heavy. We know the deep love and respect, the reverence that you hold for Gaia and the nature kingdoms. We know this. Those of you who are sending your prayers, love and light, we know who you are. If your hearts are heavy, we know that also. I would remind you today to please do your best in holding about you and your environment the energies of balance and harmony in all levels of your being and to trust and know that what we have said is true.

Bryan - *I really appreciate your message today, Master Adama. This is a difficult thing. I can't imagine being directly impacted by one of these events. It is a real tragedy for those who are experiencing the events directly and perhaps they have lost family members or their homes and all of their personal belongings.*

Adama - Believe me when I tell you we have great compassion, empathy and understanding for each and every one who is in the midst of those events. We are all connected. We are always connected and not a single one of you is ever alone. In these times of need, we ask you to call on us time and time again. Call on us a hundred times a day; it will always be our joy to assist you in any way that we can. We will hear you every time you call. We are here in your support and each and every one of you is most deeply and profoundly loved.

# Chapter 16

## Cultural Karma and New Earth

Adama - Bryan, would you like to discuss the shifts taking place in your world as they relate to various cultures and their karma?

Bryan - *Yes sir, Master Adama.*

Adama - I feel this may be a valuable conversation for you and those who will read our work. It has been given to you through some of your other lessons that different communities on Earth are subject to the same universal law of cause and effect (karma) that affects the individual. When I say communities, I am referring to your nations and countries as well as to groups of individuals who have come into embodiment in those cultures and nations. Your countries are really a 3rd dimensional construct of your current social structures. The current boundary lines of countries have come about in relatively recent Earth time history. For many thousands of years mankind has endeavored to conquer and control, to conquer new lands and territories, new resources and new subjects/people. This situation is not anything new on our planet, but it is really within these last hundreds of years that the current boundaries have come about as they are today, defining your countries. We could also very well discuss this as it applies to cultures or peoples, you see, and one of the ways in which we perceive humanity is according to their soul groups and soul families. This may not run parallel with your geographic boundaries, which have been set by governments, their political leaders and their armies. This is a part of your social structure as you know it today; and when we look at you, we often see more general groupings of individuals. Each lifestream has made a choice to come and experience that particular culture and all that it entails. They have chosen to come into and have their lifestream experience in a particular geographic location in the world. They will find themselves immersed in and subject to all the aspects that make up their chosen culture, such as spiritual or religious beliefs and understanding, human laws that govern the people of that geographic location, and all of the aspects of those cultures such as language, dress, food and tradition.

We have a situation now where there is an accelerated expansion taking place on your planet that is affecting everything. These new levels of love and light are being dispersed here among Gaia and all life equally. This disbursement is affecting all equally. It is coming to all of you in it's pure form and it will be up to the individual to decide how they wish to best utilize these energies and blessings or not. The individual is greatly influenced by his or her community, their culture, traditions, laws and spiritual understanding and so forth. So when we discuss that it is up to individuals to come into awareness for themselves, that their own spiritual attainment and understanding is their own responsibility, then we must also take into consideration the environment that each one is in.

The circumstances and environment that each one is in apply to and influence the individual yes, but they also apply to their expanded communities, race or culture. This has mostly to do with geographic location; yet in the current age, it is quite easy and achievable in most cases, for each of you to move around and relocate to other areas as you wish. This is not always the case. You still have situations such as communism or dictatorships in China, North Korea and others that limit the free will of your brothers and sisters. When we view the situation from the perspective of the project team, we take into account not only the situation of the individual lifestream level but also that of nations, cultures, races and of humanity as a whole. This is important. There are aspects of consideration here that have not been fully discussed or understood that have to do with universal law and karma as it applies not only to the individual but often to groups of people, which may be cultures or nations. So when I refer to "peoples" then what I may refer to is this group of humanity who, perhaps are of yellow skin with dark hair and dark eyes and these individuals are part of a race or cultures that are found mostly in a particular geographic location on the planet. In this example, it would be some of those in your Asia. Then, within Asia, we have a number of countries such as North and South Korea, China, Indonesia, Japan, Thailand and so on. These individual cultures make up that race or those peoples at a higher level.

It has come about through the ages, as we view the current situation, that not all peoples are on the same footing at this particular point in time. I am speaking of their levels of awareness, consciousness and God Freedom; so we see imbalance in the nature of the individual, yes, but also that of the cultures and the nations of which they are a part. Each of you has chosen to come into this embodiment and experience that which you are living now and this has always been the case; but as we look around now, we see that not every individual has the same opportunity as the other. This is, in part, due to the situation at the national or cultural level of those peoples. So, for example, we see in present day China that due to the laws of man that have been set down and are being enforced there in that place, there has come about a great control of humanity in their culture. You might say that individuals who are experiencing life in that culture do not have the same level of opportunity to achieve their own God Freedom as those of you in America do because of the social structures of man and the laws of man. In this example, we have what is, in effect, the domination and control of a great number of the population there in that political system. Individuals there are restricted in the kinds of spiritual information and activities they might seek out, as one example. However, as new waves of consciousness come to the planet in an accelerated manner, we have a great number of individuals who are beginning to shift into new levels of awareness. This is taking place in all cultures around the world and it is taking place now. We are beginning to see energetically, for example, a shift taking place for those who are in China. There are stirrings of discontent taking place now primarily at the soul level. In order for those individuals, who are your brothers and sisters, to progress forward on their path toward their own ascension, it will be a requirement that they have the freedom, the tools, the opportunities and information that will assist them in their endeavor—that is, to assist each one individually, to assist them as a culture and ultimately to assist all of you together, for this is unity consciousness. These are some of the barriers that need to be broken down, and it will happen.

Let me say, I am aware that you wish to see many big shifts take place in a short period of time; and while I can certainly appreciate your sense of urgency on behalf of your brothers and sisters,

I would remind you again that this will be a process and won't happen overnight. These big shifts must be managed in a way that provide for the highest levels of grace and ease to be experienced as the changes take place. We, the members of project team or what you refer to as the Company of Heaven, are aware of the situations existing in your world; and we have plans in place to navigate them. I tell you, yes, at some point in the not too distant future we will begin to see the dissolution of not only communism but of all man made authority and that which serves to repress the human and the human spirit. These situations and obstacles will begin to be shifted so that the path may be cleared for every single one who will make the choice to step onto the Path of Light and work to gain their own ascension. Unfortunately, the situation as it exists today is that not every lifestream has an equal opportunity and equal support in this endeavor. This is the experience that each one has chosen to come into at this time; and make no mistake, each one is playing a role according to his or her own divine blueprint. Things are happening behind the scenes that will help you navigate these situations and bring about God Freedom for all life, all of those who would choose it. Things are shifting.

One of the other and certainly more obvious situations that we are dealing with here on the planet at this time is the disharmony that has been perpetrated by certain factions or cultures in the region you refer to as the Middle East. This is a land and a culture that have been plagued by error. This is the error of their understanding and the error of their use of life force energy flowing from Creator that is flowing to all of life in every moment. So what you have and what you have had taking place in these cultures for centuries is a gross error in the use and application of Creator Law.

Similar conditions have existed throughout your recorded history with the rise and fall of various empires.

In the Middle East we have one example of an area that does have a certain amount of karma that needs to be balanced. This is an area on Gaia, a geographic area, that requires greater amounts of love and light at this time. There are deeper levels of density that have accumulated about these cultures and these peoples. These cultures and peoples have a karma that has come about through the ages. In our discussion about Gaia we spoke of her need to clear and clean discordant and trapped energies from her body. Many times the cultural karma we are discussing presents itself as a collective energy that also affects Gaia: the energies become embedded in the locations in which they are acting. We see now large groups of peoples who are locked into or have become ensnared in lower levels of consciousness. It requires greater amounts of light to break through the density of the lower vibrations of which these cultures, such as many of those in the Middle East, are experiencing now. These peoples and culture have created their own circumstance by choosing and acting in ways of violence, terrorism and the diminishment of females (taking away of the divine sovereignty of women in these cultures) and the perpetration of control, violence and fear. My point here is there is more to the story than meets the eye. So yes, each of these individuals is currently being given the same opportunities (divine dispensations) that everyone else is being given. It will be a requirement for these individuals, who have chosen to embody in these cultures, to come about some awareness of this for themselves and they will make the choice for themselves. However, we must also take into account that there are often large and imposing obstacles in the way—or lying across the path you might say––for many of these cultures, including some of those in the Middle East.

There is a collective karma for that culture. You have heard of collective karma and collective consciousness of humanity; and of course this is just the boiling up, the aggregation of each individual's consciousness and karma. We observe these situations at multiple levels, at the individual level and at the group consciousness levels. That may be a soul group or soul family or it may be a cultural or national grouping. Ultimately, as it all rolls up to the aggregate levels, we have some problem areas that we are discussing today at the cultural or group consciousness levels. Again, you have read in some of your lessons that the law of cause and effect, that of karma, may apply to groups of peoples, nations or cultures and not just individuals. The shift will need to take place such that the collective consciousness of that culture may be raised, lifted and transmuted. This is a somewhat complex subject but it is also quite reasonable. That is to say, it should not surprise you that this is the case.

As you look around your world today at different cultures, nations and groups of people, you can see that there is severe imbalance between what one group may be experiencing and what another group may be experiencing. Present day situations have been brought about through the choices, actions and activities of those who are currently residing in those nations and those who have come before them in those nations. You see certain areas and peoples around the globe who have struggled for centuries to achieve peace and create societies that are free from violence, warfare, tyranny and oppression. The case today is there are many lifestreams there who have come into these embodiments according to their choice. They understood well the experience they were stepping into. Now they are here, the veils have drawn down around them and they are living their experience in their culture. It is what they know and what they are used to. Whether it be ideal or not, it is what they know. They are there now in the present day experiencing these cultural situations that may have taken several or many generations to come about. That is the progression of consciousness or lack thereof, as the case may be, and so they find themselves here in this embodiment living under the laws of man and the constraints, beliefs and traditions of their culture.

In the bringing about of New Earth, it will be humanity who are co-creating and building the New Earth with the assistance and guidance of others. As we go through this process, it is a requirement that individuals balance a certain percentage of their own karma. It is a requirement for the forward movement and momentum on each one's path to their own enlightenment and ascension. The same is true at the cultural or national level and then again at the global level. In nations around the globe, there is karma, the result of the universal law of cause and effect from previous ages that has created the present circumstances. This karma must be released or balanced at the cultural level. We have a number of cultures or groups on the planet that will have a more difficult time of obtaining their own God Freedom because they have an added obstacle to overcome and that is the collective karma of their culture. The law of cause and effect has come to roost.

In many parts of your world individuals are heavily restricted in their choice of seeking out their own divinity, new levels of awareness, understanding and consciousness. They are extremely limited in terms of the kinds of general and particularly spiritual information they may seek out. The government does not want them to do that, for they may become less controllable if they know too much. If each one were to step fully into their divine sovereignty, certainly it would not bode well for those powers that believe they are essentially holding all of these lifestreams in some level of enslavement.

Make no mistake, this kind of activity is taking place at some level in every part of the world, including your United States. The control mechanisms may look different but they are still very much present and acting. As circumstances are allowed to shift and individuals naturally begin to expand their awareness and understanding, they will be drawn to much of the same kind of information that many of you are working with now. Each one will find their way to the wisdom teachings and messages that are in alignment with their own divine plan. As they do this, they will also need to come about the understanding and the work that is required to balance the karma of their people or nation. This is something those individuals would particularly need to be aware of; but let me say again, we are taking a holistic approach and striving for unity consciousness. In this way, we ask that each of you who have this awareness will set about your own prayers, intentions and co-creation efforts toward the balancing of all karma, both individual and collective. Intend and ask for unity consciousness. Individuals must come to this level of awareness and understanding of the need to balance their individual karma, and cultures must somehow come to this same understanding of the need to balance their cultural karma. This level of understanding will filter out to the whole, to all of humanity together in unity consciousness. We will all be working together but these are some of the challenges you face.

It is greatly beneficial then, for each lifestream who chooses, to send love and light to those they see behaving in ways that are displeasing to them or in ways they perceive not to be of a higher light and greater good but rather those of a lower, negative vibration. One of the qualities coming to your awareness now is non-judgment. Each of you will begin to have a better understanding of the situation as it is perceived from higher levels. You may look at an individual who is behaving in a way that is displeasing to you and perhaps you make the choice to move yourself away from that individual quickly and swiftly, and certainly it is your right to do so. But what will happen with new awareness is, although you may not be especially pleased with what you perceive to be lower vibrational behavior taking place, you will know innately within you that this one also contains the spark of divinity––of Creator––within him or her. This one is still a divine being having a human experience albeit perhaps they have made the choice to have a lower vibrational experience, and it is their choice to make. As levels of awareness and understanding continue to rise, you will find that you have more compassion for your brothers and sisters.

Let me say also, it is wise for each of you to establish for yourselves a perimeter and an environment that is in full support of your own development. It is each one's responsibility to create an environment for themselves in which they feel safe, secure, nourished, supported and free to pursue all that their soul is guiding them to do. It is most wise to create a sacred space around you in which your further development may take place. Do what you can to build and maintain an environment of beauty and harmony. This advice applies equally to individuals, cultures and nations.

As we move forward, perhaps what we will see is an activity taking place on two fronts: the individual and the cultural or national level. First, all of the change we are speaking of will take hold at the individual level. As new waves of consciousness continue to expand within the individual, the momentum will continue to expand to more and more of the individuals around them who make up a culture or nation. As these new energies move closer and closer to their tipping point, this light activity will come more to the forefront. As the awareness or consciousness of a particular culture grows and expands toward this tipping point, the individuals making up that culture will begin to see the importance of creating a safe space for themselves, their families and their nations. They will want it for themselves and they will want it for their brothers and sisters. In this way, change will begin taking place first at the individual level then spread to the community level and the national level and so on. There will be waves and waves of momentum in this direction and it will be taking place around the world. Each of you may participate through your intentions, prayers and your own co-creation ability. You may assist those cultures in balancing their karma by transmuting the negative and lower vibrational energies back into the light. This is one of the reasons why Master Saint Germain and many others are so intensely promoting the great transmuting benefits that come with the use and activity of the violet flame.

It will be important, going forward, for those individuals making up those cultures and who have additional challenges ahead of them, to begin to take responsibility for themselves. But also, it is the responsibility of each one of you to assist your brothers and sisters in bringing light and love to all life on the planet such that you all may move into unity consciousness and the new Golden Age together. It is the responsibility of all to endeavor for themselves and with Creator and the Company of Heaven to transmute the lower vibrational energies back into the light.

So while yes, I would encourage individuals, families and communities to create a healthy and supportive environment for themselves at all levels, realize there will be groups and cultures who are accelerating toward the light at a faster rate of speed than others. It is our hope and endeavor that as some of the cultures rise collectively, and from within those cultures as individuals raise their vibrations and their quotients for love and light, that they will assist other cultures that may be having a more difficult time of things. It will require a higher level of understanding and non-judgment. You see, it is extremely difficult for individuals to break free of the illusion of separation and elevate themselves in this kind of environment. We have plans in place to navigate these rough waters, but it is up to all of humanity to create the change you desire. When you see areas of lower vibration and darkness, you can have great sway in these situations by shining your great light on it, sending your prayers and calling for the violet flame.

What I would like to say to summarize this discussion is, as the collective consciousness continues to rise, planetary change will originate in the hearts of individuals. The soul of the individual is being stirred and this is where it begins. As the individual soul is being stirred and as more consciousness, love, light and awareness come to that individual, each one will move into higher levels of understanding, higher levels of love and light. It is from this perspective then that we will begin to see a shift among humanity out of the lower vibrations of violence, control, ego, territory, greed and dominion over others. As things continue to shift and waves of individuals come on line, a new realization and level of consciousness will begin to form. There will be new levels of consciousness––beliefs, thoughts and attitudes––within individuals that have not been experienced before and the momentum will build. You will begin to experience things like non-judgment for example, in ways that you have not experienced them before. You will begin to have a natural sense of compassion, empathy and understanding for your brothers and sisters that perhaps was not available to you previously. You will recognize the divinity that is present in each one and you will come to know that you are all equal and that all life is valuable. It is through this heart space activity that great change will come about.

As the momentum grows, there will be more and more of you who will go outside of your personal needs and wants; and you will begin working more fully toward that of the gain, success and accomplishment of all of humanity and indeed of Gaia and all life on the planet. It is my endeavor through this discussion today, that each of you may come to have a better sense of unity. If you are in a place where you have an environment set about you whereby you are safe and all of your basic needs have been met, whereby you have a family and friends who love you and so forth, I encourage you today to consider the now moment experience that many of your brothers and sisters have chosen to come into in this lifestream experience. Consider what their experience might be today. Regardless of the behaviors you see taking place, that you may approve of or not, recognize that you are all connected and all life is valuable. If you are one who is blessed, I encourage you to count your blessings this day and to be thankful and to give thanks for all that you have received. I encourage you also to shine your great light in those areas of the world that need it most.

## Addendum by Master Saint Germain

Bryan – Note; Master Saint Germain guided me to write this addendum as I was in the midst of the editing process.

In a previous discussion, Master Adama referenced certain cultures in the Middle East and other lands that are plagued by error at this time, error in use of Creator Law. Many among humanity are in almost constant error of their own use of Creator Light and life force energy that is gifted to us in every moment of every day. It sustains our lives and is present in every cell of our body. It flows through us continuously and is everywhere around us. This is the intelligent and loving presence of God. All goodness flows from God. This is our own Beloved I AM Presence. These gifts of light and love hold the power of life and creation and goodness. It comes to us with purity from the Heart of God. We then, according to our free will, place our own creations upon this pure force of creation which is always acting and always intended to be used in the light–– the Divine Will, Wisdom and Love of God.

We are creator beings and we create our experiences moment-to-moment. If we have no awareness of this fact, we may get tossed around in the storm with no way to find our bearings. We see something we don't like. That's contrast. It doesn't resonate with us. It may not be what we would choose intentionally for ourselves. This also refers to our internal guidance system, which comes from feeling, intuition and awareness. We're allowing the heart, right brain and our body's energy centers to engage and participate now. We're coming more fully into alignment with our divine nature.

Our free will choice allows us to choose the creations and experiences we desire to have for ourselves. How do I intend to qualify my portion of life force energy today? Will I set it to good use? How is my mood-energy-vibration right now? What is the vibrational request that I'm sending out to the cosmos right now? We qualify and create through our moment-to-moment feelings mostly, but also by our thoughts, beliefs, behaviors and choices. What were the thoughts and feelings we experienced throughout the day? Were they of faith and trust, hope and harmony, optimism and helping others or were they emotions and thoughts of even slight animosity and guilt, fear and judgment and a generally poor outlook on life? Throughout our normal daily living, we are either qualifying or mis-qualifying this gift of love, life and creation. The global experience we are all living today is the result of our collective co-creations and free will acting on Earth.

If we want to see change at any level, we must each take responsibility to bring the light and create through intention and prayer. We must learn to claim our divine inheritance and be our own bright lights shining in the world. Call for the light and see the splendor of your heart space as it radiates with the light and God illumination of a thousand suns.

Master Saint Germain - *Regarding your example of the Middle East, children are unfortunately being programmed with a hatred ideology from a young age. Many of the events you see taking place are not condoned in any shape or form and they will come to a stop. These activities to which we refer––terrorist acts of violence and hatred ideologies–– are in total violation of the Law. However, you cannot stamp out hatred by creating more of the same. Master Adama spoke of this and each of you might imagine that being raised in this kind of environment, it is difficult for people to shed the dark oppression and influence that surrounds them. At this time, the human is quite susceptible to programming, especially with all of the imprinting that is taking place at multiple levels. This will also come to a stop. No one is asking you, nor should any of you accept the events taking place in your world today, but realize that the way you will overcome this global epidemic is through love. It is the most powerful force in all the cosmos. Your calls, prayers and light are greatly needed at this time.*

# Chapter 17

## Food and Health Revolutions

Adama - Good afternoon, Bryan. I thought we might speak on the subject of your food supplies and the situation as it stands today in your world. There is a great deal of discussion taking place now about this topic, and it is coming more and more to the forefront of your collective awareness. This is a result of the illumination and wisdom contained within new levels of light that are flooding the planet. Several things are happening in this arena. One such topic is directly in the forefront of your own awareness and many others, and that has to do with the activity around your primary food crops. We haven't spent much time discussing the darker elements that are still present and acting in your world at this time. The results or validation of such are quite obvious for anyone who chooses to look upon it with open eyes. It is, indeed, a component of the great shift taking place now.

There is a great deal of knowledge that has been lost, hidden away or intentionally destroyed from past golden ages which is beginning to make its way back to your collective awareness. There are many topics and subject matter to which this statement applies. Many of the lost arts, lost abilities, lost knowledge and all variety of information are now allowed to be given to you again, and it is coming to you from a variety of sources. This knowledge comes forward for your great benefit, use and application. We will see a number of gains and benefits coming in with all manner of lost knowledge, and it will just continue from here on into the New Earth. Each of you will find this lost knowledge as it comes back, according to its subject matter and according to your own path. Each of you will be led in a natural way to the information that will benefit yourself and others.

Some of the new or previously lost information that is coming back has to do with a holistic approach in regard to your food supplies, dietary needs and healing modalities. There is a beautiful biodiversity present among the many plant, fungi and tree families of your world––your herbs and flowers, fruits and vegetables. Being natural means they are organic. They are in their pure form, and they have not been manipulated by mankind in any way. Their genealogy is pure and the way they grow is pure without the use of herbicides and pesticides. On the surface of your world there are an infinite variety of herbs and flowers and plants that are all actually intended to be there. They are the original gift and plan for this world such that for any illness or ailment there is a natural solution to bring one back into balance and harmony regardless of what the imbalance is. That is to say, the anatomy and chemical makeup of natural and organic plants, flowers and herbs have natural properties that your body and the intelligence within the body understand how to utilize. Your body recognizes the ingredients and chemical makeup of the herbs, for example, that you may use for a skin rash or cough, etc. Your body responds to them in a very natural way. This is a holistic and natural approach. Your body has its own intelligence. We have spoken about your body elemental. We have said that your I AM Presence is there in every cell and particle of your being. This is the active intelligence and Creator Light within your body.

We have spoken about co-creation and the use of your intention, thoughts and vibration and about the great effect to which you may apply these tools for your benefit. You can set your intention for healing and bring in those natural and organic ingredients that you know to be suited for that particular ailment. In this way, you are working holistically. Later, as more of this lost knowledge continues to come into your awareness, there will be the application also of crystals, sound and color for your healing modalities. So my point is, there was never intended to be any need for a great many of your pharmaceuticals. They are, for the most part, financial and economic constructs that are there simply for gain and profit. This is not always the case but it is the best you have had to work with, and your science has moved along at a steady rate. There have been a great many contributors to your modern medicine and what it is today. This is not to say there will not continue to be a place for your modern medicine. What I am saying is, you will find over time, an increased awareness of the quality of the foods and medicines that you take into your body. When there is imbalance, you will find that everything has already been provided to bring the body back into balance in a natural way. A great deal of that knowledge has been lost but it is coming back to you now.

Many of your pharmaceuticals are being produced with synthetics. Your science is making chemical formulas, often replicating what are otherwise natural ingredients. They are doing this in the laboratory, and these medicines are often synthetic duplicates of what science has found will assist the body in whichever imbalance it is being applied to. Often, however, modern medicine is seeking only to alleviate the symptoms and not necessarily to go further into the cause and core of the imbalance itself. We see, in many Western cultures, that medicines are often prescribed to alleviate symptoms, but the causes of the symptoms themselves are not being properly addressed. Different cultures have different approaches. Many of the Eastern cultures are often more inclined to use holistic and natural approaches in bringing the cause of the ailment back into harmony and balance. So there are differences in the way medicine, nutrition and health are approached depending on which culture you are experiencing.

As we return to the subject of your food supplies, I am speaking of food and medicine in one discussion as there are many similarities among your food supplies and your many medicines and treatments. It's really within the past 100 years or so that most of the sustenance and food supplies you consume have gone from natural and organic sources to more of a mass commercialized approach. This has been necessary, in part, to keep up with the growing populations on your planet and in an effort to have food supplies delivered to those who may not have them readily available in their own backyards or communities. Much of this has come about through necessity; but what has happened is, as a collective, you have become much more interested in simply bringing something to the table to consume, apparently with not much interest in regard to the quality of that which you have brought to the table. You all are aware of this.

Members of the animal kingdom who have agreed to nourish humanity for a time provide many of your proteins. They are being injected with chemicals. These synthetic chemicals then, have made their way into the lifestreams of those animals; and now those chemical additives, antibiotics, steroids and growth hormones are present in every cell within the body of that animal. This is being done in most cases to speed the time to market, and this means more money for those who are in a position to benefit. Where do you think these man-made synthetic chemicals end up? If you've been injecting and inoculating a baby calf for years and a cow now ends up on someone's dinner table, as I've said, when these ingredients are consumed, they are being processed and circulated out to the physical body. When you consume a hamburger, you're getting an added bonus of all of the substances that were injected into that calf over the span of its life so it could hurry up and get to market. How do you think your body will respond, and what effect will it have over time? Most of you know this already. You know it is taking place, yet it doesn't seem to bother most of you.

This is taking place at all levels of your proteins. Look at the proteins that are coming to your table: farm raised fish, red meats and white meats and so you all see what is going on. It is no surprise. Add to that the fact that there are companies who are looking to control your general crops such as your corn, soybeans and fruit supplies. There is some tampering taking place at the seed levels such that seeds are being genetically modified to withstand the spraying of herbicides and pesticides. Humanity has developed a corn seed for example, which they can spray with synthetic, chemical, man-made poisons. They can spray the corn because the seed has been genetically altered, and this corn will still grow day by day even though it is being sprayed with poisons that would otherwise end its life. They tell you this is about innovation and efficiency but really it is about getting more production out of food crops and less labor to bring it about; so again, we see it is really about the money. Not only is it just about money, but also it is about the mass control of food supplies at large for your planet. This has been taking place for some time and still is today. Humans have taken an original seed that was the creation of our Father/Mother God and now altered it according to their own desires and stemming from greed no less.

So you all, in a majority of your food supplies, are eating genetically modified organisms; GMOs is what you call them. The chemical makeup of those otherwise natural and God given food supplies have been altered in some way. Not only has the chemical makeup been altered, but also in this example of the corn stalk, it is sprayed continuously throughout its life with poison and yet it continues to grow. Does it not make sense to you then that a corn stalk producing multiple ears of corn, as it is growing and being sprayed with poisons, that the actual ears of corn, the stalk, and leaves would be taking in and absorbing that poison? Where else would it go? So now you sit down at your dinner table to eat a delicious ear of corn and you say to yourself "I'm doing so good today. I'm eating my vegetables." Well, yes you're eating your vegetables that were first grown from seeds that were genetically altered by man so that the natural God given properties that were inherent in that seed have now been altered. As a result, the presence of God and the blessing that was a natural component of the lifestream of that ear of corn is no longer present. The innate qualities of life force that were about that seed have been extremely reduced or inhibited if not removed altogether. Then, you have come along behind and sprayed that ear of corn time and time again with poison, and now here you are at your dinner table consuming that ear of corn. What do you think happens when it comes into the body to be used for nourishment and the sustaining of your own life? Do you see the incongruence and potential imbalance that is created when you bring it into the body and ask the body to process in a natural way? The body simply does not know what to do with all the synthetic chemicals and poisons. It will do the best it can. It always does. I will say, I am often surprised at just how capable the body is in adjusting and adapting to its environment, particularly this environment that most of you are living in today.

Those are some of your proteins, fruits and vegetables. Now let us talk about some of your other goods. For example, you have mass amounts of sugar being fed to the populations because sugar is addictive, and you will buy more once you get the body hooked on it. Tremendous amounts of preservatives and other synthetic chemicals are being added to your sodas, frozen foods, cookies and cereals, canned goods and so forth. In America and elsewhere, big business and the fast food industries have cultivated a way of life alongside their revenue stream. This all comes with excessive amounts of consumer waste. Perhaps we will address that in a later discussion. But now, you consume many of these kinds of goods and all of these additives, preservatives, high fructose, and these sorts of things are flooding and infiltrating the body. You know that your bodies are comprised mostly of water. Pure and clean water is an absolute necessity for life; yet we see many areas and populations adding synthetic chlorine, fluoride and other chemicals to their water supplies. Even this most fundamental and life sustaining resource has become corrupted; and this is typically a best-case scenario for most on the planet today. If we were just to look at these aspects alone, not to mention the stress of the times you are living in, we would say, "Well no wonder, no wonder the health of humanity is suffering."

The innate intelligence of the body knows what to do with natural ingredients. It often does not know how to process the synthetics that are being introduced to the body as in our examples. Because the body doesn't know how to process them, over time as they are being circulated throughout the body there are places where they become stuck. They are not releasing. Your body's functioning and systems, your immune and circulatory systems, digestion and elimination systems, electrical and energy systems, and so on are getting clogged up with chemicals that the body doesn't know how to process. This is limiting you. These substances which are now stuck somewhere in the body are limiting the amount of light and energy that the body may receive and process for its benefit. The higher levels of functioning provided by your meridians, chakra energy systems and pineal and pituitary glands are being dragged down by the weight of the synthetics that you are introducing, and often they are not just synthetics. Your industrial-medical community adds, as just one example, mercury to flu shots. Mercury is known to be a health hazard. It is poisonous to the body and particularly the brain over time, and you are being encouraged year after year to get a flu shot. Each year they inject you with more mercury. These are the kinds of activities taking place. It will shift. So again, by all means, set the intention, bring the light into your body and talk to your body. Work in cooperation with your body elemental and your beloved I AM Presence that is there present and active in every particle of your being to achieve balance and vitality. Set the intention that you are going to thrive in any and all conditions to which you are exposed, but also just realize that as you are able to eliminate toxins from your diet, you will benefit and you will see definite improvement in the functioning and feeling of your body.

Your scientists, going back 60-70 years, have clearly identified the relationships between your heavily promoted diets of proteins and dairy and your health. These have been established in your society as fundamental food groups and necessary nutrition. However, your science has clearly identified the relationship between high intake of heavy proteins and dairy with many of your current diseases such as cancer, heart disease, hypertension and others. It has been notably observed, scientifically, the effects that diet will have on these particular conditions. It is known that as you move away from heavy proteins and dairy and move toward whole and natural foods, clearly the incidence rate of these diseases, which are plaguing your society and others, will drop almost overnight as the diet is changed. This information has been known and it has been intentionally set aside from view. Your industrial and political leaders have chosen not to bring this information to light, and the reason is just as you might imagine. You have big industry running your food production and big industry running your health care. They make money by selling you the heavy protein and dairy products which are known to contribute greatly to the cause of major diseases, and they make money again when those imbalances come into the body and you go to seek health care. This is what has been taking place. These activities will come more fully into view in the days ahead.

The same kinds of activities have been taking place in your medical advancements and let me say, I am not here to speak poorly of the many wonderful advancements that scientists have made in your medical technologies particularly over the past 50-75 years. Nor is any harm intended toward the many health care workers who give of themselves to assist others in need. Great advancements have been made, and indeed those in the ascended realms have gifted you with many of these advancements. However, make no mistake, this is big business and it is being driven by business and greed and not necessarily for the general welfare of humanity or your personal best interest. It is a money game and it is also about control. As we move forward, there will be food and health care revolutions taking place, to name but a few. This is inevitable, as the old constructs will not be supported on New Earth. They will not. So what I tell you simply and plainly is, a great deal of what we see taking place in these industries does not support life, and in fact, may be in direct opposition to it. They do not support life. This is a strong statement and I stand behind it.

There will be food and health care revolutions taking place alongside any number of other changes that are inevitable between here and New Earth. More and more of you see these things taking place and you are finding them to be unacceptable. You are finding them to be infringements on your well-being, choices and freedom; so as we go forward we will have revolutions. I do not wish to put it in your thoughts of men and women taking up arms against the commercial food and medical industries. I am being a bit playful here, but great change will take place. As more and more awareness comes, most of you will find in a natural way that what is available to you today is simply unacceptable. You will begin to see things in these industries that are infringements on your human rights. Does this sound extreme? It is. Indeed it is.

In the higher realms, there are project teams in place specifically to assist you in these areas. The number one milestone will be coming into unity consciousness with each one taking a position and having compassion for your brothers and sisters. No more will you idly stand by and accept that a great many on your planet do not have their basic requirements met: food, water, shelter, clothing and God freedom to pursue their soul's calling. So these will be the first big topics that are already penetrating your awareness; and the momentum is growing by the day, bringing you further into unity consciousness. This awareness also has to do with the great amount of Divine Feminine energies that are flooding the planet at this time. They are creating in each of you a great love, compassion and empathy such that no longer may you avert your eyes from the great imbalances as they exist in your world today. As you become more aware, you will have more compassion and concern for your brothers and sisters and your greater family of humanity. Also coming into your awareness is what I will refer to as the establishment or the few who feel it is their right to pursue power, control and greed at any and all costs. They have pirated your food and medical industries and it is you who are paying the price. As this awareness comes about, change will begin to take place. As the momentum builds there will come a time when humanity will simply stand up and say, "No more, we do not accept this." This will be a part of the transition.

Another part of the transition is that there are teams in place to assist humanity in managing its food supplies. There are teams in place to assist humanity with your health, medical treatments and the management and attention of all physical body imbalances. There is a great wealth of knowledge and information coming onto the planet again. A great deal of this information has been known and it has been lost. You are moving into a time where you are ready to receive and apply high levels of new information along with that from the last Golden Age and mystery schools. You will take this information and begin to apply it now in your earthly experience;

and as you do, you will no longer have a need to do things the old way. The old paradigm is falling away and these are two major aspects of the old paradigm. Your food supplies and health care are in need of major overhauls, not just here in these United States but as a planet. Those of us in the higher realms are well aware of exactly what is taking place and we are working to correct the imbalances. We now have more dispensation and allowance to interact with you in ways that were not available to us before, and we are doing so. We are giving you our every assistance, right up to the letter of the Law, in helping you to reform all of the major elements that require it. My intention today is this be a message of hope and not one of gloom. We know what is taking place. We are aware of it and we are doing everything we can to assist you; however, I say again, it will be all of you, humanity, who will create your New Earth together. It is all of you, in unity consciousness together, who will be creating the New Earth; so while we will always be here with you every step of the way and while we will lend our support, it must be each of you individually and collectively who make these changes for the betterment of your world. This will happen. It is taking place now. I have spoken about new technologies that will be coming forth and in many cases the "new" technologies are not new at all. They have already existed here in past golden ages and we know very well how they are used and to what benefit and effect they may be. We, the project teams, are intentionally working with those lightworkers who came in with missions to help restore this lost knowledge and to bring forth new knowledge.

What I would like to describe for you then is a New Earth and a new paradigm that you are moving into. I cannot stress enough the importance of a holistic approach, which is why we have various levels of project teams all working together. In terms of your body's health and vitality, one of the very best things you can do is to control your thoughts and vibrations. If we return to our discussion on co-creation, my first suggestion, if we are discussing topics of one's health, would be to use your divine birthright of co-creation and create a healthy and vital environment for yourself. Set your intention for a healthy and vital body. It will be increasingly more important that each one of you do this; and by learning to control your thoughts, vibrations, intentions and moods, this is how you can assist yourself in navigating the days ahead and changes to come. Apply your intention and co-creation of living in your healthy, vibrant and good-feeling body regardless of the environment you are currently in. Simply set the intention and speak to your body, speak to your body elemental. "I am thriving in my environment." "I am thriving with the food supplies and all that I bring into my body."

So yes, some of the technologies that I speak of will be entirely new; and again, others have existed before in past ages. This information is coming back now; and it will include the use of crystals, light, sound and vibration, touch and energy work, and learning how to co-create perfect health within your own body, to name a few. These are modalities of the future and there will be new technologies coming about as well. As we move toward our next Golden Age, you will be living in a world where there is no disease and no physical ailments. They simply will not exist. In the not too distant future, as new technologies come forth, we will help you learn to produce your food supplies and fulfill your nutritional needs in a brand new way.

We understand this is a major concern. There are seven billion plus of you who require nutrition each day to sustain yourselves. We will help you learn to grow and produce food supplies in new ways that are greatly enhanced and much more efficient. As you are coming into your New Earth, you will be coming back more into a community setting particularly in terms of your food supplies. It will become much easier to manage your food supplies organically and without the use chemicals. This will be done at the community level such that all of your communities around the planet will have access to good and healthy foods. This is not so different than it was in past years. It's a fairly recent turn of events with the commercialization, economics, chemistry, packaging and advertising that all of this has come about. These structures as you know them today will fall away, but as I have said, it will require great effort on the part of humanity. As waves of self-awareness and consciousness build and build, it will be a natural inclination for humanity to want to choose these new ways of being and doing.

We have much here in Telos that we can share with you. We have technologies and techniques that are proven, and a great many technologies will come from our friends in the cosmos who have come to play their role in the project. These are ways of doing things that you all just have not gotten around to yet. You have not considered them yet. I want this message to be one of upliftment. As the elevated energies of the Divine Feminine continue to flood the planet there will be a greater innate drive and desire within each of you to eliminate the severe imbalances that you see taking place in your world.

Lastly, I would encourage you, as best you can, to consume whole foods. These foods are whole by themselves as they were naturally intended to be. Consume foods that have not been genetically altered by scientists. You want natural God given foods:

those that have not been sprayed by herbicides and proteins free of hormones. Just take a common sense approach as much as you can and the same way with your pharmaceuticals and health care. Do not blindly trust that your health care system has your best interest at heart, for I assure you often it does not. This is a place where you must use your discernment and decide what is right for you and your family.

You will begin to see the light being shone on some of these topics we are discussing today and some of the upset will be coming about in a relatively short period of time. So I would encourage you to do your best to eat natural ingredients and whole foods. Use your divine birthright of co-creation to create a healthy body for yourself. Each of you can do this. Also, as always, when you see things taking place in your world that you wish to change for the better, set your intention there, send your prayers and your light there. Very few of you understand just how powerful you are and just how much difference one of you can make in the world just by making your calls, sending your prayers, sending your light and setting your good intentions. For each one of you who does this there is a great ripple effect that carries out throughout the universe and it affects the consciousness of all lifestreams on the planet. What affects one affects all. Just one of you making the calls and sending your light and intentions for a better and brighter future carries a great weight and power. This is how your New Earth is to be built, you see.

# Chapter 18

## Energy Transmission

Adama - The circumstance which I had alluded to previously has come into your awareness this morning as an "Ah Ha" moment as it were. Although the concepts are not entirely new to you, you have stated this morning that "Everything is energy" and you have asked whether it is possible in the capture of a digital image that perhaps the energy of the place in which you have taken the image will stay with the image. The answer is, "Yes it does." It has crossed your mind today that you were told by Mother Mary that the images you have there in your home of several of us (Ascended Masters) who are your family and friends, that they also carry an energy and a presence. They are not simply just a picture. Lightworkers such as yourself are often drawn to our images because they help you connect with us both visually and energetically. For those of us who have these kinds of images, (and when we know individuals are obtaining them for this purpose) we will intentionally add our blessings to those images. For each one that goes out, we place our energy signatures upon the actual image such that you or anyone else who looks upon the image is connecting with us not only through the imagery and what you may perceive to be your thinking mind, but you are also connecting with us energetically through the heart space. When you place your attention on our image we receive your vibration and you receive ours. We know that you have placed your attention upon our image and our energy signature, so in this way you have "rung our doorbell" so to speak. We know that you are in that moment placing your attention upon us and we may offer you blessings, answers, clarity or however it is that we may be of assistance to you in that moment. This is a very real thing, you see.

This is coming into your awareness now and with your experiments, what you are doing and what you are setting your intention toward when you are capturing an image, is that you are in a state of grace and gratitude for Gaia and all of the beauty that she is. So when you take an image with your camera and as you are aligned with your divinity and aligned with Creator and all of us in the light, that energy through your intention is now added to the image. Perhaps as a final step, you yourself have blessed the image. You have placed your own energy signature upon the image. You have added the energy of your being to the energy of the image which now, in this example, holds the combined energies of Gaia and Creator and of you and your blessings going out into the world for all of those who would come into contact with it. In this way, you are sending out blessings as per your intentions; and these images, if you will take the time to go about this kind of a process to intentionally bring in these energies and attach them to the digital image, then those energies will follow everywhere that image goes. So even if that digital image were copied and pasted 10,000 times, each one would receive the blessings that have been added to it by your good intention.

While not quite the same, this example is also relevant to the power of the spoken word. As a divine being and one who has been given, as your divine birthright, the ability of co-creation, you are simply tapping into your divinity and the light and the love and power that you are and, through your intention, you are setting your blessings about that image. This is very similar to that of the spoken word such that you are using your divine birthright of co-creation and that of speaking into your experience that which you desire. You are setting your intention and then you are speaking it so the power of your spoken word is now being activated and directed into an activity through your intention. This is one of the reasons we encourage you to choose your words wisely, for you are creating in every moment.

This is not an entirely new process, for you have always added your good blessings and energies to your images because this is one of your soul's expressions of joy and creativity. As you participate in this activity, you are indeed expressing the love, beauty, and creativity of your very soul. You are allowing it to express also through the activity. Therefore, all of the imagery that you produce while you are in this vibration will naturally pick up and hold that vibration which you, as the creator of that image, had about you when you made it. For you, photography is a natural expression of your souls' expression and creative beauty. Just as we encourage each of you to create a beautiful and harmonious environment about you, we encourage you also to embrace your own expressions of beauty and creativity, in whatever manner they wish to be expressed. This is another way of tapping into your own innate and divine beauty and creativity; and there are many, many avenues which may be used for divine expression. Many of you are already aware of and enjoying these kinds of expressions and activities. Perhaps you enjoy painting, creative writing, gardening, restoring old automobiles, playing a musical instrument, woodworking or scrap booking. Yes, these are often your hobbies because you are naturally drawn to them, but they are also the expression of your soul's innate beauty and creativity. Consider the activities in which you lose track of time and in which you find yourself at peace. They are expressions of your own divinity and creativity being allowed to flow through you.

And so, now you are coming about the awareness that you may add additional energy or momentum or blessings––however you wish to perceive it is fine––but you may add these additional energies to that image and that image is simply acting as what you might call a capacitor. It is holding those energy signatures. You have intentionally placed it there around that thing, and that thing in this case is electronic data in the form of a digital image. The image is circulated out electronically perhaps by way of cell phones and computers, and it travels around making its way from place to place. As that digital image moves around from place to place, it carries that energy signature which you have placed upon it. This is indeed, another way to send out blessings and energy; and again, it is not entirely new. Before you left for the mountain this morning, you sent several images to your sisters. One of them was of Master Saint Germain and the violet flame. As you sent the images out to your sisters with your blessings and good intentions, in this example, you might request that Master Saint Germain bless you and your sisters through his image. You may ask that he will set his radiance and blessings about that image as it travels with you day-to-day on your cell phone. As you send the image out to your sisters, if they are also open to receive those blessings, then they will also receive the presence, in this case, of Master Saint Germain. His energy, presence and blessings will stay with that digital image; so if you carry the image on your phone, you are allowing for an open line of communication and energy flow between you and Master Saint Germain.

All of us here are most pleased when we see any of you doing something like this. It is no different than creating a sacred space in your home where you display images of your spiritual family and guides, those who you are drawn to across the veil. Through the space you have created in your home, you have used your intention to draw in the energy and the presence of that being or master who you are connecting with. When this happens, we are aware of it and we are most pleased. It is our great joy then to come to you and those of you who are participating in these activities. We will come and establish a connection through the image and the space you have created. We will indeed, radiate out our love, blessings and our guidance and all that we may do to assist you. So when you create a space like this in your home, a sacred space with images perhaps, those of us whom you are invoking and connecting with that way are indeed there with you in that place. In this example, it would be your home but it need not be such a formal thing as a dedicated, sacred space. It can be something as simple as an image posted on your social media or perhaps forwarded through your cell phones. It all works the same.

Allow me to give you another example. Let us say one of our lightworker messengers has channeled a message from one of the Ascended Masters. Perhaps the ascended master is bringing forth some new and useful information. Perhaps they have brought forth a guided meditation or perhaps an activation of some kind and then the session ends. Others may listen to that recording again at some future date. As the recording is being listened to, the actual event of the channeled message has already taken place but the recording still holds the same levels of potency if you will, of energies, blessings, activations and application as it did at the time it was created. That media, in this case, is just a form of energy that is being utilized as a source of transmission. It is being utilized to attach and hold those energies and activations, and those energies will stay attached to that recorded message, video message, or written message. It makes no difference. Even if you were to go back and listen to a session such as this that is perhaps one year, five years or ten years old it makes no difference. You will still receive the same benefit as you would have if you had been present in the now moment in which the message was being delivered. We have attached our energy signatures and the energy signatures of that particular message or activation to the actual media itself. We have done this through our intention such that it is now contained inherently within that media. Perhaps it is an image, a video recording, a voice recording, a book or a newsletter. The same applies for books. It is the same thing. It is energy. Yes, a book is made of matter and it is in the material world. You can touch it and feel it, but we also know that everything is energy. Everything is vibrating. Everything is in flux and movement even though in your 3D experience it is not always experienced to be the case. When you pull out a chair at the restaurant you don't expect the particles of matter in the chair to move or sway or dissolve on you. You simply recognize it as a physical object and you sit on the chair and everything works out okay. So it is beyond your normal perception. Your science has proven that everything is in motion and everything is energy. If that is the case, does it not make sense that we may add additional elements of energy to that which already exists as energy? As we move forward in this great shift, there will be new information around quantum physics, natural and universal law that will be coming into your awareness as new information.

You may utilize this process for yourself any time you choose. You may go about your normal processes such as prayer, use of the spoken word or sending healing energies to someone else through your intention, for example. You may also attach your energy signature and your blessings to any of these other forms of media. Even if you were to send someone a written letter, a typed email, an image in email, or even a mailed gift, you may add your energy and your blessings to those and set your good intentions along with them. If they are open to receive your blessings, indeed they will.

Bryan - *If we can use these types of media to send love and light, then wouldn't it make sense the same would be true for those who are intending nefarious purpose and energy toward humanity or individuals?*

Adama - Yes, Bryan this is true and unfortunately this is the case in many aspects of your current societies, not just yours there in the United States but in all societies. This is the use of dark magic and we see it a lot at this particular time. It is often referred to as brain washing or imprinting and it is the designing, if you will, of a culture through various forms of media and influence. This has been taking place for some time. It is now being utilized in this way at great levels. Your marketing and advertising are a common example through which advertisers look to intentionally sway your thoughts, opinions and decisions; and often they use subliminal messages to sway you in their direction. Perhaps we will go into a greater discussion at some time, but we have discussed that the subconscious mind does not always know the difference between what is real and what is not real. It just takes in the inputs you feed it and it accepts and processes those inputs. So yes, this is happening in various forms of media around the world and this is the influence and the energy that are being consciously and purposely instilled into the messages for those advertisers or for those politicians or for those elements of social structure. Perhaps they are telling you or showing you how one should live in this society and what is acceptable and what is not acceptable and so forth. These messages are coming in through your TV programs and movies, news media, advertisements, newspapers, magazines and internet.

As you know, not all of the energies which have been attached intentionally to many of these forms of media are benevolent. This is a foundational activity of those who would practice nefarious deeds against their brothers and sisters. I would caution always to be aware and to use your discernment as to what inputs you allow to come into your conscious awareness and your subconscious awareness and into your emotional and mental bodies. Use your own discernment then as to what you choose intentionally to allow to come into your space and into your being. Of course, it would always be our suggestion that you seek out those inputs and place your attention on those things around you which support love and grace, harmony, abundance, health, joy and so on. Most of you, at this time, do not have a full understanding of just how much impact and effect these various media and inputs have on all levels of your being.

As we continue forward with the rising consciousness of the planet, and this is what is taking place now, you will see this concept become more firmly engrained and understood. As more and more of you become aware of this truth and its activity and its workings, then more and more of you will choose to use your discernment about your inputs and programming. As time goes on we will see a shift in all forms of media and entertainment. What will happen is, at some point in the not so distant future, the general awareness of humanity will have risen to reflect more of a 5D state of consciousness, and as this happens you will no longer desire to participate or allow in those influences that are of a lower vibration.

Allow me to give you another example. As levels of awareness and consciousness expand more fully to align with a 5D or higher state, what will happen is humanity will come more into a natural alignment with feelings and vibrations of love, harmony and unity consciousness. At some point, you may look back at some of the inputs you have chosen, and I will use entertainment as an example. You may go back and watch a movie that you have enjoyed in the past, but what you find now is there is activity taking place in the movie that no longer resonates with you. Perhaps there is violence taking place, or perhaps there are some levels of deceit or dishonesty or what you are able to clearly see through now as falsehoods and lies. So this will be a natural transition for most of you. As your vibration rises you will no longer resonate with all that was created in a lower vibration. So in this movie example, while it was intended for entertainment, perhaps it also displays lower vibrational energies of control, violence, fear and victimhood such that now, in your new higher vibration, when you watch this movie you simply are not drawn to it because you do not resonate with it. In fact, you may feel that you simply want to move away from it, remove it from your space and not allow that input into your being. This will be the process that unfolds naturally for each one.

I will say lastly on this topic, just to provide additional clarity, that as each ones' awareness and understanding increase to higher levels of vibration, they will naturally be drawn to those things which are also in resonance with their higher vibration. They will naturally begin moving away from those things that no longer resonate with them that are of a lower vibration, and this will be the natural process. However, I wish to point out a component of this lesson and understanding. Let us say you have chosen to watch a movie and there are elements within this movie that are of a lower vibration. Perhaps this movie contains violence, lies, deceit, fear and, let us be honest, many of your current entertainments do indeed contain many elements of lower vibrational energies. When you make the decision that you will participate in this activity, you may think to yourself that you will simply somehow disregard the activities in the movie that are of a lower vibration and not to your liking. In this example, you may intend to block out that which you are going to participate in and that is the watching of the violence, greed, deceit and so on. What I wish for you to understand is that it is not within your ability to choose to disregard those aspects of a lower vibration if you have participated in the movie by watching it and placing your attention on it. You have engaged in it energetically and in that way, allowed those pictures and imagery and energies to come into your being. You are allowing yourselves to become desensitized to lower vibrational energies that are not in alignment with your pure and good nature. Your conscious mind may not register that there has been any impact of significance to your being; but what I will say to you is, indeed there has been an impact to your level of being and overall balance and health.

This effect is something that most do not understand. Time and time and time again you make the choice to engage and participate in those activities that are of lower vibration and those which you would not intentionally choose for your real world experience. You have still allowed them into your being and so those experiences and energies will gather momentum within you and they will often find a way to be expressed in your experience, you see. You are, in effect training yourself and your subconscious to resonate with those lower forms, images, sounds and activities of lower vibration that are there in the movie you are watching. It does have a great effect and impact on your overall levels of balance, harmony and health, particularly those of your emotional bodies.

This is also programming. This is the programming that you are being fed again by what I will refer to as the establishment, those that seek power, control and greed at your expense. It just so happens these kinds of programming are what a great many of you still desire at this stage in the game. This is what the majority of you still seek out and ask for at this time; and therefore all of you have participated, at some level, in the creation of the experience you see taking place today. You make the choice, or not, to accept the programming and inputs being fed to you. You can choose for yourself through your own discernment to feed this to your being or not.

Also, there is a compounding effect that takes place over time. One of your Sifus has told you very simply and plainly that if you sing the blues long enough, life will give you plenty of reasons to sing the blues. This is a part of what we are talking about today. These forms of media are energy and these energies are very much able to bring with them and to contain other energies and intentions. My encouragement then is to be aware of what it is you are feeding your subconscious mind and what it is you are feeding into your emotional and mental bodies. Use your own discernment about what you are bringing into your awareness. My encouragement is to seek out those inputs, thoughts and things that resonate with higher levels of vibration and those of beauty, love, honor, peace, integrity and harmony. So look about your world; and with your awareness and discernment, look at what you have set about your home and your surroundings. Are they peaceful and beautiful? Do they resonate with love and light, peace and harmony? Look at the influences and inputs that you are allowing to come in. Do they provide you with a sense of joy, confidence, upliftment, trust and faith; or do they break you down with energies and vibrations of lack, fear, violence, doubt, anger and hopelessness? You get to make the choice.

In this message, what I really want to bring home for you then is you must come to understand the other aspects of your being, and this takes us back again to the discussion of a holistic approach. There are many aspects of your being that are beyond your moment-to-moment conscious awareness. Your thinking mind is a tool. It is one of the parts. It is one part of the whole and this is the tool then, in this understanding, with which you may decide and apply your own discernment about those influences which you know now, despite what you see in your moment-to-moment consciousness, which you know are having some effect on the totality or fullness of your being. Once you are able to understand this holistically at some level, it begins to make some sense for you. You will find that your choice of inputs and surroundings and even those whom you choose to associate with will shift and your desire will be to surround yourself at all times with things of beauty and higher vibrational resonance.

# Chapter 19

# Transformation: the caterpillar and the butterfly

Adama - I thought we might discuss transformation today, Bryan.

I have just given you the image of a beautiful Monarch butterfly, which begins its life as a caterpillar. This is a common analogy that has been used in many cultures. It is something that you have heard and seen referenced many times because it is a wonderful example of transformation. It's not just an analogy of transformation but something real that opens our minds to possibility. Humanity is being guided now to undergo a similar transformation. In the caterpillar form, you do not know the beauty and freedom that comes from the attainment of having grown, developed and worked to earn for yourself the right to experience life in a whole new way. The caterpillar, for a good portion of its life, does not know that it has the innate potential to blossom and transform into a beautiful being, a butterfly. It is just not in the caterpillar's awareness for most of its life. This is the general condition of humanity at this time.

As you come into your embodiments, the Veils of Illusion are drawn around you, and you begin your human experience. You do not recall or remember the divinity that you truly are. You do not remember the allness or fullness of yourselves as the infinite and expansive beings of light that you are. And so, you go through your life experience typically in much the same manner as those around you. These are your family and friends; your community and country, or whatever environment you have chosen to come into. These are the clothes that you wear, the beliefs and societal rules that you inherit, the framework of what you are told is and is not possible, the education systems, or lack thereof, and so forth. It is the experience of the society and earth family that you have chosen to come into that initially sets about you the personality: the human or ego self that you know yourself to be from an early age. They are the paradigms, what you believe to be right or wrong, true and untrue, your understanding of Creator and the Cosmos, your degrees of perceived separation and so on. This all seems very natural and very normal and it is.

Unfortunately, the situation that we have today and have had for a long period of time now is that most of humanity are trapped—in this analogy—in the experience of the caterpillar, and they are struggling day-to-day to live life as the caterpillar. This is all they know. They are unaware of the life-changing transformation that is always available to them and always on offer. Even those who may become aware of the great possibility and beauty of transformation that is in store for them still may not pursue it for various reasons. Although they experience struggles in the form of the caterpillar, it is what they know and what they are used to. Transformation can be difficult and therein lies the unknown; so most are just living their lives as the caterpillar and doing the best they can with what they have or what they believe they have.

We have discussed what is taking place with new levels of light and love coming onto the planet; and we are now fully underway, accelerating forward with the rising of planetary consciousness. We have discussed that it will be all of you, humanity who will create the New Earth. The way this will come about is through each one's individual transformation. Some will choose to move forward in their transformation in this lifestream experience and some will not, and that is okay. It is each one's choice to make.

Regarding the great transformation that is possible and always on offer for each of you, it is often required that there be a great catalyst in which the human must be shaken or rattled. Often it is necessary that some event come into your human experience that will assist you in your further awakening and will assist you in the realization that transformation is always available to you. Let us establish our terminology here. I may use the terms ego, personality, human or small self to be the same; and I may use the terms real self, Higher Self or soul to be the same. Formal definitions of these terms will vary but I am attempting to illustrate for you the difference between the two in this discussion.

So we know the way of things is that you come into this human form with an ego and this is your human aspect/personality or small self. The ego is concerned primarily with your survival. In its most pure form of purpose it is here to ensure your survival. This aspect would be what you know to be your intellect, your reasoning mind and some of the other bodily systems if we look holistically. It includes recall from experience and memory or perhaps a natural reaction given by the nervous system. It may be what you perceive to be your ability to use logic, thought and reasoning based on your experience and your levels of understanding for your benefit. For most of humanity, this aspect of you is running the show. It is the aspect of you that is in alignment with your communities and societies, and it is the aspect of you that is plotting and planning how it will best survive and meet its own needs and desires.

And so we see this, it is all around you every day and this is the way of things. This is the way life happens and this aspect of you is extremely valuable. If you did not have the ego and the personality and you could not draw on recall and experience; certainly you would struggle in making your way through this lifestream experience. This is how you learn lessons. It is how you learn universal law such as cause and effect, for example. You make mistakes and you do not like the consequences that are returned to you, and your conscious mind and ego body register this and they say, "Well, we did not like that result so let us not do that again" and so on. This is the caterpillar living its caterpillar life and it knows no difference. It knows of nothing else. This is how life is and these are the confines. This is the current environment and situation, and so the ego is fighting and clawing in this caterpillar life to make the most of it and that is to accomplish the ego desires. If we think about the personality or what we refer to as the small self, the ego is primarily attuned to sensory pleasures and physical pleasures. These are material things, yes; but there are also desires that drive the ego such as control, supremacy, intellect, better than and so on. Ego desire and wanting may be any number of things depending on your personality, environment and inputs. Your ego wants more and more and more. It wants more money, it wants more love, it wants more satisfaction, it wants more recognition, it wants more authority, it wants more sugar, it wants more of the drug that makes it feel good, it wants higher status and so on and so forth. This is the human personality, the small self.

The reason this takes place is because you are working in the framework of the caterpillar. The caterpillar does not even know of the existence of the butterfly. It does not know of the beauty, joy and freedom of the butterfly. It does not even know that it is a possibility. It is simply doing the best it can with what it believes it has in this caterpillar experience. And so this is, generally speaking, the current state of humanity. And now, many in their caterpillar experience are being guided or led to some form of seeking that answers new questions arising within them. Perhaps at a young age, your family introduced you to whatever the family religion or belief system is, or perhaps you were exposed to some type of formal spiritual training that exists in your many world religions. Perhaps you had family members who brought these elements into your awareness; so often these elements of higher knowledge, elements of the real self, elements of attainment, spirituality, truth and light will also be a part of your lifestream experience. They will be a part of the caterpillar experience. Even though the caterpillar may seek to come into alignment and resonance at some level of belief or application of such subjects of study or types of experience, for the most part it is still within the caterpillar experience. That is to say the small self, the ego self is still fully in control of that caterpillar experience; so while elements such as these may be allowed in for the well-roundedness of the caterpillar experience, it is still the caterpillar and small self who are typically running the show.

What is happening now is that waves of love and light, vibration, harmonic frequencies, electro-magnetic alignments and Divine Feminine energies are flooding the planet as never before. These things are stirring your divinity, which is at the core of your being. These are the aspects of your real self—your divinity, your soul, your Higher Self and your own beloved I AM Presence. They are aspects of the fullness of the glory that you are in all of your great light and expansiveness as a divine being. All humans have the spark of divinity within them. Each of you comes in with this as your divine birthright and it is installed in you, so to speak, before you ever come into this embodiment. It is always there; however, in most cases, it lies dormant. This aspect of your being will typically become activated according to the divine blueprint that is being carried out by each one's Higher Self. When the time is right, that aspect within you will become activated. Sometimes the activation occurs through the breaking down of the small self, ego self, the personality and the human which has become so entrenched in his or her ways—what he or she knows is real and not real, what he or she knows is true and not true, what he or she knows is the right way or not the right way. This entrenchment is closely aligned to what we may refer to as the ego pride or the small self who wants to be in charge. It wants to run the show; and even despite the fact that it is trapped in this caterpillar experience, and even though it may know of the possibility of the butterfly experience, it is afraid that the butterfly experience may cause it to lose its control and grasp on what is and is not. So the ego will often rebel against transformation and change. It does not want this transformation. Often, therefore, depending on how entrenched the small self is, it will be necessary that there come some life experience that causes the ego personality and small self to shake loose of its hold. When the time is right, the Higher Self will choose this. Often an experience will come in for the human that will shake things up in the normal day-to-day life, sometimes in rather extreme ways. These experiences may be very unpleasant for the human and this is often referred to as the dark night of the soul. It makes no difference how you label it; the point is, often it is a requirement that these difficult experiences come into your awareness in order to break loose the hold of the ego. That is, to break loose the paradigm the human has been stuck in.

These are life experiences that many of you have undergone or that your friends and family have undergone. They may be disease or ailments of the body; and yes, sometimes what you will see is the disease comes into the body and the human is given only a small time from that point forward before they, according to their own design and blueprint and according to the divine will of Creator, make their transition back home. It is often very difficult, in your level of awareness and understanding, to have a greater appreciation for what is taking place in these situations. Make no mistake, we understand that pain as you experience it whether it be emotional, mental or physical pain, we understand that it is very real in your experience and we have a great understanding and compassion for you; so please do not mistake my message today as being one of non-caring or non-concern as this is not the case. But what I wish for you to know is, often there are great things happening that the human may not perceive. Even the one who is going through the experience may not have the full understanding and appreciation for what is coming about through that experience, and there are many, many reasons that it might happen this way. I will not go into the many reasons but suffice it to say, in these examples there is a divine plan. What you may find is, that through the experience of those having had serious disease for example, they may be in a position now to offer themselves and others much needed forgiveness that perhaps would not otherwise have been given had life continued in the normal day-to-day function of the caterpillar experience.

So now something has been really shaken. A big event has come about and now there is something that must be dealt with. There are deeper levels of investigation, seeking, searching, asking questions and looking for answers that will bubble up to the surface. It is through these experiences that tremendous amounts of grace may be offered to the human, and often they are simply not aware of it. It may have to do with the balancing of karma. In the example I've just used, perhaps forgiveness of themselves or another has come forth that may not have come if it were not for this experience. This person may have agreed to be in this situation and to come into this embodiment solely for the benefit of a partner. For example, let us say there is a married couple who have been together for a good while, and now one of them has been diagnosed with a life threatening disease. They will experience whatever it is they intended to experience according to their own divine blueprint, and let us say the partner succumbs to the disease. That is to say they have been called home. Now, the partner has been left here and their world has truly been shaken to the core. They are crushed. Their heart is broken. The experience is opening the heart space while simultaneously breaking down the ego control of the human.

It is through this space that grace can come in and divine love and divine light and compassion can come in. It is through this space then that the Higher Self has created an opportunity. The soul is being stirred. This may be the first time in the whole lifestream experience of the human when they find themselves asking questions and contemplating things that they've not put much thought into before. This is the soul speaking to them directly and it may be the first time they've heard or felt their soul speaking to them. This is the Higher Self and the I Am Presence. It is their divinity reaching out to them now. This is typically a process, and through this process the individual has an opportunity to view that which is offered to them. From this position they may view the opportunity and the possibility of transformation into a beautiful butterfly. This opportunity often comes into view out of the darkness, the pain and the suffering that is being experienced by the trials of life.

I have given you just one example. There are many, many more and each of you are all too aware of these kinds of experiences. They are brought about by the Higher Self so that a new perspective may be created. It is the heart of the human that has now been opened to receive and hear the message from her soul, perhaps for the first time. This may not be a requirement for every lifestream experience but often it is. The path to awakening is becoming much easier now through new levels of grace and love from our Creator. Everyone's experience is individual to them and everyone's experience will take place according to their own decisions, actions and free will, but also according to their Higher Self and the blueprint that they themselves have set about for this experience. Often a catalyst is the way this epiphany is brought about and the epiphany is that transformation is possible. Great transformation is possible. Not only is it possible, but it has been done before. The wayshowers have come before us and the wayshowers are still here. This is the transformation that brings the small self back into alignment with the real self, the soul and their divinity. It is a process. It does not happen overnight and the ego still wants to have its say and its control. These kinds of disruptive experiences are often necessary because through this space the soul emerges. The soul will nudge you to begin pondering and seeking the larger questions or meaning of your life and bring them to your awareness.

In your case, Bryan, you have experienced your dark night of the soul and at that time began your journey in earnest to bring yourself into alignment. There was a point of recognition when you understood this for yourself. You understood the transformation that was possible. You understood, in our analogy, that you had been living life as a caterpillar. You understood that it was not only possible but it was achievable for you to make your transformation into a beautiful butterfly, and in that moment you set down your intention. You had a conversation with yourself, with the ego and personality aspect of your being; and what you have said was *"Look, you have had an opportunity to run this lifestream experience for x number of years and I appreciate all that you have done and I know that you have been working in our best interest. However, as of this moment forward we are taking a much different approach. We will engage daily the guidance that is on offer from our Father/Mother God and that aspect of us which is our greater aspect, our Higher Self and our soul residing in Heaven."* You have simply made note, *"Look, you have been running the show here for some time and we've done okay but I feel we can do much better. I know there are great levels of achievement, joy and grace that are on offer for us, and I know this comes about through our alignment with our divinity and our Higher Self. From this point forward this how we are going to do things."* And so, from that point forward you set down your intention and you began doing the work in earnest. You have also come to understand that the ego or small self is also an aspect of your being and as such, it is deserving of your love. It is an aspect of your being and it has done the very best that it can to provide for you and to keep you safe. So the ego is not to be shunned but rather embraced as you might a small child.

Since that point in time your momentum has grown and grown and you have seen that great transformation has come into your own life in a very short period of time. This is significant. It is great transformation and you may say, *"Well yes but we are not done yet,"* and this is true. No, you are not done yet, but look at what has been accomplished; and in this analogy, you are, for the most part, living your life now in the experience of the butterfly. You are no longer trapped in the old paradigm of the caterpillar life. Would you agree with this?

Bryan - *Yes sir, absolutely.*

Adama - So this is what is happening now in a more or less natural way for everyone. As these waves come onto the planet, each one is beginning to stir at the soul level. Their Higher Selves are reaching out to them; and through this expansion and increased levels of awareness, this new paradigm of the butterfly experience will be a byproduct of all of that is taking place now on the planet.

As these new energies come into the four lower bodies, something begins to stir that was not there before. There begins to rise to the surface a longing, a desire, a knowing, a questioning; something new bubbles up to the awareness of the human and they begin to view things differently. With new levels of understanding, perhaps they perceive things with fresh eyes or perhaps in a way that is contrary to what they have perceived in the past. So one of the things we in the Company of Heaven are endeavoring to do—and you have received these messages from many different masters and their messengers—we are wanting and encouraging each of you to come into the recognition and remembrance of who you really are. **You are a divine being who is having a human experience.** As this comes fully into your awareness you are able to see the transformation that you can achieve. You are able to see life as a butterfly. Perhaps up until this point you weren't able to see it or acknowledge it; and now many of you are seeing it and saying, "*Wow, I have this wonderful opportunity now to go out and experience life in a whole new way as a beautiful butterfly. I don't have to* *be stuck on this tree with these little stubby legs. I can live a butterfly experience, beautiful and free to fly!"*

These new energies are coming onto the planet and, as you say, "People's love lights are turning on." Their souls are being stirred and the divinity within each one is being awakened. Of course, many are not aware of what is taking place. They may be aware that something or multiple things are happening; however, they may not quite know how to diagnose their situation or what their next step should be. Many of the messages that all of us here are giving you at this time are really with the endeavor, hope and assistance of helping all of humanity to make their transition into beautiful butterflies. It is not only possible; it is achievable. This is why you and so many of the other wayshowers are on the planet at this time to actually guide yourselves through this transformation, and of course we are here to assist you. It is our great joy to do so; and as you are able to guide yourself through this transformation, several things happen. One is that you will be able to experience the beautiful life of the butterfly and you will no longer be trapped in the caterpillar experience. When you begin to break free of the caterpillar experience and feel the expression of love, divine light, joy and harmony and peace and all of these feelings and experiences that are attuned to the butterfly experience, then in no way, shape, or form would you ever choose to go back to the life you knew before. You have a new paradigm now. You have seen it and you have experienced the many joys and benefits for yourself.

This is what is happening now for all of you who are on the forefront of this activity. The first benefit that comes is that you actually get to experience your own beautiful transformation; and secondly what happens is, as you do this, you are wayshowers and teachers for those around you. You have heard it said before that for each one of you who is undergoing this process now, you are making it easier for all of those who will follow. You are paving the road ahead for all who follow. This is true. So many of our messages are given with the endeavor and hope that those of you who are led to the messages will begin to understand all of the grace, beauty and love that is on offer for you and that you equally understand you need not be trapped in your old caterpillar paradigm. You would be the only ones holding yourselves there. If anyone is trapped it is because they have chosen to be so. I know this type of language is often difficult to be received by the human. The ego will often respond with some statement such as *"Well this is not my choice. This is what I am stuck with and there is nothing I can do about it. This is the way it is for me"*. That is an ego response, you see. That is the small self maintaining its status quo. Yes, I will say, there is effort and work involved in bringing about transformation for yourself. Those of you who have done this and continue to do this work for yourselves know all too well that there is some actual work involved. It does take some of your energy and intention and some of your thought and time to gather the understanding that you need for your own forward momentum on your own chosen path.

I will say also as you are thinking about it. It is not always a requirement that a major life-shifting event take place before this awareness and these levels of transformation can begin. That is not the case. Sometimes it is a requirement, depending on how entrenched the ego personality and small self are in the human experience. Depending on their own path, many will not be required to experience painful lessons or earth shattering events to help them wake up more fully. Each one's path is unique to them. Many are simply at a place where they are able to allow, open and receive these new levels of awareness and expansion as they come to them. Many are able to move into new levels of growth and transformation with a fair amount of grace and ease. That is the experience that one person is having. Perhaps it is similar to yours, perhaps not. I just wish to make this note, that what you often refer to as the proverbial dark night of the soul is not always a required catalyst for transformation. Also let me say, it is not a requirement at all that this transformation even be made. It is something that is on offer for each of you; and I would pose to you that in this analogy, the butterfly experience is much more fulfilling in all manner of ways. It is much more delicious, enticing, fulfilling and joyful than the caterpillar experience. That's just my encouragement. There will be many who will choose to remain in their caterpillar experience throughout this embodiment. The choice is yours. If you choose not to make your transformation in this lifestream experience, there will be other opportunities available to you.

When you come to this place where you have some conscious understanding that you have been living a caterpillar's existence and you know there is an offer available for you to live a more beautiful, peaceful, abundant and harmonious butterfly life, you will also understand that one of the reasons you are not currently living the butterfly experience is because you have been choosing to live in separation. You have chosen to live disconnected, to some extent, from Creator, your soul, your Higher Self and the Company of Heaven. Said another way, you have simply allowed your ego and small self to run the show of your earthly experience. When you come to this level of understanding for yourself, perhaps you will make the conscious decision and set your intention that you are going to make your own transformation. You may declare something to the effect of; *"I AM moving out of the old caterpillar paradigm. I AM moving into a beautiful, new butterfly paradigm and experience. I know there are greater things in store for me, and I surrender in full faith now to my higher guidance."*

In that moment when you have fully had this understanding and you have made this declaration for yourself, the last component will be that you ask for assistance. Look up to the heavens and Father/Mother God in whichever way you perceive them and ask for help. Let me tell you––I pause here for effect––let me say it is beyond your current imagining and understanding the great magnitude and the great force of light, the great number of beings, those of your family in Heaven who will all come rushing in to be by your side in that moment. For truly, in that moment, you have the full support of the Company of Heaven by your side. This is where your transformation begins. This is where you can begin to build a new momentum. This is where you can make a fresh start and be reborn. This is the place where you will begin to heal all within you that requires healing, forgive all that requires forgiveness and begin learning self-love in a new way. This is the place where you begin to open your heart and your mind to new levels of understanding and possibility, new levels of assistance and guidance that have always been available to you yet perhaps unseen. This might be referred to as the tipping point for the individual where, through a variety of influences and experiences there has been a compounding effect and culmination such that the human now sits on the precipice with some level of understanding. This is where the decision is made that they are going to leave behind the old shell, the old form of the caterpillar, and they will go now into their cocoon.

There is work that must be done in the transformation. It does not happen in a flash but in each one's awareness, here in this tipping point moment, they understand the truth and the beauty of the butterfly experience. They know there is work to be done and perhaps further discomfort along the way. They step out of that that is familiar. They step into this experience of the cocoon and herein lie the stages of the greatest transformation. They will find lessons of self-love, compassion, forgiveness and more. There are messages being given to humanity now in many different forms and by many different messengers to guide the way. These are also the messages that have been given by many great avatars who have come in the past. This is where they will step into the cocoon, essentially having made the decision now to surrender in full faith to God and the divinity that they are, asking that they be guided and led each step of the way. With faith and trust, simply to go and do those things that perhaps they thought they wouldn't or couldn't do, to begin taking the time to look at themselves deeply and truly and to begin the work in earnest.

Once that decision has been made, I say again, it is incomprehensible how much assistance, grace and love, how many beautiful beings of light will come in support of the one having made the call. This is similar to some of the events and ceremonies taking place within various religions and spiritual traditions around the world when someone has come to that point of recognition––perhaps it is this tipping point that I am speaking of and perhaps not–– they have come to that place where they want more. They want to know more. They want to receive more. They want to embody more light, love and illumination. Their soul is guiding them to come further into alignment. They are seeking a greater connection to the love and goodness of their Creator. When the time is right, they will emerge from the cocoon and leave the old ways behind. This is a part of our message, and you see a common theme from many messengers from those of us in the ascended master realms and those of us working on the New Earth project with Creator. The message is that you do not walk alone. You need not do it alone. The love and support of Heaven are with you always and are always available to you. I invite each of you to contemplate now what your life might look like in the fullness of love and grace that is the experience of the beautiful and free butterfly.

# Chapter 20

# Clearing and Foundations for Co-Creation

Adama - I would like to speak on the topic of co-creation today. There is a great deal of information circulating on the topics of manifestation and co-creation, and I believe this topic may be of interest to our readers.

Bryan - *Yes sir, there is. It's something we all want to learn how to do.*

Adama - Of course this is a topic of great interest because each of you has your own hopes, dreams and endeavors. Each of you has within you an innate drive for expansion and growth. This is your nature. At some level, most everyone desires to have the same kinds of things. Everyone wants to be happy, to feel loved, to be appreciated and to have the freedom to do and be what they want to be. Everyone wants a safe and stable home environment along with all the basic necessities of life. There is always the innate drive to have, to see, to know, to achieve more. Let's say you want something for yourself and you have been able to bring this thing about. Pretty soon you want something else and it need not be a material object. Perhaps you want to travel someplace new or you want to learn a new skill. If that goal is achieved then pretty soon you have another one that you're going after. This is the nature of life and an innate quality that is present in all life. It is the nature of our Creator. There is always expansion and growth. There is always creation. It never stops. What I would like to speak about today is this innate drive or quality within the human; and that is the innate desire for expansion, experience and growth, to do more, to see more, to learn more, to experience more.

There is much information present now and much more coming forth about manifesting or co-creating your experience, so let us speak about this today. There are really two levels in which this may take place. We have, what I will refer to as the real self. The real self is your divinity, the greater aspects of you now residing in Heaven (higher dimensions). It is your soul, your Higher Selves and your own beloved I AM Presence. These are aspects that make up your higher level of being, and there is much more we could say about it. It is the expansiveness and the divinity that you are, each and every one of you. Whether you are aware of it or not, your soul's greatest desire for your achievement is for you to earn your ascension. Ascension is your victory in the light. It is returning HOME to where you came from. It is coming fully back into your divinity and coming back home fully then in the presence of Creator and having full awareness and unity consciousness with all beings of light with whom you are connected and who are your family. The experience of the ascension is more magnificent and grand and exciting and fulfilling and pleasing––there are not enough words in your vocabulary to express the grandeur of this event; and make no mistake, whether you are aware of it or not, this is your soul's greatest desire for your achievement. That is for you to come into your full awareness and knowing and to step onto the path of initiation with the momentum of your own soul. This comes about through the nudging of the soul whereby a space opens within you and the light and guidance of your Higher Self and your soul begin guiding you to step firmly onto the path of initiation or Path of Light. As this happens, you begin moving confidently in the direction of seeking your greater awareness, seeking higher levels of understanding and consciousness, remembering who and all that you are and what it is you came here to do.

Certainly, there are obstacles, tests and experiences to be had along the way. This is moving out of the caterpillar experience and moving into the butterfly experience. Another analogy that has been used is climbing the mountain one step at a time as you ascend to reach the heights of the summit. You earn your ascension step by step, day by day and moment by moment. It is the soul's greatest desire to elevate itself out of the rounds of reincarnation and karma in which the human has been trapped for so long.

As we discussed earlier, you have come into this embodiment with the Veils of Illusion around you; and you have, for the moment, forgotten all that you really are. You have forgotten all that you have known and all that you have done. You've forgotten the great wisdom you have accumulated through countless embodiments here on Earth as well as many other experiences throughout the cosmos. You have forgotten the purity and the fullness of divine love; for as you have dropped down into this embodiment, not only have the Veils of Illusion been placed around you but your ability to connect with and commune with Creator Light and the Company of Heaven has been greatly diminished. So here you are in this human embodiment and your personality and ego develop along the way. This is the experience you are having as the human. You go through life and stages of learning and as you come into adulthood, your ego is firmly set, and for the most part your personality is set. This is the world you're living in and the world as you know it to be.

Most of you, understandably, are very attached to the 3rd dimensional lifestream experience that you are having now. Often in the case of those who are primarily working in the ego, when the topic of manifestation comes up, they desire things of the material world, those things which they see, feel and know here in the 3rd dimensional experience of duality of your current earthly experience. This is not always a bad thing. This is not intended to be a negative statement. It just is, and often it is necessary and valuable. If you are someone on the planet now who is having the experience of a refugee or castaway with no home, you endeavor to manifest about you that which you need to survive and to make yourself more comfortable. Perhaps you desire to manifest a beautiful home, safety and all that you need to live a comfortable and joyful life. Perhaps you wish to create a life of unlimited beauty, bounty and abundance. This is natural and it is your divine birthright to do so. Then perhaps at the other end of the spectrum, we see cases where the ego has been allowed to run rampant and the ego desire may be for such things as more power, money, fame and fortune. There are all manner and variety of desire and endeavor in between. Many great sages and masters of the past have spoken about walking the middle way or middle path. It applies to a number of circumstances of the human experience, but we are speaking today on the subject of co-creation/manifestation. As higher vibrational waves of love and light flood the planet, individual souls are beginning to nudge the human and they are waking up. They begin the inevitable process of seeking who they are––their truth and divinity. This is what each one's soul will propel them to do and indeed this is what is taking place.

What I would like to speak about today is this concept of manifestation and co-creation. We use both of these words. You see them being used to mean the same thing; however, look at the word "co-creation." I will say that it is possible, through the application of universal law alone to achieve results through the activity of the lower self and ego if that one has reached an understanding of universal law and the application of those laws. That one may indeed become a powerful manifestor. They may manifest a great number of experiences or material objects or whatever it is they are endeavoring to bring about, and they may do this within the framework of the lower self. This is possible and there are many who have and are demonstrating this in your world now. You see them all around you, individuals who have accomplished great feats in the material world. They may have great power or fame. Perhaps they have amassed great fortunes. Perhaps they have many homes and servants tending to their every need, and perhaps they have entire warehouses full of brand new automobiles. We do not encourage anyone to pass judgment on your brothers and sisters, for you know that you are all children of God and all are created equally in the eyes of God. Often though, when you see some of these individuals, you may observe their behavior and perceive they may have achieved these things in the material world without the benefit of love and light, fairness, integrity, honor and truth. So yes, they may achieve great things, often through manners of the ego and that of control, domination, perhaps trickery and manipulation, perhaps dishonesty and so on; yet they have achieved those results. In one way or another, they have applied universal law alongside their human error and they have still managed to achieve seemingly great results. So this is possible; however, I would not encourage it as your best choice. The reason is that universal laws of Creator are always in effect, and your soul's greatest desire is to earn your ascension, your victory in the light. Just as the universal law of attraction is always in play, so too is the universal law of cause and effect or karma. So one of my main points here today and my encouragement for each of you is to, as our Brother Jesus said, "Seek ye first the kingdom of God, and his righteousness, and all things shall be added unto you." This will be more or less a natural process for most of you as you go through this shift.

As you clean and clear lower vibrations and as higher levels of light and wisdom come into your four lower bodies, you will begin to recognize the stirrings of discontent. The soul will nudge you to move in the direction of seeking out your own divinity. The other word we use in place of manifestation is co-creation. Why do you suspect it is called co-creation? Certainly you have seen evidence that it is possible for those who are not in alignment with the guidance and presence of their Higher Self, that they may still, in the fullness of the small self and ego, go out and create great results in the material plane. However, ask yourself. Have they created great results in terms of their spiritual development or of climbing the mountain to reach the summit, of earning their ascension in the light and of breaking free of rounds and rounds of reincarnation in which they have been trapped for so long? Perhaps not. I dare say some of these individuals may be sorely disappointed after they have been called home and have their life reviews to see the net result of their choices in this lifetime.

So my encouragement then, is to use a balanced and middle way approach in the bringing about of the experiences you choose to have for yourself. It is our Creator's great delight to see his children whole, happy, successful and joyful and having the experiences they choose to create. You see, when you learn to co-create, you are creating what you choose to have for your earthly experience with a balanced approach. You are experiencing life as the human here in the 3rd dimensional earth plane. This is where you are. This is where you wake up each day and go to sleep each night. You are having an earthly human experience; so when that aspect of you is able to work alongside your divinity and Higher Self, tapping into your divine birthright of manifestation, which is co-creation with our Father/Mother God, then you are much more likely to gain momentum and see the results you desire. Furthermore let me say, if you will strive first to come into alignment with your divinity––and there are any number of sub-topics we could discuss––but as you step firmly on the path of the initiate and seek out your divine birthright, your divinity and all that you are, your soul will guide you day by day to come further and further into alignment.

You will begin to be led naturally to clean, clear and move out the lower vibrational energies. These are energies of the old 3D paradigm that no longer serve you. They are the programs, patterns, beliefs and memories that may be from your childhood or even from past lives. You may have residual karma that has been accumulated in this lifetime or others past that require balancing. You will be led naturally to clear and fully release the stagnant energies of fear, the sad memories and all that no longer serves you as you begin moving into the 5D New Earth paradigm. As you come more fully into alignment you will begin clearing out the lower vibrational energies from your four lower bodies. This, in turn, makes room for you to receive and embody more light and higher vibrational energies. It is not just light; it is innate wisdom and knowledge. This light brings the activation of your dormant DNA and the activation of previously dormant light packets of wisdom contained within your being to name but a few examples. We have discussed some of the many benefits of coming into alignment in our last chapter about transformation. As you do this work, your soul will guide you every day closer and closer to your alignment. Think of it as grace. The closer you come into alignment, the more grace and beauty you will see taking place in your world and experience, you see. As you go through the process of clearing old patterns, energies and beliefs, you will find yourself coming more into vibrations of harmony, peace, acceptance, forgiveness, love and understanding. This is a very necessary step for you to make any real progress in the activity of co-creation. This is a vital step that is not being fully discussed or perhaps it is being glossed over in much of the information that exists on this important topic at this time. So one of the points I would like to highlight in this discussion today, is not only the great benefit but the requirement then that these levels of work be done first or at least alongside of your serious manifestation/co-creation projects.

You know through the teachings that thoughts are things. Thoughts are energy vibration that you transmit out to the cosmos. According to your vibration and the law of attraction, whatever it is that you are feeling and thinking about and whatever levels you are vibrating at, is what is being drawn into your experience. You all have seen this and you know this; but often, in my opinion, there is not enough emphasis being placed on what I would call this section of work, which is really preliminary. This is the beginners work really that needs to take place if you're going to have any real success with your co-creation projects. You must learn to walk the middle way. You must learn to have some control over your emotional state and your thoughts by coming more fully into self-awareness. This means you are aware of what you are feeling and thinking moment-to-moment rather than simply allowing the old programs to run. Many of you are still fast asleep and the programs are just running in the background. You are on autopilot and you don't even know it. The programs are running, so the world around you and the circumstances around you are shifting you to and fro like a sail in the wind. Your emotional states and mental states are swinging to and fro according to the whims of life around you, and perhaps you feel that you don't have any control over it. Well, in these kinds of situations perhaps you do not have much control over it. What are you doing intentionally to change or better your situation? Perhaps you're not aware of these principles or the applications or how you would go about creating the experience you desire. We are talking about coming into self-awareness. "*How am I feeling right now, not yesterday or tomorrow but this now moment? What am I feeling? Am I trusting in my divine plan and higher guidance or am I choosing fear and frustration? Can I be in acceptance of how things are in this moment or am I struggling against it?*"

This moving into a place of self-awareness goes hand in hand with this work of clearing and cleaning all of that which no longer serves you. All of the lower vibrational energies, painful memories and limiting beliefs must be cleared and moved out of the way so that greater amounts of love and light, knowledge and wisdom may come in. I really want to emphasize today the importance of this step, and it's not just one step. Many of you reading this material know that often the work and discipline involved in coming more fully into self-awareness does not happen overnight. Those of you who are intentionally doing this kind of work or process for yourselves know this already. You know what it has taken to come to this place where you are now; it likely didn't happen in a day. This is a vital component. It is an absolute foundational component if you are one who is wanting to become proficient at co-creating your own experience. It may take some time but it is necessary. Ask that you be shown and led to your next steps and so you will. What happens over time is, you will come to have a greater range of control and influence over your moment-to-moment experience by controlling the vibration that you are feeling and therefore sending out as your energy signature to the cosmos. As you begin to step into your self-mastery and you begin to have not only a theoretical understanding of these topics but you begin to have some application in your own life, you will begin to see the many benefits coming into your experience. One benefit for example, is being able to make the choice to move into a state of happiness rather than a state of sadness or choosing trust over fear. It may take some time and work to actually come to the place where you may have some real world application of these concepts. As you do so, you will be well prepared and poised for success in the next steps or process you choose to bring your co-creations into their full manifestation. Having taken a serious look at that which your soul desires, and now from this place of further alignment, you may look across the spectrum of your being and decide what you really want for yourself. What do you want in terms of your spiritual attainment and what do you want for your earthly experience?

The rules are changing. We are moving firmly into the next Golden Age of New Earth and the results of manifestation and co-creation will begin to pick up speed. In fact it already has. What is happening now is, often your creations return back to you almost instantaneously so you can see the result of what you have just created. This momentum will continue to expand moving forward so that you will have a greater opportunity to bring about your manifestations. However, again, let me say, it is important that this groundwork be done; for if you are not in control of your energies, vibrations and thoughts then not only is it possible that this would slow down the speed of your manifestation but you could also inadvertently bring about manifestations and experiences that you did not want in the first place. You did not choose them intentionally, but you brought them into your experience inadvertently because you were not aware of the universal laws and you were not self-aware of what you were vibrating and sending out to the cosmos. There are a great many who are living this condition now.

Another foundational piece of understanding is that you and you alone are responsible for the experiences you are living today. You are not being punished. You brought them about. Now granted, I will say there are times when your own divine blueprint and your Higher Self may lead you to situations and events which are indeed for your highest growth and greatest good, but often in your human experience you may not always perceive them this way. We will acknowledge this as a component of your earthly experience, but aside from that and still within the framework of this discussion, it is still your responsibility. You signed off on your divine blueprint prior to your embodiment here. You knew what was going to happen. You agreed to it. You created it in fact. So whatever it is that you are experiencing here, make no mistake, it is your creation and your responsibility. You may experience conditions that have been brought about by the Higher Self and the blueprint that you created for this embodiment AND/OR you may be experiencing what you have created here in this lifetime through universal law and that which you have been sending out to the cosmos. That is your vibration. This is a foundational component of this discussion. Once you have begun doing the work of clearing and cleaning and you come to some level of understanding and self-awareness, you will come to see and know that you are now poised to create a beautiful, harmonious experience of your choosing and to absolutely bring in those conditions of the human experience and the material world which you choose to have for yourself.

My encouragement is that whatever it is that you're asking for, just ask that it be for the greatest good of all. As long as you are in alignment with the greatest good of all then please believe me when I say that our Father/Mother God and each and every one of us in the Company of Heaven want nothing more than to see you living the fullness of your own creation. It is your divine birthright to go forth and create. We want to see your dreams come true. We want to see you in your joy, laughing and fulfilled at all levels. We want to see you find the path of service that nurtures your soul. It is our great joy to assist you in your endeavors to bring about the hopes and dreams you have for yourself and again I say, the rules have changed. Things that may not have been possible or easily attainable in days past are now not only possible, but they are here for you now. The rules have changed and your manifestations will begin coming to you more quickly now so it is important that you not try to rush and bypass these foundational steps for these are the requirements for the proper application of universal law. As you strive to bring yourself into alignment, balance and harmony what you will find is that many of the aspects you want to have in your experience will simply begin to just show up without a great deal of effort. Through this foundational work of moving into further alignment you will begin to walk in grace. Let me assure you, when you begin to have this experience and recognition for yourself, that you are moving out of your old paradigm and have now grown and expanded to a place where you are walking daily in harmony and grace, you will never want to go back. The state of balance and grace and peace within you is invaluable and I encourage you to see for yourself. As you begin feeling whole within yourself and begin feeling self-love, coming into resonance and balance and walking in grace then I suspect this will become the most important thing to you.

We want to see you create a beautiful life for yourself, whatever that means for you. To do this is the expression of your own divinity and that is to go out into the world and co-create with our Father/Mother God. This is the way your creations will most readily and most easily come about. This is a path of self-awareness and alignment and that of doing what you can to clear and clean all that is no longer serving you, all that is of a lower resonance and vibration, and to move those out of your four lower bodies to bring in greater levels of light and love.

We have not discussed any of the processes, methods of details that you may use to go about your intentional co-creations and manifestations. Again, there is a wealth of information coming onto the planet in this regard. There are any number of processes that you may use to bring about your desired experience so we will not go into those details. I am, primarily, wanting to stress the use of a balanced approach and walking the middle way. Seek your spiritual development and follow the guidance of your soul while contemplating what it is the personality/human would like to see, have and experience for yourselves throughout the balance of the time that you have here in this embodiment. This is walking the middle way, and as you begin to do this and incorporate this holistic and balanced approach what you will see, I believe, is that you will feel better all the way around in your body, your essence and your being. Also, the experiences you desire will flow more easily and readily into your now moment experience and their full manifestation, you see.

So my two main points here today are first, the encouragement of walking the middle way. Sure, you may go out and create on your own but I assure you, you will have much greater success with the momentum of Creator and the momentum of your families in Heaven behind you. Beauty, Bounty and Abundance are your divine birthright and this is what we endeavor to see each and every one of you living for yourselves. Secondly, is to stress the importance of the path of self-mastery and self-awareness. Strive to further understand and bring yourself into alignment with the application of universal law and the natural flow of your divine guidance. Being aware of and being able to control ones thoughts, vibrations and emotions is an absolute key component in the establishment and bringing about of the experiences you choose to have. It is a process. It is all a process, but I can assure you that if you will be diligent and if you will come to know and accept this as your truth, then these things are indeed possible for you. If you will continue to do the work and continue to trust, if you will continue to follow your own inner guidance, I assure you that within a relatively short period of time you will begin to see real changes taking place in the world around you. You will be walking in grace. As you begin to recognize the many positive changes that you have co-created for yourself, you will never choose to return to the old ways of being and doing.

# Chapter 21

# Animal Kingdoms in Telos and 5D

Adama - Would you like to discuss the Fields of Telos and the animals that are here with us? We will also discuss how the transition will take place for the animals there on the surface.

Bryan - *Yes sir, I have a great love for the animal world and therefore an interest in this topic.*

Adama - We will discuss it today and I agree that it may be an interesting topic for our readers as well.

We have had some discussion of the animal kingdoms and the understanding that they are also in the midst of their evolution and expansion at this time. These new levels of light and vibration are affecting all life here including the animal kingdoms. So let us begin our discussion by saying there are many, many levels of life and consciousness both in our universe and many others. As the manifestation of Creator's ever expanding energies, creation and love go forth into the cosmos, it is the Elohim who are the builders of form. They work with many other levels of being to create new worlds, new stars and new life forms. This evolutionary process, the process of creation and expansion never stops; and so under this umbrella of all of life existing everywhere, we have a great, wide range and variety of life.

We have discussed various levels of beings that have consciousness that is a group consciousness. They are cared for by the Elohim, Archangels, Devic angel kingdoms and the elemental kingdoms. Examples include the crystal kingdoms, plant and tree kingdoms and many species of lower levels of independent consciousness from the animal kingdoms. Many levels of being from the animal kingdom that humanity often label as non-sentient are not only aware of themselves but also connected at all times to their group consciousness. This level of consciousness has the ability to send and receive information, and this is one of the primary roles that is played by the Devic angels, the elementals and the Elohim. For example, there are several forms of group consciousness within the family of crystal beings, but it is also possible for an individual crystal to have, what I will say, is some sense of independent consciousness. I understand this is complex and it is somewhat difficult for me to describe in a way that will be pleasing for you and others.

We shall return to one of our previous discussions. You have a variety of specimens from the crystal kingdoms with you in your home; and I have informed you that if you will take one of those crystals in your hands so that your energy, thoughts and intentions are being allowed to transmit back and forth, that crystal will receive it at some level. In this example, there is a blending of the individual consciousness of that particular crystal with the group consciousness of that group or that kind of crystal. So there is some understanding taking place there. Coming back to you will be some kind of emanation or energetic response from that individual crystal but with a blending then of its group consciousness. Let us say you are holding an amethyst. The collective consciousness of the amethyst families are now radiating out through the crystal you're holding. So that crystal, being an amethyst, is always attached to and connected with those of her amethyst families around the world, and this is the group consciousness of the amethyst crystal family. As you hold the crystal and send your intention and vibration, the energy from your body is flowing into the crystal and this is what is activating that particular crystal to receive your energies and vibrations and to emit back out to you then, specifically those vibrations and attributes that are inherent within the amethyst crystal families. Those energies and attributes radiate back to you specifically though the crystal that you are working with.

Within your plant kingdoms of trees, grasses and flowers, etc., we also have collective levels of consciousness that are essentially governing the species found within those families. In the case of a tree for example, if you were to actually touch a tree and set your energy about that tree, and let us say you send prayers and blessings and good will toward that tree and the tree families, what happens then is the collective consciousness of that tree family will receive your blessings. As you have blessed one, you have blessed all. This is an important note. We are all connected.

Gaia's animal kingdoms include an incredible diversity of life with many levels of consciousness and thought. You share your world with a wonderful variety of amphibians, reptiles, birds, fishes and mammals; and each species, or their closely related family, have a group consciousness. Many forms of life such as insects, fishes and birds are still working primarily at the group consciousness level. As we view the spectrum of animal life, we move from those species or levels that are primarily working within their group consciousness to those groups that exhibit higher levels of independent consciousness. They may act independently; but for the most part they are still acting within the framework of their group consciousness. Some of your herd animals might be an example. As we continue moving up the scale, we begin to see species like your beloved dogs and cats, rabbits, horses and elephants. We see parrots and macaws from the bird families and dolphins and whales from the mammal families in your oceans. Now we are describing some of the species or forms of life that you might consider to have higher cognitive awareness. They have independent consciousness, thought, awareness and feeling within themselves; yet they are also working within a group consciousness just as humanity is. So let us say we want to discuss dogs and cats. We know they have their group consciousness, but we also know that each of them have their own distinct personalities. They have the ability to have feelings and thoughts independent of their group consciousness. They are, however, still working within the framework of their group consciousness. This will always be a part of them for they are born with certain traits, characteristics and ways of being if you will. This is what allows them to find food, work together for survival and to be fearful of things that might be dangerous to them. While they are tied into their group consciousness, they also express their own divinity or their own individual expression.

We are speaking again in a holistic manner. Over the ages there has been a shift in the boiling up of the collective consciousness of humanity, for example. There has been a shift in the density of the consciousness of humanity and that is what is now contained within the collective consciousness of humanity. You see it is different now than it was at any other point in time. It is always changing and shifting according to that which is being placed upon it. The collective consciousness of humanity as it exists here in your earth plane, is always changing, and we have another great shift that is taking place now. So, if we were to look at the collective consciousness of humanity say at the time of the last Golden Age, what you would see is the aura or the color and vibration of that collective consciousness was much, much different at that time. It was a much higher vibration. It was a more pure and loving vibration. Your collective consciousness now looks much different than it did then.

The same is true for all life on our planet. All life is in a constant state of shifting, moving, flux, cycles, patterns of evolution and change. If we were to view some of the animal kingdoms that were present in our last Golden Age and make the observation between their collective consciousness then and now, we would see that the collective consciousness within the animal kingdoms were also much more elevated at the time of our last Golden Age. We will use your beloved dogs and cats as an example. We would observe different behaviors at the individual levels of expression and being within the canine and feline families who were also present with us at that time. Each one would be moving and behaving in their levels of being at a higher vibration. They were actually living, moving and behaving, at that point in time, in a $5^{th}$ dimensional vibration or level of consciousness. As we have discussed previously, the lower levels of vibration will simply not be allowed to exist in the $5^{th}$ dimensional and higher vibrations of New Earth.

In Telos, the minimum requirement for entry is a lower $5^{th}$ dimensional consciousness and vibration, and we have many beings from the higher dimensions visiting us frequently. The animals who are present with us here in Telos are vibrating at a minimum of a lower 5$^{th}$ dimensional frequency; so in those frequency ranges of 5D and higher we know that negative vibrations such as fear, worry, doubt, control, anger, domination and so on are simply not present. Any life form that you will observe here in Telos has reached and is operating at a 5D level of being. This was the case in the last Golden Age; and in our example of canines and felines, they also had expanded abilities which they no longer have. Their innate wisdom and their ability to send and receive telepathic messages and to perceive energy and vibration more readily were much more advanced at that time than it is today. When we came out of the last Golden Age and the great fall, all life forms and all consciousness on the planet fell into density. The animal kingdoms that share your home with you also fell into density. This is the current state of things and this is the world as you know it today.

Let us discuss then how these changes will take place. As I have said, this is a bit complex. Certainly there are aspects of this discussion that may seem confusing; however, it need not be as complex as we might make it out to be. As new levels of energy and light come to the planet, all life here is being affected; and within every life form, the densities are moving out and new levels of light and vibration are moving in. Each life form is being expanded in whatever level of consciousness they are currently working at. It is all being expanded. Everyone and everything is evolving and expanding now at an accelerated rate of speed.

So let us stay with these examples. If you have a dog or a cat that is a member of your family, make no mistake, they are feeling the shifts that are taking place within their level of being, and they are being affected by these new energies just as you are. Some of you may have noticed this change in your pets and members of the animal kingdoms who share your home. You may have noticed some shifts in their energy or perhaps you are finding that, as you go about your daily practice of meditation, stillness, listening to uplifting music, etc., that your animal family is joining you in that space. In those times when you are settling in to balance your energies, expand your consciousness, bring in love, light and prana or to find your place of peace and calmness, you may perceive that they are also enjoying the experience with you. You may perceive that they are also receiving some benefit in settling into a guided meditation or music or whatever it is, and indeed they are. Although they may not be consciously aware of why they are especially drawn to you in that space and although they may not be aware of the words that are being spoken in a guided meditation, let me assure you they are receiving benefit. At some level of their consciousness as they are experiencing it, they are also being drawn to the higher vibrations of peace and stillness, harmony and love. They are feeling the energies and they are being led, in their own way to move in that direction. It is happening naturally. It is a natural process that is unfolding with all life on the planet. You have heard of the 100$^{th}$ monkey effect and this is similar to how the transition will take place. The vibration of all life on Earth is rising. The lower levels of density are being allowed to fall off and fall away, and they are being replaced by higher levels of consciousness, those of unity consciousness, Christ consciousness and the Divine Feminine energies of love, peace and harmony. So make no mistake, the animal kingdoms at all levels are feeling the shift. They are undergoing the shift and they will be moving right alongside all of you, humanity and Gaia as you all go about your collective and holistic efforts of creating your New Earth.

There is also a great range of lifespan within the animal kingdoms. Some may only live a few hours or a few days and others may live to be quite old. Some animals may live a decade or longer and some may even live to be many decades old in this experience. What will happen is the same natural process of evolution, except that now it is being greatly accelerated. It will be similar to this notion of the 100th monkey effect in that, through just a very few generations, you will see a complete shift in the consciousness of all lifestreams on your planet and that includes the animal kingdoms. Humans, along with many members of the animal kingdom, are known to be predators. Your beloved cats and dogs are predators, and this is the way they were designed or at least the way they are naturally functioning at this time. There are many animal species on your planet that are predators; and as it stands today, this is still a requirement for sustaining life. What will begin happening in a relatively short period of time, as your carbon based bodies are transitioning to crystalline-based light bodies, is you will find that you no longer crave the same types of sustenance you craved before. It will not be long, perhaps another generation or two, before the human desire to eat meat and lower vibrational foods, of which there are many on your planet today, will simply fall away. Those desires will no longer be there because your physical bodies are changing and shifting as you move more into your crystalline-based light bodies. Your body will no longer need or desire the lower vibrational foods that you have relied on for so long. It will just shift naturally. The exact same process will take place within the animal kingdoms. They will not have this change in the forefront of their minds and awareness as you do, but the shifts will be taking place in almost exactly the same way. Their bodies are changing and their vibrations are moving from lower vibrational bodies to higher vibrational bodies. They are moving from forms of greater density into forms of lesser density. All life will move into a place where much of your sustenance will come from light and the life force energy of Creator contained within that light. Your bodies (humanity and the animal kingdoms) are shifting and adjusting such that they can receive more light and the energy that is prana or chi, the life force energy that is always available to us. It is the gift of life from Creator and it is what sustains life. Your bodies will naturally begin, more or less, to function on light alone. There will still be supplemental food sources like those we enjoy here in Telos, but this is very much the path that all life is on.

What will happen in the animal kingdoms is that their bodies will evolve over a number of generations as they continue to evolve more into their light bodies. They will begin to take in most of what they need through forms of light and plant food sources, so it will no longer be a requirement for predators to have a predatory diet. It will no longer be necessary to have meat and protein to sustain themselves and therefore the desire, or those innate behaviors that drive that activity are going to shift. They are going to slowly fall away. Things are happening in a holistic way. You are all moving into your New Earth together. All forms of life are moving together. In a relatively short period of time, you will see these shifts coming about more or less in a natural way. By the time you are fully living in your New Earth environment, you will have all manner of beautiful life forms sharing the planet as you do now, but all of them will have evolved into higher levels of consciousness and vibration. For example, the group consciousness of the lion is also receiving higher vibrations of love and light. Even the predators are moving into unity consciousness. This will be their new nature. It is not anything they are going to have to think about or choose for themselves; no, this is all going to take place naturally. It will not happen overnight but I assure you it has already begun.

These shifts are taking place now. Within a matter of several of your human generations, which could be considerably more generations for most animals, you will have moved firmly into your New Earth environment. The lions and lion consciousness will still be there, but they will no longer be predators. Your New Earth will truly be a place where the lions lie with the lambs in harmony and peace.

It will be humanity's responsibility to be good stewards of the planet and all life on the planet. This was originally all of our responsibility. That responsibility was taken away from humanity at the time of the last great shift. As you move back into unity consciousness and reestablish your daily communion with Creator, the light, your brothers and sisters in the light, then you will be given stewardship again of your planet and all life upon it. When this comes about, all life will be living in a minimum of lower 5$^{th}$ dimensional frequency. At that time, you will have the ability not only to communicate telepathically to each other, and there will be a variety of levels on which this will occur, but in many ways you will also have the ability to communicate telepathically with various members of the animal kingdom. By that time, each of you will have control of your thoughts, energies and behaviors. You will be masters. Self-mastery will be what you live; and so you will then become true stewards of Mother Gaia, your environment and all life that is here sharing your home with you. It will be all of you who are leading the way and setting the example for all life here and you will be the stewards of all the other kingdoms and manifestations of life here on the planet. Humanity will have dominion over the animal kingdoms, crystal kingdoms, plant kingdoms and so on; but because you are all working in unity consciousness, you will be working holistically with these other kingdoms and only in ways that are for the greatest good of all.

When you arrive firmly planted in your New Earth it will be very similar to what you see and experience here in the Fields of Telos where there are a great variety of animals present whose company and companionship we enjoy so very much. We are able to communicate telepathically with a great many of them, as you have witnessed, and truly this is a place where the lions lie with the lambs. All are in harmony. Yes friends, this is a wonderful and most beautiful experience. It is quite exciting for all of you to imagine your world in this way and I assure you this is where you are headed. In regards to the other forms of life, the animal kingdoms, the fishes, birds, insects, the plant and crystal kingdoms, all of them are evolving right alongside of you. The elemental kingdoms are also evolving alongside of you. All of you who are here with Gaia today are undergoing the same great shift and transformation together. You are all in this together.

We, the project team, are working this in a holistic manner and we have many teams here who are specifically working with Gaia. We have teams who are working specifically with the elemental kingdoms and we have teams who are working with all plant life and biology on the planet. We have teams who are working with the various animal kingdoms and we have many teams who are working with humanity. It truly is a holistic approach and this is why I believe each of you will have some appreciation for the analogy of the project plan, for truly this is a monumental project. There are many divisions of work and many milestones to achieve. There are many sub-projects taking place under the umbrella of the overall grand project. I encourage each of you to envision for yourself how this New Earth might look; for truly, truly the rules are changing. You are stepping out of your old paradigm and moving into a whole brand new way of living, a new way of being, a brand new paradigm that has long since been forgotten but it is being remembered now. Many of you––in fact I would say most of you who are drawn to read this material––are beginning to remember and have an inner knowing that you have experienced life in past, great golden ages. You just know you were there. In some ways, we are returning to the glory of past golden ages long forgotten; but we are also creating a world that is new, unique and radiantly beautiful. It is a wondrous vision to behold! I assure you the day will come when humanity will walk and commune side by side with the lions and tigers and any other animal, form of life, or beings that you can think of. All will be working in cooperation and all experiencing divine love. You and the generations to come will perceive the shifts within the animal kingdoms coming about more or less in a natural way. It is our endeavor to bring this great shift about with as much grace and ease as possible for all of you.

Bryan - *Master Adama, I would like to know if Telosians share their homes with animals as we do?*

Adama - Yes, Bryan, we do. We have a wide variety of family members from the animal kingdom.

Bryan - *Would you be willing to speak on this for a minute?*

Adama - Yes, we have a great many of the same animals in Telos that you have there on the surface. They would look very familiar or perhaps even exactly the same; but keep in mind, as we have discussed, all of the animal kingdoms here are living in 5D. We also have a number of animal species that are not known to humanity. Perhaps they have had embodiments on other planets and it has come about now that some of them have come to be here with us. Many species that have been lost on the surface in previous ages are with us now also. We also enjoy the companionship of our cats and dogs, as well as rabbits, birds and a wide variety of members of the animal kingdom according to the preference of those who are here. It is really more of a mutual agreement because we have the ability to communicate back and forth with the animal kingdoms. This is a different experience from that which you have in your world today. We usually have a joint agreement, you see. Let us say a family has a fondness for a particular canine. That canine also has a choice as to whether or not they feel they resonate and belong with that family. We are all always in communion with our higher guidance, you see, so this process comes about in an easy and natural way for us. So yes, we enjoy our family members of the animal kingdoms very much, and certainly it is a part of our culture, especially for our children. Our children, as is the case with many of your own, have a special love and affinity for members of the animal kingdoms; so yes, this is a part our culture as well.

# Chapter 22
## Legends and Myths

Adama - Would you like to talk about some of the stories and mythology you've read recently about the mountain?

Bryan - Yes, *indeed, Master Adama. We have stories. JC Brown and Abraham Mansfield have provided two of the most recognized accounts. Also, can you share any information about these creatures we know as Bigfoot? They are a big deal here in Northern CA and I'm curious about them.*

Adama – Yes, Bryan, there are many stories and accounts through what I will call recent history, that of the past 150 years or so. There have been a number of accounts of humans here on the mountain who have encountered us, and I can tell you that at least some of the accounts are based in truth. There is usually a reason why legends become legends and myths become myths. They often have some element of truth to them and this is no different. For although it is obvious and true that we have chosen to keep our existence here in secrecy for the most part, there have been multiple occasions when we have come out of the mountain and made ourselves known to those who were ready or those who simply required some assistance.

One of your most recognized accounts is from a gentlemen known as J. C. Brown who stumbled across one of our tunnels. He discovered an entrance to a tunnel network that leads to the city. We simply had no expectation that it would have ever have been found in this location. This gentleman was prospecting for gold, and he stumbled across the entrance. Some of the Native Americans, the indigenous peoples of this region, have also been aware of us. They have held in their oral traditions a great respect and sacredness for this mountain, and they know that it is truly a special and magical place. There have been times throughout our history when we have come out and shown ourselves to the natives here and we have communed with them. There have been occasions when we have come out of the mountain and we have sat and spoken face to face with the leaders of these peoples here; we have told them of our history, which is of course also your history. Of course, their reference points in their own culture and language may be a bit different from that which you or others might perceive; but the point remains that we have, from time to time, come and made ourselves known to the native people, these people of the mountain. One of the reasons, and there are several, is to assist them in continuing their oral traditions in holding the mountain as sacred lands. We have given them knowledge about the mountain and the importance of its location on Gaia; this is one of her primary energy centers. Also, we have given them information, as I have said, about our history and theirs so they will have the benefit of a greater understanding of who they are. Many of these occasions are still remembered to this day, and the sacredness and beauty of this place are still held in high esteem and reverence among the indigenous peoples of this area. We understood that it was what I will call "safe" for us to make ourselves known and to share openly with them. We knew they would accept us and hold our truth sacred. In this way, we have worked together and our presence has benefited them and their presence and understanding has also benefited us.

There are also a number of non-indigenous peoples who have had experiences here on the mountain. J. C. Brown did stumble upon a cave and what he has relayed in his story was mostly accurate. At that time, we were not ready to step forward with full disclosure of our existence here in the mountain. As you know from the story, he was driven in his belief of our existence and he was prepared. He had assembled a large search party and he had his maps upon which he had made note of his discovery years prior. The intention was to bring a large group back to the mountain on an exploratory mission in an attempt to discover the truth of our existence. By Heaven's decree, none may interfere with your free will. To be clear, we did not interfere with his free will; however he was visited by one of our council members the night prior to the expedition, and our situation was explained to him. We asked him, after giving him an explanation from our perspective, that he not move forward with the search party; and there are a number of other ways we could have managed this. We could have simply hidden the cave such that it would not have been located again, and this would have been a relatively easy thing for us to do. However, our concern was twofold. One was for the safety of the search party and two was just to alleviate, as best we could, the fanfare around the search that would have most certainly taken place. We felt this would have led to more of the same, so it was our intention to bypass this kind of activity. An offer was made to Mr. Brown whereby we invited him and him alone to come and join us in Telos. He was told that he would not be allowed to return to the surface if our offer was accepted.

As would be expected, he had mixed emotions about these choices. On one hand, he had a great desire to provide evidence to others for his accounts and to show them that his story was true. He wished to share this remarkable discovery as well for its historical and archeological significance, so we will say his heart was in the right place. Had it not been, he would not have been invited into the mountain. So while he did have some sincere regret about leaving behind the search party with no word or explanation, he did make the choice to accept our offer and he was brought here to the city. We helped him to become acclimated to our higher levels of vibration––we have ways that we can do this. We have special chambers and temples of healing whereby we were able, over a relatively short period of time and mostly in his sleep time during this transition, to raise his vibration and to assist his physical body in preparing itself for this new experience. This is what we did. He lived here among us for a number of years before his passing for he was still very much in his human form. None of that changed. We simply raised his vibration and frequency and such that he was attuned to life in Telos. We assisted him in releasing density and coming more fully into his light body and higher states of awareness. This is similar to the process that you are going through now. In making your trips to this portal, you are becoming synchronized with this frequency. And so this is what we did and he lived out the remainder of his life here in good health and with great joy. He was a natural adventurer and seeker so this was an opportunity that he could not pass up. He was quite happy in all that he saw and learned and did here in our city and we were most happy to have him here with us. I will tell you that while this has only ever happened a small handful of times, he was not the only human to have been invited into Telos and extended an offer to stay with us. There are other accounts as well.

Yes, the account of Abraham Mansfield which you are reading now talks about the Queen of Etrucia and her six sons. He is relaying in his accounts that he is one of the chosen six overseeing a 30 year period as a God of the Lemurians. This is not such a complex issue; even though there are many levels of understanding that are not made known in his account, there are elements of truth here. However, if we were to recount this story for ourselves, we would revise the context, language and phrasing to provide the reader with additional information. Remnants of the history and existence of Mu span far and wide. There are a great many lineages and cultures present today that still remember the Lands of Mu. Our shared history has been lost to you. Indeed, he was one of the descendants of the great Queen of Etrucia, and when his time came that this should come into his awareness, then it did. I would not necessarily agree to every detail and description as it is written––and I do not intend any harm or damage to the author by this statement––just to say again, I might recount things a bit differently. But it is true that he had a lineage back to the Queen of Etrucia and it is also true that she was a ruler in the last Golden Age. She was a most wise and gracious leader. She was most radiant and beautiful. She was of course living in unity consciousness and in constant communion with her guides and teachers of light across the veil. She was a spiritual leader, not a political ruler. You have many negative emotions around this word "ruler" and rightly so. So what I would like to say here is that in his service, he provided what I will call a link from the past to the future. He was here to establish what you might call an energetic link in a chain, and it was important that this link be established. It was a part of the energetic interdimensional timeline between your past and your future, and he himself was aware of this in some way and at some level. This is what propelled him to take the actions, have the experience and recount his story when he did. So again, he is kind of coming into the picture, so to speak, by way of the indigenous peoples that I have spoken of a few minutes ago.

The indigenous peoples knew of the sacredness of that which was here and of our existence and they understood this all very well. They kept the information hidden and protected to outsiders with the exception of Mansfield, about whom the Chief was given a vision, so he knew this man had a role to play. Through a course of events that were being guided by higher light and truth, he was led to this chief who had been given the vision, and the chief in turn recognized this man as someone who was playing an integral part in our story. This is how that came about. You must remember that up until just a short time ago, less than 200 years or so, the indigenous peoples were really the only ones living here. It was only in what we would call the mid to late $19^{th}$ century that non-indigenous peoples began moving into this region, driven primarily by the gold rush and later for its natural resources. A new population inhabited this region to make it what it is today.

Through these years, there have been a number of accounts by individuals who have seen us. We have shown ourselves for one reason or another to those individuals and many of them have told their friends, family and community of their encounter. My point is there have been a few handfuls of encounters that were never brought forward in a published manner. This is where a lot of the legend and myth comes from. It is through these handfuls of accounts here and there of those to whom we have shown ourselves. Others indeed, have stumbled across some of the petroglyphs in the area you know as the Crags, where there are markings of our first visits long ago to this region. They are our markings. This area was a mining region at one time. There were Etruscians, Lemurians and Atlanteans here mining gold in this region, so the detail you have there about mining tunnels stretching for hundreds of miles in the mountains is true.

It is still true today. We have overhauled the interior, of course, many times. We have made many modifications to the mountain in the thousands of years that we have been here. Obviously this is no longer a mining district. Mining stopped at the time of the last great shift. So we knew this region, and of course this mountain was known to us. We were guided specifically to come here and to build our city. This would be one of numerous locations around the planet where we would go to reestablish ourselves. It was beneficial to us that this mining work in this area had been done, for it provided us with a foundation by which we could further build our city. It is also true, as has been noted, that before the great shift the ocean was much closer to the mountain. We understood, even at that time, that this mountain was a power center for Gaia.

While there was gold mining taking place in this region, I wish to let you know that it was done with great reverence and respect and in a way that was not harmful to the sacredness and energy of the mountain. Over the years we have sealed and hidden away most of the exterior entrances into the tunnels of the mining systems. There are still several exterior entrances remaining here on the mountain and you have seen one in your vision. Before you were entering through this portal, you were guided to enter through your meditation a portal on the backside of the mountain. You are aware of one entrance that is still open and remaining to this day, albeit extremely difficult to locate and access. There are still several entrances to Telos, but we will keep these hidden from view until such time as we are able to discuss this information with you openly.

As we have discussed before, we are not yet at a time when we are comfortable and ready to do this for a number of reasons. It is true that I have made myself known to a number of individuals in this area. I have shown myself to select others in a physical way, and there is always a reason for me to do this. It most likely has to do with what I will call the mission or the purpose of that individual that I am showing myself to. It is for their benefit and to bolster their confidence in what they already know, and these individuals have been instrumental in their path as it relates to us and also to each of you. As I have said, sometimes there are bigger things taking place behind the scenes. What you may perceive as an account that is perhaps obscure or curious and you wonder why this situation played out as it did, you know there is often more to the story, so to speak. There have been a number of reasons why and when we have come out to make ourselves known. Let me be clear, we will not come out of the mountain to make a spectacle of ourselves; but when there is an opportunity for mutual benefit, whereby we may jointly contribute to the project plan as it were, and for the greatest good of all involved, we may do so. We have never desired that our memory would die out completely. We have always wanted to keep the thought and the mystery and the myth alive particularly within this region and particularly with those of you who are called to the mountain. We have wanted to keep our existence in the forefront of some of your minds at some level such that when this time came that we are entering into now, there would be more of you who would be open to accept and work with us. But also, when this grand day and event comes, whereby we may come out of the mountain and show ourselves to you, it is our intention that you will be prepared to receive us. Because of the legends and mythology of our existence, it will not be such a great surprise to you when we are able to come out and make ourselves known to you on a larger scale.

Bryan - *Thank you, this is fascinating. Do you wish to comment on this creature that is known as Bigfoot, Sasquatch and Yeti?*

Adama - Yes, your Bigfoot is also that of legend and mythology, and again there is often a reason why legends hold or why they simply do not pass away. Your mythology of dragons and unicorns are still quite prevalent in most of your societies. You may not have any real understanding or recorded history of their actual existence, yet somehow they are still there widely prevalent in your mythology. You have come to know, through the course of this project and your own experience, the truth of their existence and much more than that, some of which we have shared in this book. There will be more forthcoming.

This creature that you all call Bigfoot is very real. These beings also come from the time of the last great shift. There were Lemurians, Atlanteans and Etruscians and others that survived the last great shift. We left our homes and journeyed to places that we were told would be safe havens for us such as this city of Telos. This happened in other geographic locations around the world as our great civilizations were undergoing the great cataclysms and shifts, and so there were a number of beings there. It was not just the Lemurians and Atlanteans you see. It was a much different world at that time and there were other species here with us as well. You have heard stories of those other beings that were more of a humanoid type of species. They were not exactly as we were (Lemurians, Atlanteans, Etrucians) but they were still of a human type nature. At that time they were a lesser-evolved species that were there with us. There were many, many forms of life and levels of being there co-existing with us. There were others which you are not yet familiar with. Some of these beings, such as the dragons were higher dimensional or multi-dimensional beings. Others were not. Our world was much different then.

These mammals then, which you refer to as Bigfoot, were one of the species that was there at that time and they were able to survive. They were a small number. They were not a heavy population and this was a species that came about through experimentation by some of those there at the time (Atlanteans). We will not go into a great detail here. They are some of the giants that are referred to in various places in your mythology and also some of the material you have read regarding our civilization. You are not likely to find this in one of your high school textbooks, but you have heard it said there were giants existing there. They were giants and they were not the only ones. There were others. They were well suited for heavy work and protection or guardianship. They were not highly evolved and they exist today in a similar state as they did at that time. In fact, rather than evolving, they have actually lessened what we will call their levels of awareness and consciousness over the span of time here. These beings live significantly longer than humans and they may live for hundreds of years. While they are not as highly evolved as they were at that time, in many ways they still have innately within them, ability and knowledge that even humans do not have at this time. They were also subject to the great fall. We refer to this species as the Koondra. They were not a large population to begin with and they were not taken specifically to these locations such as modern day Egypt and Tibet or our mountain here to which limited numbers of us were able to escape and rebuild our civilizations. We were not able to include them, so they were left scattered across the Lands of Mu to fend for themselves just as many of our own brothers and sisters were. There was no way for us to save the entire civilization. These are some of the painful memories that many of you have observed coming to the surface of your remembrance at this time.

At what we would call the intellectual level, the Koondra were not a very advanced species in that they do not have the same level of consciousness or cognitive awareness that humanity has. However, they do have other skills and abilities that benefit them obviously. They have at some levels, higher ability and skill related to their nature and survival. This has suited them well as they are still among us today, albeit in very small numbers. As I have said, they have undergone the fall also, so some of the abilities which they possessed at that time have been greatly diminished and there are relatively few of them on the planet now. They exist on multiple continents, and they have always been here with you since the great shift. They have been able to survive, but obviously they have not thrived. Their level of consciousness or what you perceive as intellect may be viewed to be something higher than your primates but still short of humanity. In some ways they are advanced and able to speak to each other telepathically. Their preference is to be sole wanderers and gatherers. They do not live in families. They will come together for the purposes of mating and there may be some time spent there in what you will refer to as a family unit; pretty soon, however, they are out living their individual existence again. It is their nature. They have great sensory abilities along with their telepathic abilities. Their sensories are in some ways expanded over the human and this is not uncommon. For example, you know that a dog has an infinitely greater ability to perceive smells than a human does. The Koondra have many of these kinds of sensory abilities that humans don't have. This makes them quite efficient in living the lifestyle they choose, which is one of secrecy. They do not wish to have any contact with humanity. They are a gentle species. They are not aggressors or at least this is not their inherent nature. They are gentle in their nature and they always have been. They have undergone the fall just as you all have, and they are making their shifts back into a higher level of awareness and vibration just as all life on the planet are. Yes, they are real and they have been with you through the ages and I suspect they will continue to be. There will be more information coming to the surface around these topics and many others. We endeavor to assist you in reestablishing your true history. The Koondra have intuitively been afraid of humanity, as it was their fear they would not be accepted or that they would be hunted or end up in your cages on display. They do not wish to have this experience for themselves so they live in remote places to stay hidden.

# Chapter 23

# Lenticular clouds and ships

Bryan - *I saw my first lenticular cloud over the mountain just now, Master Adama.*

Adama - Yes, we have seen it too. This is an interesting phenomenon that takes place here on the mountain. This is one of the trademarks of this sacred location, if you will. You will see more of them. You have wondered when you saw this lenticular cloud if a ship was coming into the mountain. It was not. We do not require the camouflage of a lenticular cloud for visitors to travel to and from our city. That is of no consequence to us. It is easily within our technology to bring our ships into the atmosphere, onto the planet and into the city of Telos without your instrumentation registering it. You would never know we were here. It will be a big surprise to many on the planet when the day comes that we, according to the project plan and the meeting of appropriate milestones, that both Lemurians and those of your star nation brothers and sisters, will make ourselves known to you. There will come a day in the not too distant future when humanity will have the opportunity to see ships and visit with their inhabitants from other star nations. It has not yet been determined which of the star nations will make first contact with you. We've talked about waves and waves of consciousness flooding the planet at this time and these waves are sweeping through humanity now. As milestones are achieved and as we move along in our project, there will indeed come a day when not only we, the Lemurians in the mountain, but also numerous others of your star nation family will come and make themselves known to you.

Many of your star nation families are here now assisting humanity, Gaia and all life here in making their transition into New Earth. We will be guiding you and assisting you in many ways through new technologies and new levels of understanding in various areas such as science and physics, astronomy and history, healing, energy, food production and so forth. We have much to teach you. But we must wait until such time as humanity is in a state of awareness when they are open to receive us as your star nation family and friends. You see, we do not wish to create setbacks unnecessarily; and at this particular time if these events were to take place, we perceive that humanity as a whole is not yet open or ready to receive this truth. It is not our intention to create further disturbance, disharmony or stress on top of all that is already taking place in your world today. With the current situation being what it is, we fear this could trigger events that would be more in alignment with your current and past paradigms and the masculine energies of domination, control, territory and defensive positions. If our first contact is not managed appropriately, it could lead to a course of events which would actually create further misalignment, disharmony or perhaps even further levels of destruction on your planet, you see. This is not the course of action we will take.

We are working according to the grand project plan where milestones must be met along the way. As you would expect, some of the milestones have to do with the general awareness, consciousness and receptivity of all of humanity. It is more complex and detailed than that in the actual blueprints of the project plan, but that is the general scope of the situation today. It is my hope that you will see these events coming about in the not too distant future, and I strongly suspect that you will. We will be discussing this again. Let me remind you, at this point in time nothing is set in stone in regards to the timing of events that may come forward. You have heard through other messengers and you and I have discussed that in many areas we are well ahead of the project plan. We still need to catch up in some areas but this is to be expected. We are generally pleased with current progress; yet there is still much work to be done so we will not take our foot off the gas so to speak. We will continue moving boldly and confidently forward according to the plan, but it is difficult to predict when certain events may come about. It is our hope that you will have the opportunity to experience our first contacts in the not too distant future and certainly within the time many of you have remaining here. It could take place even in a matter of a few short years. We will continue on our path according to the project plan and we will continue to push forward for the best success. At this particular time, many of humanity are still struggling in the 3rd dimensional paradigm, which is the old paradigm. Those of you, lightworkers and pioneers who are doing your work are well ahead of most of your brothers and sisters. Indeed, this is why each of you is here––to be the wayshowers––so please understand that it will take some time to move the mass consciousness forward a bit more.

There are a number of situations that must be resolved before the time will come when we may show ourselves to you. There are a number of events that must take place, so this is not so much a timing issue as it is an event driven plan. When we are reviewing the milestones of our project plans, milestones are tangible accomplishments; and we have ways of monitoring and registering them. We are interested in the accomplishment and success of the milestones in the order in which they are included on the project plan and not so much the timing of particular events. We are not working within the linear construct of time that exists in your world, so we are not working to time schedules; we are working to milestones. As we have discussed, it is often difficult for us to lay down the linear time construct over top of what we perceive to be event driven activity. You and many others already have some awareness of how this concept applies in your own lifestream experience as it relates to your co-creations and the work you're doing to manifest the results you desire. In this regard, we have a very similar scenario between what is happening with each of you individually and what is happening globally. Your individual divine blueprint is, what we might say, the equivalent of your personal project plan and there are milestones along the path of your individual project plan or your divine blueprint that must be accomplished. One level, timeline, or event must be attained before you may move on to the next level of experience. A particular circumstance may need to come about and be experienced; perhaps it is a lesson or an initiation or perhaps it is simply an experience that needed to take place, and often this event or experience must be accomplished before the next one can come into play.

There are many parallels in the way you might perceive your own project plan and that of our larger grand scale project plan for Gaia, humanity and all of life here on the planet. So the very best course of action individually––both in looking at your individual divine blueprint and at the greater project plan of the whole––is we would encourage each of you to simply follow your soul's guidance. This is your divine guidance from your Higher Self. Use your emotions as your guidance system and follow your joy. Follow your fulfillment and follow those experiences, people, events and surroundings that bring you to a place of peace and joy. Following your inner guidance is what we endeavor to assist you with. This is happening in a natural way as new and higher levels of light flood the planet. Many of those who are not aware of the changes taking place may begin acting out in some way. Their programs are running in the background and all energies are being amplified. Many individuals may struggle through this change until they can self-correct through the seeking out of their own internal balance and harmony. There are bumps and roadblocks and challenges along the way, but each one is being led to a greater connection with their divinity and their Higher Self. As this takes place, each one will come more into alignment and begin recognizing their own internal guidance system. This is the moving away from the ego, the personality and the lower self and acknowledging and embracing your own divinity. As these shifts come about, each one will be led naturally to follow his or her own inner guidance. Listen with your heart and pay attention to what your emotions are telling you. In this way, each of you will more readily accomplish the tasks and milestones ahead of you. Your New Earth will be created through the recognition and embracing of each ones divinity. At the individual level, it is just a matter of doing your best to remain still in your moment-to-moment choices and experience. Go inside, be still and feel. Listen to your inner guidance or feel into your inner guidance to make those decisions that feel to you like you like you are following your joy or your best choice. It will feel like the right decision.

This is a bit of a roundabout answer; but yes, my friend, it is our hope and endeavor that we will accomplish our milestones in such a way that we can come to these events in a relatively short period of time and that could be even as soon as a few years. I will not make that prediction. All of you together are co-creating your collective experience moment by moment. It will come about as we move forward on our project plan.

Can you imagine what an exciting day this will be when either we, the Lemurians here in Telos, or one of the other star nations, will finally be able to come forward and make ourselves known to humanity again? We must ensure that humanity is in a place where you are able to accept us as your brothers and sisters of the cosmos. You must be closer to unity consciousness and also with an expanded awareness of various truths as they exist here in the cosmos. If we were to come and have these events today, we see it could trigger all manner of fear and chaos or perhaps even defensive positions taken against us. We must wait until such time as humanity is at some stage of readiness to embrace and acknowledge us as your neighbors, as your family in the light. When this day comes it will be very exciting. It will certainly be cause for celebration and we are very much looking forward to it.

This reunion will be a major shift forward in the project plan and for the forward momentum of your world, for when this happens there will be a number of things taking place. This event will be of great assistance to those who find themselves stuck in the old paradigm, those who perhaps are having some trouble releasing all of the old ways and old patterns. It will assist them in moving forward in the new paradigm for it will be right there plainly for everyone to see. This will be a monumental event and it will offer assistance to those who may be just a bit behind the curve, so to speak. It will help people to step into the New Earth paradigm and unity consciousness and it will also be the beginning of a more grand cooperative effort taking place between humanity and those of us who have come to assist you at this time. This will be the event that opens up a wealth of opportunity for the exchange of knowledge and technology that will assist you all in moving forward. But we still have much work to do, my friends. We will get there. You will see these events. It is a most exciting proposition and certainly it is something to endeavor and strive for. We have great anticipation for these events just as you do. We also long to reconnect with you, our family. Let us continue our work and see where we go.

# Chapter 24

## Journeys with Tabiananti and her merkaba

Bryan – Note: These journeys took place on March 29 and April 5, 2017 as I drew near to the completion of this book. There are lots of interesting conversations taking place in Mt. Shasta City, and many of them have to do with Master Adama and the Lemurians of Telos. Everyone around here is at least aware of the legend of the Lemurians in the mountain. Others are being asked specifically to come and participate in a bigger way. Lots of people I spoke with on the trail or the parking lot last summer just came to be on the mountain and they weren't sure why. They just came. Until these experiences took place, I had intentionally avoided others who are here working with Telos because I didn't want to be influenced by someone else's work or experience.

A dear friend of mine called and told me of her experience with a facilitated "Journey to Telos." My friend is also becoming more aware of her Lemurian family and this experience had facilitated a new level of connection for her. She was really excited about it. This gathering takes place every Wednesday night in Mt. Shasta. I was aware of it but didn't know anything about it. My friend invited me to give it a try and said she didn't think it would interfere with my work. I said okay.

The Journey to Telos gatherings are facilitated by Maqua Iqua. Maqua was traveling the world and after living in Hawaii for seven years, she was called to reconnect with her Lemurian roots and Adama in Telos. She did a great job of providing us with information and setting the stage so that each one would have a successful session, whatever that was going to be for them.

I didn't realize it at the time, but I had been led to this weekly gathering for a reason. It had been a while since I had visited with Tabiananti, who I refer to as my "Ambassador to Telos", and I thought this might be a good opportunity for us to enjoy a visit. I wish to share an authentic view of the experience; therefore, I'm choosing to leave them in essentially the raw, story-telling style in which they were taken down. Points of clarification have been added here and there for your benefit.

After the second journey, it dawned on me that perhaps I had been "set up," so I went to visit Master Adama and Tabiananti in the Great Hall. It turns out these experiences had indeed been planned for my great enjoyment and yours. Master Adama, the High Council of Telos and our friend Tabiananti also wish to end our book on a high note and to give us all a better view of this wondrous world that I refer to as Middle Earth. May these journeys delight you and stir your own sense of wonder.

## 3-29-17 Maqua Journey to Telos

Maqua holds a "Journey to Telos" guided meditation here every Wednesday night and I thought I would give it a try tonight. Earlier today I spoke to Tabiananti; I was not in meditation and therefore not immediately aware of her response. I asked her if she wanted to have a visit and said I would go to the portal later that evening.

Maqua's huge drum was beating steadily to the rhythm of the heartbeat, and the journey may have lasted 45-55 minutes. I am not accustomed to meditating with drums or with others for that matter, so it took me a few minutes to really settle in before I traveled to the portal. When I got there, however, I could see that the drums and energy of the eight or so people present were assisting me greatly with my connection and clarity. Several Lemurians had joined us in the space also.

Tabiananti was waiting when I got there. It's been a while since we've seen each other and it was great to see her again. We walked out to the natural platform and I took a look at the city off to the left. The parking garage appears to me to be under Shastina and this is where we were looking back toward Telos, which I perceived to be quite a ways off to the East. I say several, maybe 5 miles away. The space or geographic landscape view is completely different down here. Space and distance don't match the surface at all. I saw a brilliance of color with several large spires standing here and there throughout the city. There is a huge archway crystal over the main entrance to the city that glows white and blue. Everything around the city as far as the eye can see is lush and green with different landscape features about.

We jumped into the merkaba and she drove us over the city. Some of the streets were lit up with the golden glow I've seen before on the streets and the tunnel shaft we've just come through from the physical portal. The seven flames of the Creator rays were shooting far into the air and putting off a magnificent soft glow. It felt like late afternoon. As we were above the city I could see there were two or three suburbs a short distance away. We were moving quickly and she veered left as we approached the far side of the city. She took me over huge fields where there were two large crystal domes. They may have been a quarter or half mile each in diameter. She said it's where they grow their food. They're essentially greenhouses. The fields themselves were full of crops and vegetation, so they're using a combination of growing systems. People were working and moving about in the fields. We turned west again and traveled very quickly. Sometimes I could see the landscape but when she accelerated quickly I couldn't make anything out.

The agricultural landscape quickly faded to one that reminded me of the Sierra Nevadas. Later, as I was describing my experience to the group, I said it reminded me of Yosemite. The mountains were rugged and beautiful. I was surprised to see that we were also flying into a Redwood forest that extended out as far as I could see. We landed on a rock outcrop and began walking down a trail. She said they were a mix of Redwoods and Sequoyas. She said she brought me here today because she knows how much I enjoy them. She said they have plans to re-establish the tree giants on the surface when the time is right and that I need not have concern about it. This Redwood grove looked very much like the ones I've visited here in California. There were oddities though. There was a flower that was ten times the size of our garden-variety flowers, and it was shaped differently. There was a main trumpet stem going straight into the air and then from the top and traveling down the stem, there were four trumpets at the same point with each one facing a different direction. This configuration continued down the stem so that it made one large flower that stood about five feet tall. The colors were soft orange and white, and the flower emitted a soft glow.

After what seemed like a short distance we came to a stream and she precipitated (produced from thin air) a thick, white blanket. We sat face to face by the stream. She asked if I wished for her to assist me in further awakening my Lemurian DNA and I gladly accepted. We sat quietly for a moment and I enjoyed her beauty and radiance, her calm and soothing energy. We were, of course, already connected telepathically and now we opened our heart space to each other. I asked my I AM Presence to come forth and flow the highest purity of light the human was capable of and to direct that sweet love to her. I felt warmth and generosity and acceptance and grace and all that good stuff radiating back to me in return. She held her hands out for me and then surrounded us in a golden bubble of light. She asked me to relax and simply to still the mind and allow the energies to work. I could definitely feel the energies and that was awesome, but I was still excited about all that I had seen in these past minutes. I couldn't help but wonder what else I might see. I did my best to settle in. A few minutes later we stood up and walked into the stream where I sat on a rock that had obviously been used for this purpose before. It had a natural seat just off the water. She reached down and got a handful of water and poured it gently over my head. She did this three times.

I see Tabiananti as a little over seven feet tall with long white hair. It's not the same as the white hair we're all familiar with. Hers has a special quality or brilliance about it. Her face and body structure are very petite but with soft muscle definition. Her eyes are just ever so slightly wider than ours and they beam love to whatever they see. They are soft to medium blue and they have a sparkle... no joke. She has full lips and her skin tone is what we would consider to be a pale Caucasian. She is captivatingly beautiful.

She told me it was time to go and we began walking back. In a short distance, we were walking through an otherwise typical and beautiful Redwood grove, and about twenty yards away, I saw a bull moose with two cows farther away still. That was all fine except that his back was about eight feet tall, which meant the top of his antlers may have been fourteen feet off the ground. I don't know. I was alarmed. Master Adama had talked about the animals in 5D but it was another thing to be standing in the forest looking at one this big. Tabiananti assured me we were perfectly safe. I just couldn't believe the size of this freaking moose. He must have picked up on my vibration because he stopped and turned his head back to me for a second or two before walking off again.

We arrived back at the rock outcrop and I could see Telos off even further in the distance. It looked like it could have been twenty miles away. We were high in the mountains looking way down into a valley. Like I said, it reminded me of some of the views in Yosemite. The drum tempo changed and it was time to come back. Tabiananti and I jumped in the merkaba and within a second or two we were back at the portal entrance. I thanked her for showing me around and for the great energy lift. It was awesome!

## 4-5-17 Journey to Ahatana with Tabiananti

I went back to Maqua's "Journey to Telos" tonight. I had spoken to Tabiananti earlier to let her know I was coming and to see if she would meet me there. I said if I didn't find her at the portal, I would travel to the Great Hall and see if anyone was there. If not, I would come back; no big deal. It was easier to get into the rhythm of the drumming this time, and I traveled easily to the portal. She was there waiting for me. We walked through the tunnel to the area I call the parking garage, and I saw more ships there tonight than I have ever seen. I couldn't make out the details but I sensed there were quite a few ships ranging from what I would call small to medium in size. I don't know anything about spacecraft, but I perceived that some of them were large enough to easily facilitate a crew of a couple of hundred or more. She told me that Telos was hosting a meeting regarding the project plan and there were seven star nations represented. She didn't share any details about what the meeting was about.

From this location, I could see the skyline of Telos off to the left. She said she had a surprise for me and we got into her merkaba. Instead of traveling towards the city we traveled in between ships hovering in this monstrous cavern, traveling down near the bottom and toward the back or to the west. We entered a tunnel that wasn't that much larger than our vehicle, and light was just flashing by. We were moving very quickly, and she said we were going to Ahatana.

When we stopped a few seconds later, I could see that we were in a developed area in front of a massive temple. The environment looked and felt like you would expect it to in Hawaii. It was very tropical with all kinds of lush vegetation in and throughout the city. There was a blending of urban development and nature. Telos contains beautiful lights and crystal structures, domes and spires with a wonderful vibrancy and color. This city looks ancient and has a much different feel. It's difficult to describe but it reminded me of nonpyramidal Egyptian or Incan architecture. The buildings were made of stone but all very meticulous in their design and with different colors and textures of stone so it all felt very natural. It is a paradise. The stone walls and buildings had many different tones and shades, mostly tans but with a range of really deep and dark to almost white like some of the architecture in Italy and Greece.

The shape or footprint of this huge temple very much reminded me of the Navaho symbol for the sun. There were four extremely large entrances facing what I assumed to be the cardinal directions, whatever that means here, and there were no doors. Twenty people at a time could pass through each entrance without any problem. You simply walked in from the sidewalk and into this huge temple; it was all open air. Things were moving fast and I was just trying to keep up as it was all taking place, so when I provide estimates of distance and space, I'm just doing the best I can to frame up the experience. I would guess that the footprint of the Illumination Temple consumes ten or twelve acres of land. It was by far the largest structure that I saw on my visit. There was a ceremonial stone structure in the center with the Golden Flame of Illumination shooting straight into the air. The circumference of the flame may have been sixty or seventy five feet. It is literally massive. The temple and the surrounding area were filled with the golden luminescence and soft glow of the sun and the illumination flame.

There were two large pools in the shape of thin rectangles near the sides of the temple. Tabiananti said that Gaia along with their elders had especially blessed the waters and that to bathe here would leave you feeling very serene but with a slight lift of energy and joy. A man walked forward and introduced himself as Kala. He said he is one of the elders of Ahatana and that he was well aware of me and the work I'm doing with Adama. He thanked me for following my guidance to the mountain and for all the good work I'm doing. He said he recognizes that I am drawn to their city and that I will visit Hawaii one day soon. He said the dolphin collective there are well aware of my desire to visit with them; and they, the dolphins and the elders of Ahatana, will be awaiting me when I arrive.

He said he had something to show me and turned to walk. I followed him to one of the back walls of the temple where he somehow made a door appear in the stone wall. We stepped through and walked down some stairs to what I could see was another entire level of rooms, halls and corridors. We stepped through another doorway and we were in a great hall similar to the one in Telos. However, there was no marble or gold here. There were huge banners with lots of color and design hanging from the ceiling against the walls. They added elements of color and elegance to the hall. The walls were a polished stone with a tan color that may have been sandstone. Centered in the room was a large circular table made of emerald. The table is made from one solid crystal that is perhaps fifteen feet in diameter and four feet thick. What a sight to behold. I asked him if this crystal was a part of Gaia or if it came from somewhere else. He said they brought it to Lemuria thousands of years ago. He said this is one of the powerful crystals that was relocated and saved before the last great shift. He said the temple we are standing in now is the Temple of Illumination and this crystal represents and is used for the healing of Gaia and humanity. Many of the community elders are oriented in service to the golden ray of illumination and the green ray of healing. He said the table, along with their intention, provides great healing energies for the world. They have also awaited this day and the coming age for a long time. They are excited that things are expanding in a new way for us all now and that they may begin to make themselves known to us again. Kala said they have other rooms here that are used for training and study. We walked back up to the main floor; and as we stepped through the door, I could see a large black panther walking up to me. He was about four feet tall. He said "Hello" to me telepathically. I said, "Hello, this is all so interesting, I haven't been here before." He gave me a look and said, "Yes, I can see that." I said, "You are an aware being." He said, "Indeed I am." He said, "I see that you are wanting to know if you can, what you refer to as pet me, and you may do so if you wish." I kneeled down and stroked the back of his head and ran my hand down his back almost to his tail. He said, "I trust that you will enjoy your visit with us today," and as he walked off he put his weight against me like cats often do.

We stepped back onto the street and I noticed then that other animal beings were scattered about among the citizens. I saw a couple of canines and some birds that resembled peacocks. There were others that I couldn't make out. Lemurian light language symbols were prevalent on much of the architecture, especially the temple. Although the feel of this place was truly ancient, everything was still perfect in form and everything pristine clean. This is what Master Adama was talking about when he said the elders built their city and brought with them the beauty and feeling of the original surface city of Ahatana. Tabiananti said they have all the same technology that exists in Telos, but it's not as noticeable. They prefer their environment to have a more natural feeling.

The buildings and temples of Ahatana seemed to blend naturally with Gaia and the natural world. There was no separation, if that makes sense. Mother Nature and the animal kingdoms along with small pockets of urbanization all blended together so beautifully that it was hard to know where one stopped and the other began. Tabiananti invited me to get back into the merkaba and we traveled a short distance to the top of a mountain. When we stopped, I was awestruck to find myself looking out over an ocean. It looked just like our oceans. This confused me greatly so I asked Tabiananti about it. She said that Inner Earth is made up of worlds within worlds and this one contains an ocean teaming with life. Of course I had more questions but it wasn't the time to try to get into all of that. There was a large clear crystal placed strategically on this viewpoint looking out over the ocean. It looked like an eight or ten foot boulder with a definite shape that I didn't recognize. It's obviously significant but I didn't get around to asking what it's used for.

Looking down through the valleys and out toward the ocean, I could see that Ahatana is not a continuous city. There were small pockets of urbanization scattered here and there among the forest, with small roadways and paths connecting them all. It was like a group of very small suburbs all connected together back to the main hub which houses the Temple of Illumination. I was completely fascinated by it all. We were sitting together looking out over the ocean when Maqua sounded the drum that it was time to come back. Tabiananti took me back to the physical portal in Telos and walked me back to the entrance. I told her how much I had enjoyed my experience and thanked her for showing it all to me.

# Dedications

Please allow me to make a few dedications for this book.

First, I dedicate this work to God and pray that his Light shine through me.

To my beautiful parents who, seemingly without effort, appear to me to be two of the most enlightened people on the planet. I could not have asked for better parents and I would have been lost in the world without them. Even though they may not always agree with or understand some of the weird stuff I'm so interested in these days, not once have they uttered a discouraging word or doubt about my chosen path. They have and continue to offer their full love and support in the fulfillment of my passion and joy. Thank you Mom and Dad for everything. I love you.

Thank you to Archangel Michael for truly I cannot say what my path would have been had he not come and gotten me that day. When I say he came and got me, this experience led directly to my understanding of the necessity and of my great inherent longing and desire to return home, to earn my ascension in the light. I have come to know many of my angel brothers by name and I have seen them fill the cosmic landscape before me in numbers far too great to count. If only I could somehow express the truth of this and the overwhelming and astounding love that they hold for each of us. I promise you the world would change in an instant. Indeed, he has become my best friend and most trusted ally. I feel his presence with me now always; the energies of Shasta have assisted me in this way. It doesn't feel like an intrusion in any way yet his presence remains in the background. As I set my attention to him I can feel his presence beside me even before I finish speaking his name. I hope this makes some sense for you. His love for humanity and each of us is quite literally beyond our understanding. I asked him once; "Archangel Michael, aren't you tired? You have been here watching over humanity beyond time that I can comprehend and there are so many of us calling out to you each day for help." He told me that he is omnipresent and as such, it is within his ability that he could have a unique and personal interaction with every human being on planet today at the very same time, and it would not even begin to tax his ability. In fact, he said this is his great hope and that he would love nothing more than for every single one present to call on him now or at any time of their choosing. I invite you to see for yourself the blessings, friendship and guidance that are always on offer to you from our Beloved Archangel Michael.

My great gratitude to Master Adama for offering me the best "job" on the planet. Since my arrival to the mountain, we've had the opportunity to spend a great deal of time together. As I have allowed myself to relax and connect more fully with him and the energies of Telos, I see more and more the great blessings that come to me as a result. He has come to be one of my most trusted friends and advisors, not only on spiritual matters but those of a personal nature as well. He continues to be ever gracious and supportive as I allow myself to open to this expansion and the role I am here to play. I long for the day when the Lemurians come to make themselves known to us. I long for the day when humanity will experience the harmony and grandeur of life as I perceive it to be in Telos. The love and warmth that I feel from Master Adama and our family in Telos is something that I value greatly. I cannot wait to see where this project takes us.

Love and blessings to my Heaven Family; Lord Jesus, Blessed Mother Mary, Archangel Ariel, Master Saint Germain, Master El Moyra, Master Hilarion, Archangel Uriel, Archangel Raphael, Beloved Quan Yin, the mighty Elohim Astrea, first ray angel brothers, the Mighty Blue Dragons of Venus, Tabiananti in Telos and so many more. Our Blessed Mother Mary has given me lessons in what I think of as the unified field where she's shown me timelines and events as bright highways of light and energy running and connecting in the most astounding ways. Master Saint Germain provides a foundational piece of my understanding through his many teachings in book form and otherwise. He was the second of my family to appear and speak to me. At first, I thought he looked like the figure I recognize as Father Time. Later I came to understand that he is the Master Saint Germain. From time to time, he would show himself to me as Merlin and remind me that we knew each other at that time also. There is so much more I could say about each one. These and so many more are your family also and they long to connect with you again. I love and appreciate Y'all so much. Thank you.

Much gratitude to my spiritual sister, friend and mentor Carolyn A. Jones. She is an incredibly gifted channel, healer and guide. I describe the catalyst experience given to me by Archangel Michael. However, there was a great deal of work and attainment that needed to take place in the roughly three years between that event and my coming to the mountain. There is no textbook for how these changes will come about for an individual and I found many questions along the way. Carolyn and our Heaven Family guided and supported my growth at each step. She taught me about Reiki and other energy healing modalities where I learned new ways of sensing and working with energy for the benefit of myself and others. A part of our agreement for this lifetime was that she help me wake up and indeed she has. She remains my very dear friend and ally. I cannot thank her enough for the wisdom, love and light that she brings to the world.

Off and on through the years, I have received great benefit by participating in the study of martial arts. I have been blessed with two great and masterful teachers. I intend no disrespect by the omission of their names. I received impulses on several occasions not to include them and I have chosen to follow that guidance. My teachers are also my friends and each of them is aware of my appreciation and affection for them. These statements are shared for their recognition and for the many friends made along the way. Each of them also, has contributed to my learning and growth.

In my late twenties, in Colorado, Sifu would offer wisdom teachings that often shook my paradigm and opened my eyes to concepts that I had not considered or been exposed to previously. He gave a lecture once about ancient civilizations and a book titled "The Lost Continent of Mu" by Col. James Churchward. I read it and was fascinated. That was nearly twenty years ago and now I find myself in Mt. Shasta doing this work. I can't help but wonder about this strange coincidence. His words still return from time to time, as "AH HA" moments of understanding. My Sifu is a wise man and he has had a profound and positive influence on my life. I am grateful.

Later, in Tennessee, I had the opportunity to study Tai Chi and Chi Kung for a time. I began learning how to feel and work with energy in a very real way, and this continues to be of great benefit to my daily living and spiritual practice. Sigung is a wise and gracious man. Among other things, I am grateful for his caring and patience as he assisted me and others in the process of learning and applying these new skills. New gifts continue to come forward by way of his teachings. I am grateful.

Lastly, a dedication to my dear friend Abby. Abby is a golden retriever who was my loyal friend and companion for fifteen years. I often told people that if they wanted to experience the sweetest energy existing on the planet today, to simply spend a minute or two with this kind soul and beautiful being of light. She went to work with me every day for twelve years. She was one of many "Love

Ambassadors" for the pet products company we worked for. Archangel Michael has relayed to me that she has earned her wings and now resides with the angels. He tells me she often accompanies me on my trips to the mountain and that she is able to understand directly any thought vibrations I might send to her. I will see my old friend again someday.

# Acknowledgments

In the co-creation of this book, it was necessary that I rely on the expertise of others in the community and I would like to acknowledge them for the important role they played in bringing it about.

## JoyAn Tucker - Editor

My deep gratitude to JoyAn for not only editing this book but for her friendship as well. When I arrived in Mt. Shasta, JoyAn gave me a room for rent until I could find a home of my own. She showed me around and began introducing me to some of her friends in town. I'm grateful for all that she's done and all that she continues to do for me and others. She is also an author.

www.joyrisingranch.com

## Mei Drucker - Cover art

Mt. Shasta is a small town and one of the first places I visited was Mei Drucker's Art Gallery. Mei moved here from China some years ago and those traditions are evident in her work. I was especially drawn to the bright colors and vibrancy of her work. To walk into her shop and appreciate the art she brings forth is an uplifting and joyful experience. I was most pleased when she agreed to do the cover design for this book, and I know that her kind and joyful energies will also travel with the book. I gave her a list of visual elements that I wanted to include on the cover and then got out of her way so she could create something that was inspired and beautiful. I believe she's done just that.

www.meidruckerart.com

### Lisa Diane - Designer

Thanks to another new friend in town, Lisa Diane for assisting with the project. Lisa helped me on the back end of the project. We spoke about the future vision and branding of the greater Lemurian project which I found to be very beneficial. Among other things, she took the original light language drawings from Michael and created the page layouts used in this book. She's been a valuable asset to this project and I'm grateful.

www.lucid9design.com

### Maqua Iqua - Facilitator/Healer. *Journey to Telos* guided meditations

I'm so grateful to Maqua for having facilitated the journeys that were shared with you in the last chapter and for all the good work she's doing with our friends in Telos.

www.journeytotelos.com

### Michael Lott - Artist, Lemurian Light Language

www.MichaelLottArt.com

Allow me to express my sincere gratitude to Michael Lott, the gifted artist and channel who brought forth these Lemurian light language symbols for us.

We had been introduced by mutual friends and decided to get together for a practice session. In my experience, it's not nearly as easy to hold a connection to Master Adama, for example, if I also need to be more present with my surroundings and consciously interacting with others. It represents another level of growth and so this was a good opportunity for us both.

We got settled and I led him to the Great Hall in Telos where Master Adama was waiting for us. Right away, I could see that their connection was strong and easy. I started cracking up and said something to the effect of, "Apparently my communication skills aren't required here today." Master Adama spoke with Michael about his personal history in the times of Lemuria and other topics. In turn, Michael brought some messages to me that were noteworthy and beneficial.

A week or two later, Michael gave a talk at the Silk Road Chai Shop here in town. His amazing art was displayed there at the time and I made the comment that I saw elements of light language in his work. I don't recall what his thoughts were about it. Because he's such a talented artist and his connection with Master Adama was so strong, I had the idea (or was given the idea) to see if we could bring through some examples of Lemurian light language for you. The three of us agreed it was something we wanted to do, so we set another meeting and returned to the Great Hall.

Michael and I were sitting across from each other at the ruby table in the Great Hall. Master Adama stood behind Michael's right shoulder and looked on. Back on the couch, I was aware that the symbols were flowing out of him with ease. I would let Master Adama know which word we wanted next. Michael would wait a few seconds for the transmission to come through clearly and then just allow it to flow. Once he began there was no hesitation and each symbol was completed quickly. Master Adama confirmed with us along the way that each one was coming through accurately.

As Master Adama was guiding Michael, he said that a Lemurian light language symbol may have far greater meaning and understanding than can be fully translated to a single word in our English language. He said there are nuances also in the symbols that may lead to different ideas being expressed. Michael was given the symbol for Divine Love. He was told that nuances could have changed the symbol to reflect family or romantic love for example. These symbols express powerful energies of the beautiful things they represent. They carry Master Adama's blessings as well as Michael's and my own. May each one bless you with the highest Love and Light!

# Bibliography


## Prologue

Herman, Ronna.

*Scripting Your Destiny.* Star Quest Publishing, 2008.

*Your Sacred Quest.* Star Quest Publishing, 2004

www.starquestmastery.com

Jones, Aurelia Louise.

*Telos Volume 1: Revelations of the New Lemuria.* Mount Shasta Light Publishing, 2004.

*Telos Volume 2: Messages for the Enlightenment of Humanity in Transformation.* Mount Shasta Light Publishing, 2004

*Telos Volume 3: Protocols of the Fifth Dimension.* Mount Shasta Light Publishing, 2006

www.mslpublishing.com

## Chapter 6: Returning to Balance

Swetlishoff, Marlene. *The Hilarion Connection: Book One.* Symphonies of Grace Publishing, 2015. www.symphoniesofgrace.com

## Chapter 9: The Seven Rays

Herman, Ronna. *Scripting Your Destiny.* Star Quest Publishing, 2008.

Jones, Aurelia Louise. *Telos Volume 3: Protocols of the Fifth Dimension.* Mount Shasta Light Publishing, 2006

## Chapter 10: Lemurian DNA Activation

Carroll, Lee. *Kryon: The Twelve Layers of DNA (An Esoteric Study of the Mastery Within)*. Platinum Publishing House, 2010

51210173R00214

Made in the USA
San Bernardino, CA
16 July 2017